DATE DUE
DISCARDED
261 2500
Printed in USA

Tales from the Pewter Shop

Tales from the *Pewter Shop*

RAYMOND E. GIBSON

PETER E. RANDALL PUBLISHER
PORTSMOUTH, NEW HAMPSHIRE
1999

To Cyrus, Mark, Christopher, Lauren and Jonathan
Laborare est orare.

Peter E. Randall Publisher
Box 4726
Portsmouth, New Hampshire 03802-4726

Distributed by University Press of New England
Hanover and London

Library of Congress Card Number: 98-92264

ISBN: 0-914339-81-8

Contents

BECOMING KNOWN

SPECIAL MEMORIES

Foreword

I first "met" Raymond Gibson (not in person but through his work) as the sole juror of the 17th Annual Juried exhibition of the League of New Hampshire Craftsmen in 1992. As the old saying goes "by their works ye shall know them." Judging Gibson by his work, I gave him the Stevens Metal Award of Excellence at that exhibition. By looking at his work I surmised that Gibson was a sincere, mature man of spiritual depth. His pewter bowl spoke quietly but with eloquence. His work was clear, open, traditional, and expressive of a reverence for the past, yet it embodied a distinct acknowledgment of personal investment in the design sensibilities of the late twentieth century. Gibson's approach to spatial divisions, volume, edges, and texture, and his refined love of surface finish, yielded an astonishing vitality and purity to his spun pewter. I could imagine that this artist had enjoyed long training under an apprenticeship system that led to his mastery of the medium. His work seemed to be something from the past blended with the present.

How could I know that Gibson was a retired Congregational minister, who taught himself how to work out the technical difficulties of his art through the sheer love of pewter and what could be made with it? Imagine my surprise when this modern master stopped by my office at the Museum of Fine Arts, Boston, and briefly explained his background. I was so impressed with his works, his life story, and his joy with the art of workmanship that in October 1992 I acquired for the collections of the Museum the very same prize-winning pewter fruit bowl plus a small (3 3/4" high) elegant beaker, the interior of which displays the impress of the grain of the birch wood of the chuck on Gibson's lathe. Both were donated to the Museum from the artist in honor of Arthur Barnes, an elderly pewterer of Norwich, Connecticut, who generously passed on to Gibson all that he could teach him.

Thus the Museum's important collection of antique pewter was notably enhanced with works by an acknowledged contemporary master. Raymond Gibson and his pewter-artist son, Jonathan, have kept us informed about their remarkable careers. As a result the Museum's data folders on Gibson pewter bulge with information about their lives and their works which are now superbly documented in this book.

Tales from the Pewter Shop is a remarkable record. It transcends a mere autobiography for it offers the reader insight into how and why the work of Gibson's hand, heart, and mind have been transformative experiences. Those who work with raw material and transform it or shape it into things useful and beautiful feel the magical power art has in their lives. Some artists and craftsmen have identified this experience with the poetry of the physical. Art is a profound shaper of life. Artists discover that as they shape their works, they also shape their inner selves. Gibson's narrative offers the reader insight into such experience. His vision of connections—bridges between things that might not to everyone seem connected—is the metal which joins this narrative. Undoubtedly, the flowing wonders of forming, skimming, trimming, and finishing metal on his spinning lathe are coupled with the joy Gibson shares with those who come to admire his excellence of design and workmanship. The Gibson shop, his work, and his life all flow seamlessly together through the insights offered in this eloquent account.

Reader beware: after perusing this book you will want to take a journey to Hillsborough Centre, New Hampshire, to meet the "spinning Parson" and his family, and to acquire the works made by his remarkable son, Jonathan.

Jonathan L. Fairbanks
Katharine Lane Weems Curator of American Decorative Arts and Sculpture
Museum of Fine Arts, Boston

Acknowledgments

Thanks are owed to so many for so long that I am glad for the opportunity at last to record my many debts. The late Arthur Barnes, teacher and mentor, was also an inspiration. His achievements in his hobbies of woodworking, pewter, and photography, all practiced in his retirement after a distinguished business career, no doubt contributed to the length of his life that reached ninety-four years. Daniel Fairchild and Edwin Morgan of the Fram Corporation gave encouragement and special help in acquiring the basic, major tools for the craft. Daniel Hingston, a neighbor and authority on antiques, has been a ready reference for knowledge of old pewter, and a warm and supportive friend. Ruth Burt, a leader and guardian of standards in the League of New Hampshire Craftsmen, gave much friendly advice and patient help as I struggled to master the finishing processes required in the craft, and rejoiced with me when they were achieved.

Apprentices, some of whom lived with us during the summer before our retirement brought us to New Hampshire year round, have been special to us through the years. Some served for several years and were like family, and have continued as special friends, visiting to see what is new in both the product and machinery. I have devoted a chapter to some special memories about them, though to tell their complete story would fill a small book.

Customers, many visiting and often bringing friends year after year, become a community of human sharing that begins with the craft and then ranges far beyond it. Their stories, too many to be told, and their friendship, special in the uniqueness of each, provides a richness we treasure.

Jonathan Fairbanks, whose most recent kindness has been to write the Foreword for this book, has been a continuing inspiration to us to achieve in our time and in our craft, pewter worthy of the best traditions of our early American forebears.

Thanks are given to our publisher, Peter E. Randall, for his wise guidance, and to the copyeditor, Doris Troy, for many helpful suggestions.

Finally, family. Working together in such a variety of ways in the pewter enterprise has been a powerfully bonding experience for us all. Each has made different and special contributions to the endeavor. All have found meaningful rewards in their work. I count the sharing with them in this, as in other things, among the deepest and most meaningful of my experiences in life.

A final special word of thanks goes to Susan, without whose help this book could not have been written. Her wise judgments and critique, and her patient help through all the exacting requirements of manuscript preparation, have been a godsend.

Background and Setting

INTRODUCTION

The call came sometime past midafternoon, during the time of day when, if the work in the pewter shop was going well, I could feel good about it as I glanced at the clock to measure the time left to work. Or, if the day was going badly, the clock could give an early reprieve, or the promise that something of worth might still be wrested from the day. I cannot remember what kind of day it was, only that the call laid down a significant marker in the afternoon of my life.

The caller was an assistant in the curator's office at the Museum of Fine Arts in Boston. "This is not an official call," she told me. "You will get a letter from the director of the museum in a week or so. I just wanted to tell you that the committee met this afternoon and voted unanimously to take your two pieces into the museum's collection." I thanked her quickly. I had known the committee would be meeting sometime during the week, but not when or how I would hear. "We're so pleased in this office that your work was accepted," the assistant continued. "The curator wrote a strong letter in support of that decision. I'm glad to give you the news."

Could I find words to voice the waves of elation I felt? Eight years until the end of the century, and my two pieces would be the first from this century to be added to the pewter collection of one of the finest museums in the nation.

I told Jonathan, our youngest son and my partner. He had driven us to the opening of the juried show in which one of the two pieces had won the prestigious Stevens Metal Award. He had also driven us to the museum the day we met with the curator, Jonathan Fairbanks, to present the pieces for consideration. Now, in the pewter shop, we stood in the midst of lathes on which were partially formed works in progress, smiling and seeking words that would express our joy at this recognition and affirmation.

Long ago I had copied a passage from a favorite psalm, a kind of "mantra" tacked to the wall over a workbench central to our shop. It is one of a number of places where the Scriptures affirm the work of the hands.

> Let the favor of the Lord our God be upon us; and establish Thou the work of our hands upon us; yea, the work of our hands, establish Thou it.

There was someone else to be told the good news from Boston. I hurried down the back stairs of the barn and crossed the walkway to the back door of the wooden ell of our home to find Susan, my partner in marriage for forty-seven years. Again came the struggle to give expression to the feelings about what had occurred. We can speak of a milestone, but that does not tell us what the miles themselves mean: a pinnacle maybe, but one from which to look forward or back? Do we learn more from the heights than from the depths? In Zion National Park, for instance, a visitor views the canyon from the floor, looking up at the massive heights of stone. Bryce Canyon, on the other hand, is viewed from vantage points along a road around the rim, so a visitor looks down into it. Both are impressive; neither is definitive. Is there a vantage point from which to look at important things that happen to us? Do we ever see the way the many parts join to form the whole?

I can name other elements of significant meaning that had been scattered across the threescore and eight years of my life. Personal growth and achievements, family sharing, ministry and teaching, numerous causes for social justice, civil rights, and world peace, writing, and other things had crowded the years.

Born in 1924, I grew up on a diversified farm in Kentucky, attended Berea College, and enlisted in the Navy V-12 officer's training program during World War II, preparing to become a chaplain. The war ended before my training was complete and I remained in Union Theological Seminary in New York City. After graduation, I continued study for a Ph.D. in the philosophy of religion at Columbia University. My doctoral dissertation was published with the title *God, Man and Time.*

My professional career included a small rural parish for eighteen months, a city parish for eleven years, and a final ministry in a large urban parish for twenty-seven years, during the last dozen years of which I held a visiting ecumenical lectureship at the graduate and undergraduate levels in a Catholic college affiliated with the Dominican Order. In all the years of ministry, I was engaged in social action, civil rights, programs for the elderly, hospice, and the various theological transitions taking place during those four decades, and published occasional essays in scholarly journals.

The day after commencement, in 1945, I married Susan Cochran, a Berea College classmate. We both studied at Union and Columbia. During the second pastorate, four sons and a daughter were born. The long third parish tenure provided a settled base for their growing up. And despite the tensions and social upheavals in the sixties and seventies, there was enough love and respect for each other to make it possible to survive the usual tensions and conflicts mixed in with the growing pains. Summers were close

Picture taken before leaving hilltop campground in central Germany in the Autumn of 1970.

and bonding as we worked together on our farm in New Hampshire. Skills that I had learned from my father and others were shared with our children. From the mid-sixties onward, much of our summer activity was devoted to a growing mastery of the craft of pewtermaking. In addition to the excitement of gaining competence in the medium, there was a special joy in sharing the craft with our children as we worked together in the new enterprise. The increasing number of product offerings and the production itself were enhanced as each of us developed special skills that together resembled an informal assembly line. At a time noted for generational tensions and conflicts in the culture at large, our working together daily in the pewter shop was a powerful unifying experience. Watching our family grow and share with each other and with me was one of the most satisfying experiences that I can recall.

The year after Woodstock, the seven of us shared a family safari of more than five months, through ten countries in Europe, traveling in a station wagon, pulling a caravan designed with a tent attachment to be added when we camped. The sabbatical, given by our church, was partially financed by a grant from the Danforth Foundation. It allowed me to study religious groups that engaged the world seeking social change, or that withdrew from the world into monastic settings for contemplation and prayer. My study was to ask what happens to the personal awareness or consciousness of God at these polar opposites of religious group life and personal religious experience. Studying the experiences of others drove me ever deeper into the analysis of my own.

The travel also allowed us to study various national traditions in pewter. We watched a pewterer in Delfshaven casting small porringers in a historic shop that had among its many molds one dating from 1425. We were pleased when we discovered pewter in museums and shops, and purchased a few pieces for our collection.

From the sabbatical until my retirement seventeen years later, the internal dialogue about the two sides of my own religious quest continued with varying degrees of intensity. Much of my life was devoted to the functions of institutional religion, to public issues, human rights, and social justice; and to correct ancient wrongs, seek justice and peace, and to foster healing and understanding among the Catholic, Jewish, and Protestant traditions. Another part of me wanted to pursue a more personal interior journey of spiritual discovery.

Through the years, in a very public ministry, I had found myself intrigued by the Desert Fathers, who lived in the early Christian centuries. They had tried to shut out the world and give their entire attention to God. I recalled the passage in John Donne's meditations in which he confesses how hard it was for him in his private devotions to keep his mind focused on God. A straw under his knee, a fly buzzing about his head, countless distractions intervened; if asked, he could not tell when he had stopped thinking about God or praying to God. I could identify with that, and with kindred problems. Yet the very difficulty made the effort appear more valuable. The pressure of work, the evident needs of the parish and its people left me saying to myself, "Some day," and eventually to add, "Someday, when I retire!"

One part of my life did much to sustain me through all the intense and draining work of those years: the work with my hands, the fragments of time devoted to creative growth in a very special craft. It was there, as real as the dirt and grime that had to be washed from the hands with special soap. It was challenging, with a rich history to inspire and an open future to bring my own designs and creations to reality. It provided the meeting place for art and hard, careful work. It demanded a concentration of the mind and the hands working together. Intuitive moments fostered new designs and sometimes new techniques in their creation.

The call from the museum would, I knew, raise yet again the question that had followed me from my childhood on that Kentucky farm. It was a marker, a vantage point from which to look back and forward, to find again traces of the wonder of the heights and awareness of the depths. The years, like the canyons, had given me not answers but larger questions and the conviction, sometimes, that it was better that way. The wonder and mysteries of the world, even the small world of our own existence, and the lives of those whose existences are intertwined with our own, like the incredibly larger wonders of the Divine that surround and environ all things, are simply too much to know, and far too important not to think about. Life is a strange and wonderful mix of the head, the heart, and the hands—of reflection, feeling, and creating.

This book is about part of the journey, some of the thought, and the craft of pewter, which, for me, so often holds a mirror to the craft of life itself.

NEW HAMPSHIRE SUMMERS

In our family, the end of the academic year and the beginning of the summer could be likened to the opening of a bottle of wine. Pressure built during final exams, term papers, and the last games of spring sports—in our case, lacrosse. Then, pop, the pressure was off, and we could enjoy the fine wine of summer.

We lived in two worlds, and there was a world of difference between the summer and the rest of the year. During the "school year" we lived in Providence, the capital and principal city of Rhode Island, rightly called the Ocean State, with most of its cities on, or near, the coast. Our summer world was in the country, in a small, hilltop village of a dozen homes, a one-room school, a clubhouse, and two churches.

With both parents working and five children in school, our lives were of necessity structured during this time. In summer, however, the pace was often intense, always busy, but generally free in form, and we improvised our schedule to suit the tasks or recreation at hand. In the city there was a large house, a two-car garage, and a lawn to care for. In the country, we had a Colonial brick house with a wooden ell and woodshed attached, a barn, open fields, and a hundred acres of woodlands to tend and manage. Moving from one world to the other required careful orchestration.

We gathered our gear, each responsible for the special belongings needed for summer in the country, loaded our utility trailer and the station wagon that would pull it, then traveled the 135 miles to the farm in Hillsborough Centre, New Hampshire.

The duties of opening, airing, and connecting became rituals in which each of us had a special responsibility. Water and electricity must be turned on; the water system, drained during the freezing months, would now have all valves closed, and we had to prime and start the pumps. Pipes throughout the system needed to be checked for breaks that could occur if water had remained in a pipe and frozen over the winter. Then, when the pump was working well, one outdoor faucet was allowed to run until rust and sediment were flushed from the system and the water came clear.

Overnight trips to the country in spring provided a chance to rake leaves, gather the limbs and sticks broken and blown from trees, and uncover the perennial beds. During the final weeks of May, when pressure of work kept us in Providence, the grass would grow uncut in the country. We owned two kinds of mowers, one for the fields, another for the lawns. But the field mower had to be called into duty to cut the tall grass on the lawns for a first mowing. We then removed the cuttings and mowed the lawns again.

Storm windows had to be taken down and stored in the loft of the barn, and screens installed. The garden would be turned with the rotary plow on the Gravely tractor, then rototilled smooth before we planted our vegetables. We spent rainy days indoors, organizing the barn or restacking the wood in the woodshed to make it accessible to the door leading into the kitchen.

The woodshed, more than a hundred years old, stores two sizes of wood: larger for the fireplace, shorter and smaller for the kitchen range and the Franklin stoves. A shingle bin in one corner of the woodshed holds kindling. Green wood, freshly cut and split, is stacked in the shed along the west wall, dries and cures before it is restacked on the east side, along the walkway leading to the kitchen. Normally, no wood is burned until it has cured for two years.

Above the woodshed is a second floor. Half is used for storage and the other is a closed room that we called from the beginning the "boys' dorm." Four single beds and a desk and chair crowded it a bit but it suited them. "Their" music could be played at their volume and their hours without infringing on their parents' space or sensibilities.

From the woodshed there's a short hallway and then you're into the kitchen, and here, more than any other place on the farm, we live with the legacy of the past. The "Quaker Social" woodstove is a marvel of early engineering, with its broad top cooking surface, the firebox to the left, the oven in the center, and water reservoir on the right. The stove pipe rises and bends to enter the brick chimney, with a damper to control the flow of air and therefore the rate of burn and heat level. Beside the woodstove is the wood box, refilled as necessary from the woodshed only a few steps away.

The kitchen contains a remnant of early technology with its copper Athol pump and soapstone sink. Water during the colonial period was from a stream, a spring, a cistern, or a well. The stream and spring could be a problem in winter. The cistern, a reservoir created to collect rainwater, could have maintenance problems and provided water that was not always fresh. A well was the preferred source. On our screened-in porch is a well from the earliest days, reportedly never to have gone dry. It was used by the one-room school nearby, from which students were sent with a bucket to fetch fresh water. It is fifteen feet deep, with three to six feet of fresh water always available. The water could be lifted by a bucket on a rope, or pumped up and into the kitchen with the Athol pump.

To work, the pump has to be primed; that is, enough water is poured in at the top while someone works the handle. This creates a vacuum and fills the pipe with water from the well. Then water will flow out of the spout and you can pump as much as needed. In winter, we must save enough water at night for the next priming, and let the water run down, or flow back down the pipe into the well to keep the pipe from freezing. During the summer, we can keep the prime overnight. Anyone can walk by, pump the handle a few times, and draw up fresh water to drink from the copper cup we keep hanging on the wall behind the pump. We may marvel at the ingenuity of the colonial folk, and while it is easy to understand how the mechanism operates, it is not always easy to keep it working. Eventually, we learned the necessary fine-tuning.

The kitchen, connected to the dining room, forms the oldest part of the house, dating from c1770. The dining room, with its post-and-beam frame and large summer beam, the fireplace, paneling, and Indian shutters on the windows, suggests stories from the past. That original building was a dwelling for about forty-five years, until a brick house in the Georgian style was added across one end of it in 1815. The old and new are attached in such a way that the original front door is the connecting door into the back hall of the "Brick House," as it is known locally.

The backdrop to the house is the one barn remaining from the days when it was a working farm with two large barns, a freestanding toolshed, and an attached shed. Our barn, nearly 200 years old, is now the home of the pewter shop. It has many reminders of the old days when it was part of the working farm. The stanchions were still in place with oak bars that held the cow's head during milking. The large sliding doors and center aisle of the barn allowed the hay wagons to roll in and be unloaded into the loft on either side for the cattle's winter food.

Reminders of older times are everywhere. Ox yokes hang on walls, and scythes with long blades hang over beams. A well-worn grindstone built on a frame allowed the farmer to sit and turn the stone with a foot pedal, leaving both hands free to hold the blade. The grindstone is near the south end of the center nave of the barn, where, when the double doors are swung out in summer, a near view of the garden and fields is backed up by a view of Crotched Mountain to the south and the peaks of Gibson and Riley to the southwest. We could imagine the farmer of old sharpening a blade and glancing out at the fields where the scythe would be used, or watch the birds flying in and out of the garden.

The tools for shoeing horses are still there. I can look at or handle those tools and remember scenes from my childhood, when my father shoed both the riding and work horses on our farm. I could hold the shoes from the box, look at the special nails, and recall my anxiety as I saw nails like these being driven into our horses' hooves.

On one beam of the west loft are hung two large augers, their bits the size of the holes made in the beams of the barn for pegging them together. Like other barns made two centuries ago, the lengthwise frame of this post-and-beam construction had been cut, fitted, and pegged together on the ground, and then on barn-raising day, when friends and neighbors gathered to help, these were lifted, joined, and held by the cross beams that had been precut to size for this final joining. To identify the pieces to be mated, circles and slashes were cut into the wooden beams at the joints. They remain today, showing how the barn builders were guided in the assembly of the many beams. Among the items remaining in the barn I found the tool used to make those symbols.

We learn of other times and other people by studying and trying to use their tools. In the loft of the barn we found a low, ruggedly built stone boat, used in early times when clearing fields. On it large stones were carried to stone walls or to cairns, sometimes piled on large boulders that could not be moved. Lacking oxen, we managed to use it to good effect on a number of occasions by pulling it with our Jeep.

Another ancient contrivance puzzled us until an elderly farmer explained its use. It is a tripod of strong hemlock poles, bolted together at the top with a hook hanging below when it is set up. "You'll find a lifting device," said the farmer, "some kind of ratchet, and a strong chain. It was used for pulling stumps or lifting large rocks out of the ground so they could be dragged off with the stone boat." The wisdom was timely. We had a diseased cherry tree by the corner of our terrace that the forester had told us to cut down and burn, adding that we should dig out the roots and burn them as well.

It was not easy, or quick. We dug around the large taproot as far as we could, fitted the chain, and arranged the tripod above with the ratchet. With each pull of the long lever, we lifted by one length of the chain, or one inch. The chain tightened, slipped a little, then took hold and the root began to move. Inch by slow inch, we brought the root above ground and carefully carried it to the pyre we had built for the wood of the diseased tree.

A bonus from that summer remains in our possession today. An elderly guest brought her easel and oils. Sitting on our terrace, she painted a scene with the tripod in the foreground, the stone walls and hills in the background. It is a pleasing reminder of the last summer that the tripod was used before we returned it to its place in the rafters of the barn.

The woods were another source of wonder and adventure. A previous owner had made and marked trails to special places. There was an older trail wide enough for a horse-drawn cart, going down to the ruins of a sap house where maple sugaring had been done. The woods around still contained large maples that years before would have been tapped in early spring. The rusted remains of the firebox, with RUTLAND, VERMONT stamped on it, were surrounded by the ruins of walls that once enclosed the operation. The years had rotted the wood and rusted the iron. The heavy fall of leaves had turned to soil, and we could see the hand of nature steadily erasing these traces of earlier human activity to reclaim the wildness of the woods.

Beyond the sap house was a treasure that we all enjoyed, but one that became special to the children. It was called Battleship Rock for good reason. A huge boulder, fractured in such a way that it resembles the oncoming prow of a battleship, had been skidded into place during the glacier age, with several small boulders on either side like waves rolling aside as the prow cuts through the water. The "battleship" has sheer walls more than a dozen feet high, and a flat top. Throwing a rope over the top, we could scale the walls. When the rope was pulled up, the fortress was secure from pirates and other marauders. The games were limited only be a failure of imagination.

Another trail wound deeper and downward toward the north corner of the woods, where a small natural marsh had been enlarged over the years by a succession of beaver families. Evidence of their work, old and new, was everywhere. Their engineering in wood and mud had dammed a small stream. Then, as the marsh spread, they built larger dams until there was enough water to build a "fortress" home of sticks protected on all sides by water. Approaching silently, we might find them working and watch a while. If one became aware and troubled by our presence, it would slap its broad tail on the water as a warning to the others, then dive out of sight and swim to the underwater entrance and the safety of the den.

Encounters in the woods are various: some creatures are seen frequently and without surprise; others are met so seldom that their sightings are reported and shared with family and friends. "You won't believe what I saw," we'd say. It might be a porcupine ambling along in his armor of quills, or in a tree munching on leaves; wild turkeys, almost never seen singly; deer, singly or in pairs or groups, sometimes spotted when flushed out of a secluded resting place; gray and red squirrels, the latter ready to chatter their disapproval of someone's presence in their domain. Moose, always larger than we expect them to be, are occasionally seen at the edge of the woods or crossing a pasture in their continual ranging over their wide territory; perhaps we'd spot the tracks of bear, though never in our experience was there an actual encounter. The fox, in field or forest, is always hunting birds and rodents, often making the same rounds on a daily trip; woodchucks, on the edges of woods, in the fields, or under rock piles, forage for clover and grass, or our garden in season. Raccoons, with fur rings around their bushy tail, are seen at dusk or dawn, the limits of their nocturnal ventures. Coyotes, sometimes seen at the edge of the woods, peering into the fields or meadows. Singly and together, the creatures form a society of nature of which we rejoice to be a part.

Birds are a special joy, with daily reminders of their presence providing unlimited possibilities for learning. Like our human neighbors, some are year-rounders; others go south, or far south, for winter. Watching their staging up for the journey in the fall, and their appearances as the spring progresses, imparts a measure of the passage of the seasons. We eagerly anticipate the bluebird's arrival in spring. For years, Susan offered a cash reward to the children for the first confirmed sighting. With a half-dozen special boxes ready for them, the daily watch would then begin, to see whether a pair would settle, then defend their holding in the inevitable contest with tree swallows. These rogues arrived soon after in much greater numbers than the bluebirds and harassed them incessantly, seeking to drive them away.

Seasonal visits occur when migrating Canada geese alight on our pond for a brief respite on their journey north or south. They are large birds for a small pond; the wonder is in their taking off, that they can be airborne in so short a distance. The landing of the great blue heron is the most spectacular—circling the pond like a large transport plane with its flaps down, slowing as it comes to rest on the dam at the south end of the pond, then taking its short walk on stiltlike legs into the shallows of the water to fish for trout or, rarely, to catch a frog.

If our primary goal in summer was a break from demanding schedules and to achieve physical and spiritual renewal, much of the pace and form of our summers was dictated by the needs of the place itself. Lawn care was important, but the fields made their claims on us as well. There was mowing to be done and the edges had to be cleared of bushes trying to work their way into all the fields from the stone walls outward. Tall plants like goldenrod, St.-John's-wort and meadowsweet were brought low by the long, curving blade of the scythe. I had learned how to use a scythe back on the Kentucky farm, and taught my children as my father had taught me. "Keep the blade low and level and cut through at a low angle, taking only an inch or so at a swing." The instinct is to swing down, at ninety degrees to the cut, and the result is hard work with practically nothing to show for it. Done properly, though, much is accomplished for the effort spent.

Once, early in our New Hampshire experience, I saw an elderly neighbor scything the tall grass in his blueberry patch midmorning on a sunny day and stopped for a brief visit. "Been doin' it for years," he said, wiping the perspiration from his forehead with a faded blue bandanna. "You got to know how. And you got to keep the blade sharp." Whereupon he stood the scythe straight up on its handle, took a whetstone from his back pocket, and began whipping it back and forth along the blade as deftly as a chef putting a fine edge on his carving knife.

From early June until the end of July, nature sends up its plants at full throttle; just keeping up is a constant contest. Once I wrote a poem called *July*; part of it describes the struggle.

The baking earth-smell
dries in the nostrils
while water grows and runs
on face and back;
glistens, like the blade
long curving through
the falling hay
as the scythe swings.

Slow rhythm; severed stems,
soldiers in line, lying straight,
graceful in death;
the Appomattox growing
in circles 'round my feet.
Each year the war is waged again:
July is battle time.

There is mowing inside the yards, too, and Susan's constant attention is needed to tend the large perennial beds; some plants have been there for half a century or even longer: peonies, clumps of lemon lilies, tiger lilies, and some old roses, not to mention the ancient lilac bushes.

August comes with fewer rains and much more sun. Growth slows and mowing is spaced at longer intervals. The vegetable garden and flowers need watering. The woods are cool and more free of blackflies and mosquitoes, so this is the time for clearing any encroachments on the trails. Trees, especially the apple trees, need care—cutting out deadwood and pruning suckers. Grapevines must have protection from the Japanese beetles that cluster on them. These pests also like the ampelopsis vines climbing the house, and taller flowers in the perennial beds. We avoid pesticide sprays, so it takes time to capture the beetles by brushing them off the leaves into a can of water.

August and the autumn months are for projects. A new house requires maintenance; an old house requires that, plus thoughtful and loving care. In New Hampshire, with the onset of long and sometimes severe winters, the owner develops the habit of getting ready for the onslaught by checking everything from windows to walkways and repairing what needs mending, to avoid having to do repairs later in the cold and snow.

On occasion throughout summer and fall there comes a day so special in its weather that it would be wasted if not used for climbing a mountain. We called them "High Posted" days, a term we got from an elderly New England friend who had used it for decades and was not sure where the expression came from or just what it meant. We wondered: Because it was a cloudless, clear, bright day, perhaps the sky seemed higher, like the raised canopy over a four-poster bed favored by the affluent in colonial days.

The day was usually recognized very early and preparations began right away. As breakfast was readied, lunches would be packed, and gear assembled. Discussion then began about "which mountain." For us the options were Kearsarge, Monadnock, and Lovewell. Of the three, Lovewell is not in a state

The stairsteps: Raymond, Susan, Cyrus, Mark, Christopher, Lauren and Jonathan. "Bunky," our white labrador, is part of the family.

park, did not have a year-round access road, had a trail that was tended by volunteers, and was, therefore, far less utilized. In some way that increased its attractiveness.

Monadnock became, after a time, the mountain of choice for a reason that turned on its line-of-sight connection to the farm. I was staying home on a climbing day, and asked what time the family expected to get to the summit. Noon, was the confident answer. I told them to expect to see me flashing a mirror starting at noon at intervals for half an hour while I was having lunch. Could you see it at thirty-five miles? We would find out.

At noon, I balanced a large circular mirror on the wooden arms of a terrace chair. To target the mountaintop, I selected a dark cluster of tall pines two hundred yards away and directly in line with the summit. Catching the sun and beaming the spot on those trees, it was possible to line it up accurately. Then I would repeatedly raise the spot to flash the mountaintop and then lower it to check my alignment.

It worked. The family reached the summit at five after twelve to find a group of people studying the light flashes and discussing whether it could be someone signaling for help or trying to send a message. "That's our dad," said our kids and then explained the experiment. After the first success, it became a ritual for future climbs.

In New Hampshire summers, we found wonderment at three levels: things close at hand, the background distances, and the far reaches of the incredible star-filled nights. Things close might be planting seeds in spring or setting out onion shoots; having breakfast on the terrace and watching the birds come from the mulberry tree to the birdbath; or lying on my stomach looking through the barrel lens of my camera at the petals of a flower inches away and seeing them magnified as I focused, knowing that when the slide was projected, it would fill an entire screen. The lilacs and apple blossoms in spring; the clover, daisies, and devil's paintbrush all across the meadow in summer; the fruits of trees and garden in autumn; the incredible colors of fall; the icicles on the eaves and the juncos at the bird feeder in winter: Was it not something like this that prompted the writer of Genesis to exclaim that "God saw everything that He had made, and behold, it was very good"?

Then there are the background distances. I look up from my work in a field and see the rim of trees, growing right up to the stone wall that borders the field. If I look for a minute and focus on what I'm seeing, new things will appear—birds and wildlife. Sometimes a wild creature will be looking back at me from the perimeter—a fox on a boulder beside the stone wall, a hawk in a treetop, an owl sitting on a dead branch, its body still, head rotating left and right.

The longer background distances are the hills that ring us. They all have names, and one of them, Gibson, recalling an early settler, is in our line of sight midway between Monadnock and Crotched. Living on a hill means that we see more hills around than does the valley dweller. Between our terrace and Monadnock I can count five ranges of hills.

Hills and mountains have always been celebrated. Religions around the world have built holy places on the heights. If the ring of hills is the view in between, then the view from the mountaintop, in letting us see all around and far away, becomes the bridge to the farthest view of all, the stars at night.

From very early in our New Hampshire experience, the stars and planets became an active and vital part of our environment. Years ago we had a

Our dining room, dating from 1770s with table of our pewter and older pieces on the mantel.

"children's telescope," made by the company that made the erector sets, which had been our children's first introduction to building with girders, nuts, and bolts. That little 'scope could, if properly positioned, manage to see two, sometimes three, of the moons of Jupiter. Its field of vision was small, which created two problems: It was difficult to find the faraway planet, and the rotation of the earth would rather quickly take it out of the picture.

A friend, learning of our interest in the heavens, gave us an Astroscan, made by the Edmund Co. A reflector telescope, it gives a powerful view of the moon, four of the moons of Jupiter, and a feeling of "approach" as you look at stars like Antares, the red star in Scorpio; it's as if you had journeyed partway there and were getting a better look.

I had taken a college astronomy course, and still possess the term paper that I wrote and illustrated on the major constellations and their mythological stories. I taught these to our children as we looked at the stars; viewing the stars as a family is a regular part of our being together. When there are meteor showers predicted, we spread blankets on the lawn, settle ourselves to watch, and soon the exclamations begin: "There!" "See that?" "Wow!"

When the children have guests, they often ask me to point out the constellations, which means our standing together in the south yard, close together, as I use the beam of a strong light as a pointer to direct their attention to the constellations in view and the major stars whose names they will already know. The majesty and the magnitude of the heavens enhance the wonder of the world and the mystery of creation. Perhaps, in such times, we resemble the characters in Robert Frost's poem, *The Star Splitter*. One night, when two men have looked at the heavens through a telescope, one of them, the narrator of the poem, sums up the meaning of their experience with the line, "and said some of the wisest things we ever said."

Beginning in the mid-1960s and continuing to the present, summers in New Hampshire have had an increasingly intense focus on the craft of pewter and on the development of Gibson Pewter, a cottage industry that has grown in output and in reputation. From 1967 until 1988, it was primarily a summer operation. Then Susan and I retired and moved permanently to Hillsborough Centre, at which point the pewter shop was open year-round. In 1991, Jonathan and his wife, Camille, moved to New Hampshire. Of all the Gibson siblings, Jonathan spent the greatest number of summers in the shop. Now he joined me on a part-time basis. In 1993, a partnership was formed, and since then, Jonathan has given full time and effort to the development of the business. It remains a cottage industry. As the curator of the London Guild, in an early letter, noted about us, "You resemble the family firms existing in the London area in the 1700s."

Thus, we are in New Hampshire year-round, no longer just the summers. We have full exposure to the beauty and rigors of New Hampshire winters. The pewter shop in the barn is snugly insulated and heated. Work continues, and visitors come throughout the year. We are blessed with the changing beauty of the seasons as we experience the joy and challenge of the craft. *Tales from the Pewter Shop* seeks to share both with you.

SUNAPEE I — AND WEAVING

In the early 1960s, we acquired a sixty-acre tree farm in Warner, New Hampshire, which placed us in easy visiting distance of one of the oldest and largest annual craft fairs in the country. Our five children ranged from eleven to three years of age when we attended the Sunapee Craftsmen's Fair for the first time. We liked it, and it became a yearly outing.

Situated on the gentle incline of a long sloping area at the foot of the ski slopes of Mt. Sunapee State Park, with acres of parking, the ski lodge, and dozens of large tents, the facilities were ideal. The New Hampshire League of Craftsmen sponsored this nine-day event as a service to its members and as a major source of income for its yearlong programs. The dates were always the first two weekends in August and the weekdays between, generally a season of fair, warm weather and a time when many vacationers were in the area.

All the crafts were represented, some of them with several individuals doing their own variations and designs in wood, pottery, leather, jewelry, fiber and metal. A hundred or more booths showed the work in creative displays. One large central area was set aside for demonstrations, from blacksmithing to totem-pole carving, from spinning yarn and weaving to woodcarving, pewter spinning, hand forming in clay, and throwing pots

Joe Tucker, the blacksmith, a wiry, wizened, wisp of a man with bright blue eyes, gave playful descriptions of his work, keeping us riveted - the children in particular - as he placed a large spike in the fire, started the bellows, moved the large nail to the hottest part of the fire, then took it out, holding the glowing yellow-orange piece in his tongs, placed it across the horn of his anvil, and hammered it into the shape of a coiled snake. There would be a great hiss when he doused it in a bucket of water, and if he handed it to you for your inspection, you would marvel both at how he had turned the long, straight spike into the coiled snake and how something that had so recently been red hot was now so cool in your hand. Joe Tucker remains a vivid memory for the seven of us, and though he has been succeeded by a series of able blacksmiths over the years since his death, his is the only blacksmith's name that comes quickly to mind.

Susan and I had a favorite who became a friend and correspondent with whom we stayed in touch, through our annual family Christmas letter, for many years. Thelma Brackett was a librarian at the University of New Hampshire, and a longtime and distinguished weaver who practiced all aspects of her craft, from carding and spinning, to dyeing and weaving. We visited her studio in Durham and marveled at the finished work, as well as the incredible store of yarns she had spun and dyed in readiness for future projects. She demonstrated spinning on an old, perfectly balanced wheel and looked as if she had just stepped out of a picture from colonial times.

I had a particular reason to value this friendship. At Berea College, where students engage in a work program to help earn their tuition, I had spent two semesters under the guidance of a Swedish weaver who had come to the United States for an international craft exposition and found it unsafe to return home because of World War II. I was assigned a large four-posted loom with a hanging beater and throw shuttle. I wove a strong homespun woolen cloth that required a firm hand on the beater and a quick wrist in throwing the shuttle, and the coordination and rhythm that could keep a continuous motion. The skills learned there lay dormant for two decades, until they were revived in New Hampshire.

I met Miss Helen Barnes at her home in Lowell, Massachusetts, after conducting the funeral of her brother Hammond in Providence and the committal in the family plot in Lowell. While there, we discovered that we were summer neighbors in New Hampshire, and agreed that we would visit when we were in Warner and she in Hillsborough Centre. It was the beginning of a wonderful friendship that deepened through the remaining years of her life.

When I went to see her in Hillsborough Centre, a hilltop village that is part of the Historical Register and in which the thirteen houses date from just before or after 1800, she gave me a tour of her house and barn. In the barn I noticed a number of large oak beams standing in the corner of the loft and asked about them. Helen said they were the parts of a large blanket loom; she thought the loom might be as much as two hundred years old and did not know when it had last been set up or used. It reminded me of my Berea experience, and when I told Helen about having woven while in college, she suggested that when we moved up for our summer vacation, I take the loom to Warner and use it for the season. When summer came and we moved to Warner, I kept the U-Haul trailer an extra day, went to Hillsborough Centre with son Mark as helper and brought back the pieces of the loom to Warner. Pulling it in the trailer reminded me that this loom may well have had many journeys before. It was the practice in colonial times for weavers to take their loom to a village, where they would set up in a room large enough for their work. They were housed and fed by the families of the village, and spent as long as was necessary to weave the accumulated yarns the village women had spun on their spinning wheels. The loom would have been taken apart and pulled in a cart as the weaver went from one village to the next. The loom was pegged together and I had found a very old wooden measure holding the pegs. Doubtless that had belonged to the weaver and was used when carting the loom to its next temporary stopping place.

The children helped me carry the pieces of the loom into the large screened-in porch at Warner. Matching the pieces was not easy, though Cyrus, eleven, who would one day become a builder of post-and-beam houses, and Mark, nine, who would one day be an engineer, were a great help. After a few false starts, we decided to put together the sides, then fit the crossbeams. We figured out that some markings incised in the wood were a code telling the proper matching at each corner. After that discovery, it came together nicely. A wooden mallet set the hardwood pegs firmly and stabilized the frame.

It was the simplest of looms: two harnesses, two heddle bars, two foot pedals. The reeds were made of split bamboo, a few of which were broken. The heddle bars did not have wire guides for the threads but, rather, string tied with loops, a testimony to the age of the loom. The strings were rotting. On the hanging beater there were no mechanisms for a throw shuttle, another mark of its age. The loom had been used by a weaver who leaned forward from his seat at the edge of the frame, spread the warp with a foot peddle, then pushed through by hand a long stick around which he had wrapped, end to end, the yarn he was weaving. The width of the cloth could have been a maximum of forty-two inches. It would have taken quite a reach to put the long stick through from one side, reverse the pedals, beat the warp, then enter the stick from the other side. That would have been slow work indeed. With two heddle bars, the design would have been limited to simple over-under weaving. I decided to update the loom by a hundred years. I would add two pedals and heddle bars, wire guides for the threads, putting in lams for design possibilities, and add a throw shuttle like the one I had had on the loom in Berea.

While I was assembling the parts, I called a friend who was president of a large knitting mill, looking for yarns for weaving. I welcomed the two large boxes that were dropped off at my house in Providence the following day, containing enough yarn to keep me busy more than a summer. They were end-of-run leftovers from the mill and a great boost to my project.

When the parts came and were added to the loom, I set up a trial run by preparing a twelve-foot warp and threading it through the dents in the reed to spread the threads properly as the warp was rolled onto the eight-inch-diameter roller at the back of the loom. Then I pulled the individual threads through the wire heddles and the dent and anchored them with equal pressure at the front of the loom so that, as I wove the cloth, it could be advanced and rolled onto a beam at the front of the loom. I adjusted the tension on the warp, tried the treadles to see if the warp would separate, practiced throwing the shuttle, and adjusted the release of the thread on the bobbin inside it. When all was in balance, I was ready to weave.

It is said that you can't unlearn how to ride a bicycle. Once you know how, the knowledge of how it is done resides in your reflexes, which come quickly to life when you try your skills after a long absence from the practice. I wondered how it would be with the coordination between the throw shuttle and the beater, a rhythmic alternation between the hands as you laid down the thread and the other "beat" it firmly against the growing cloth being made, strand by strand. The feet were coordinated in the action, pressing first one treadle, then the other, to spread the warp for the shuttle to race through.

I spent two days on the trial or training warp, using samples of most of the yarns my friend had provided, studying their colors and their sturdiness. What was created by those random selections of threads, each used for at least one whole bobbin, was something akin to Joseph's coat of many colors in the biblical story of his brothers' treachery. While I wove that practice piece, I was planning the big project for the summer. It was a blanket loom, so I would make blankets. I would weave one for each of our children. I also chose the yarn for the project, a light blue mohair with an acrylic fiber core for strength. It would be harder to comb and beat, and more difficult to spread with the foot treadles, but it was the color and strength that I wanted.

The remainder of the vacation was given, in bits and pieces, to preparing for and weaving six blankets, one each for the children and another for the church bazaar to be held in the fall. Between times, we worked in the woods, climbed mountains, swam in the river below the covered bridge at the foot of our hill, and entertained "Aunt Helen," who was becoming an important part of our family.

The most noteworthy memory of that summer's weaving was the challenge I put to myself as I finished the third blanket. I wondered how much I could do in a day if I did nothing but weave. Actually, the question formed itself more as a challenge. Could I weave a blanket in one day? I decided to try on a clear, bright Sunday in August.

After a good breakfast, I began work and kept at it steadily for the morning. I did not rush, and I was especially concerned to preserve the power in the beating arm and shoulder, the right one in my case, as being left-handed I used the left hand for the throw shuttle. During the afternoon I worked in half-hour runs with a short break between to walk around and loosen my shoulder muscles. By supper it appeared that I would complete the blanket by eight or nine o'clock. I ate a light meal, had a welcomed massage of my back and shoulders, then finished the blanket. It was eight-thirty when I got up from the loom, every muscle thoroughly fatigued, shoulders and arms giving me signals of how sore they would be the next day.

That experience made me wonder what it was like so long ago, when the weaver worked all day, every day, as long as the light lasted. What were the yarns like that the women had spun on their spinning wheels? Did they break easily? The experiment made our visits to the Sunapee Craftmen's Fair more meaningful to me as I watched Thelma Brackett at work with her spinning wheel and viewed the work of other weavers. I know that visiting the fair gave significant impetus to my interest in, and the desire to pursue, a craft. At that time it was weaving; it would become, in a very few years, pewter. In neither case would it occur to me that one day my son and I would be demonstrating there for nine full days with an aggregate attendance of more than forty-five thousand visitors.

When we returned to Providence and prepared for the church fair, a *Providence Journal* reporter came to our house to interview me about the blanket that would be sold at the fair. Seven-year-old Christopher was home with a cold, so he sat on the couch, the blanket carefully draped about his shoulders, for the large picture that appeared with the article.

The next, and final, project with the loom came after the loom went back to Hillsborough Centre, when that lovely place became our home. So close had we become with Aunt Helen, and so like family, that she proposed we be given the first option to acquire her place when she died. Her will would set terms that would make it possible for us to make the transition. We had all recognized that the house at Warner would not be a good place for us in retirement. Clearly, the house in Hillsborough Centre would. Helen, who was seventy-six, said it would give her great pleasure to know that we would be there, and that our children would grow up there. After her death, brought about by a fast-moving cancer, we spent our first summer in Hillsborough Centre in 1966.

The loom had been upgraded with lams so that I could do complex patterns, and it was set up on the first floor of the barn. I designed drapes for the four living room windows and wove eight drapes, using the Chariot Wheel design for the border, a pattern that requires ninety-six threads to complete. Lauren sat beside me on the seat of the loom, read the pattern, and marked the place in the progress if a string broke, then she picked it up, after the repair, and guided me through the rest of the pattern.

It proved to be the final project on the loom. My apprenticeship with Helen's brother Arthur would begin in the fall. Another summer would find the loom moved back into the loft of the barn, and the first tools moved into the bay that would become the forming or spinning area of the pewter shop.

With that transition, trips to the Sunapee Fair would find me continuing to look at and admire the work of the weavers, but focusing on a succession of pewterers. Most memorable would be Lindsey Shuford and Fred Pulsifer, two very different—but very accomplished—craftsmen.

TEACHER AND MENTOR

Looking back at the life-changing moments and events in my life, I am amazed at how often they came upon me without warning, and in ways totally unforeseen. It never occurred to me to be a pewterer or, for that matter, even to consider pewter as a craft of interest, until I met Arthur Bradley Barnes, who became my teacher and mentor. I became acquainted with the craft through him, and without him that part of my life would never have unfolded.

Arthur lived in Norwich, Connecticut, an hour's drive from our home in Rhode Island. I met him first after conducting the funeral of his brother, Hammond, a member of my parish in Providence. I met him again after the death of his sister, Helen. This time, when I visited him in Norwich, the pewter saga began.

I quickly discovered that this retired industrialist was a superb craftsman and, despite his Yankee dignity and reserve, a warm human being. He worked in wood and metal. In wood, there were inlaid pieces that were simply stunning. He also made a variety of carefully crafted works in pewter. When I commented on the pewter, he said, "Yes, I spin it." For me, spinning suggested fiber, and the image that came to mind was the flax wheel and much larger spinning wheels I had seen at craft demonstrations. In response to my confusion, he took me to his basement, where I was astonished at the complexity and organization of his workshop. Every inch of floor space, and every wall, had been set up to hold a wide array of power and hand tools, workbenches, and specialized machinery.

For the first time, I saw the spinning of metal. He placed a pewter disk

Arthur Barnes at the buffing wheel in his shop.

against a form on the headstock or power side of the lathe, held it in place by a following block centered on the tailstock, and tightened until the pewter could turn, remaining centered as it rotated more than two thousand times a minute. In front of the spinning metal was a cross bar or tool rest with holes in it, allowing him to move an anchor pin along the cross bar as he formed the metal into the shape of the form, or chuck, he had selected. He placed a wooden tool over the cross bar, against the anchor pin, and with the leverage this provided, he stroked the fast-turning metal from the center outward.

I watched transfixed as the metal began to "move." In a matter of minutes he had transformed the flat, circular disk into a small bowl. It was one of the most exciting craft moments I had ever experienced. I heard myself saying, "I'd love to be able to do that!" Arthur turned to me. "I'd like to teach you," he said, "and pass it along to someone before I die." The offer was sincere, and my response immediate.

Arthur was seventy-four. Pewter was a hobby he had taken up after retirement from a business career. He had learned what he knew from Frances Felton, a world-famous teacher and an inspiration and moving force in the craft renascence following World War II.

So began a friendship that lasted until Arthur's death twenty years later. For the first few years, I commuted to my teacher and mentor two evenings a month, going late Sunday afternoon, after my clerical duties were finished for the day. We would have a sandwich supper, then work in his shop until eleven, so that I arrived home after midnight—tired, but happy at what I was learning.

Arthur was a remarkable teacher: relaxed, steady, encouraging. He was warm in his praise, and patient when things did not go well. He had said at the beginning, "We'll see if you can do it." Two months later, as we were completing a lesson, he said, "You're going to be all right." He said it matter-of-factly. I did not understand the meaning of those two comments at the time, and that is perhaps why I remembered them. It was years later that I realized from experience what he meant. The knowledge came in watching others try to learn the craft. Not everyone can do it. Some learn quickly, others learn slowly; some just can't get it at all. There is a sensitivity to the metal that must be understood by both the head and the hands before mastery can be achieved.

It reminded me of a comment by my father as we worked with animals on the bluegrass farm in Kentucky: "Not everyone can train horses." That seemed perfectly reasonable to someone who had grown up with horses. You had to understand, or be sensitive to, what was happening with the animal, and whatever the horse's response was to what was being asked or required. It was another matter when it was not a horse but, rather, metal. Still, I could not deny the truth of it. I have often thought, and sometime said, to the perplexity of my listeners, "The metal is often my teacher."

After one or two sessions learning the rudiments of spinning, Arthur set me upon a series of projects that would introduce me to procedures from which I would learn the skills I needed. He had a natural way of explaining things, and would watch me work and make suggestions. He never took a tool out of my hands to show me a technique, but would coach my movements as I worked, pointing out variations on what I was doing that were invariably helpful.

One of the wisest instructions he gave mystified me at first: "Try to imagine what the metal is feeling." No other admonition has proved as helpful, so often, as that simple direction, especially in forming the pewter in the spinning process. An abrupt motion with the spinning tool can cause a ripple, or even a tear that destroys the piece. Uneven pressure will leave one part thin and another part thicker. The craftsman is in touch with the metal as it turns, just as the potter's hands are on the revolving clay as the piece takes shape. If you watch a master spinner at work, the impression grows that the master and the metal are working together. The pewter seems to cooperate in the formation of the shape it is destined to take on.

I did not know it then, but I was to learn with the years of growing competence that part of the knowledge would reside in the hands rather than the head. If you were to heed Arthur's advice about sensing what was "happening in the metal," you'd realize that the hands are always the most direct connection with the metal and are the first to know what is happening with it. Of the individuals I have sought to teach the spinning craft, the dividing line between those who learned and those who have had difficulty is simply this: The successful ones appeared to have a form of "knowledge" in the hands. Arthur may well have seen or sensed such a development in me that prompted his judgment that I would be "all right."

My first project was to make a simple six-inch plate. The metal was moved only a little, as far as the rim of the plate is raised from the table. But even this simple project had its pitfalls. The curve of the booge—the short bend in the metal between the bottom and the inner edge of the flat rim—needed to be a steady curve with no variations in the bend. The flat rim had to be truly flat, with no waves in it. Bringing the flat disk around that simple curve and laying it down smoothly and evenly so that it is flat requires a steadiness of touch and pressure, or control from the hands, that a novice learns only with experience, by seeing small failures in forming a steady curve or smooth rim, and improving on the next attempt.

My second project was a small bowl. From one of many chucks that Arthur had turned out of rock maple—a hard wood, with almost no grain to distort the surface of the metal that would be pressed against it—I selected a chuck, or spinning form, over which it would be shaped. Here the lesson was twofold: to move the metal in a continuous curve up the side of the bowl, and to roll the edge at the top to form a strong rim. The long curve—or booge—was like an extension of the small curve done on the plate, which meant that the control of the line was the lesson to be learned. The rolled edge is a maneuver that requires rather precisely applied pressure in a continuous motion that will make the metal roll back upon itself. Neither the

The first group picture of our pewter was made into a postcard. The porringer and centerpiece vase continue to be popular items.

rolled edge nor the curved side of the bowl I produced was the work of a master, but the apprentice that I was felt rewarded that I could have formed them at all.

My third project was a warm-up for a long-term and complex project that was to follow. I was to make a short beaker, not by spinning but by hammering. I would cut out the pewter in the shape of a fan, hammer it over a mandrel—any one of a variety of shapes, over which metal can be formed with a paper, or hard rubber mallet—into the beaker shape, solder the seam, and then fit and solder a bottom onto it. It was a lot of work for a small result, but it was excellent training. Hammering was new to me, and the rubber and paper mallets that are used to bend the pewter sheet around the tapered steel mandrel were more effective than I had expected. Once it was formed, I tied the curved piece with fine, flexible, iron wire. With the joint carefully aligned, I suspended it in air, placed small pieces of solder on the inside of the seam that had been fluxed with a liquid agent to aid the solder to flow into the joint. Then, with some trepidation, I applied the acetylene torch below, moving it back and forth. The flux boiled, and the solder, or at least most of it, flowed into the joint. A pewter circle, slightly larger than the bottom of the beaker, was soldered onto it, and the edge and excess pewter and solder were cut and filed away.

My fourth project stretched over many weeks, as I made a set of six footed goblets. The top of each would be hammered over a mandrel and the seam would be beveled and soldered. The footing was of two spun pieces: the upper one to curve inward from the bottom of the goblet, the bottom one to curve outward and down to provide the footing. Between them was a flat disk to which they were joined by solder. It resembled a slightly tapered beaker placed on a flattened hourglass. I soldered the base pieces to each other, then joined them to the bottom of the goblet. These procedures involved many of the elementary skills: cutting, hammering, and soldering the top; spinning, fitting, and soldering the bottom; then finishing the entire piece. Arthur had me complete a matched set of six, doing each step of the formation on all six pieces, so that I would get practice on each of the lessons I was learning.

After the goblets were completed, most of the projects that followed were variations on part or all of the fundamentals. There was a compote, the top a medium-size bowl with a rolled edge, soldered to a base that flared outward and down.

Two years into my training, I began to taper off the instruction. Over the following years the visits were not frequent, but the sharing was deeply meaningful. Arthur's daughter, Ann, who lived with him in the closing years of his life, became a lasting and dear friend of our family. After Arthur's death, much of his shop equipment came to us and is still part of our continuing work, valued both for its usefulness and for the memories it evokes.

The memory of Arthur, and of those learning years, is both a resource and a blessing. I keep a picture of him working at his buffing wheel, bending slightly forward, his white hair above a firm but gentle expression, his thick glasses aiding his aging eyes. Below is another, taken in the earliest days of our fledgling enterprise, a photograph of me and our youngest son, Jonathan. In it, I am watching him perform a simple task. Now, nearly thirty years later, the two pictures suggest a generational lineage: the seventy-something teacher, the forty-five-year-old pupil, and the pupil's seven-year-old son who will one day be his father's partner in Gibson Pewter and the hope of its future. As this is written, I am nearly Arthur's age when he began teaching me, and Jonathan is in his mid-thirties.

Turning from those pictures to the shelves on which are displayed

Porringers, beakers, plates, and candleholders were the early pieces as we developed the craft.

nearly a hundred items we have made and seek to keep in stock, it seems a very long way from the day in Arthur's living room when I asked about his pewter pieces and he said, "Come down to my basement and I will show you."

Getting Started

TOOLS AND MACHINERY

> Man is a tool-using animal. Without tools he is nothing, with tools he is all." —*Thomas Carlyle*

I often have to explain my tools to those who come to the pewter shop, particularly when the visitor is a craftsman. "What is this?" "How do you use this?" And occasionally, "Where in the world did you find this?" This is particularly true of the large lathes on which production depends and the place where most of the forming of our pieces occurs. For us, as I suspect for most craftsmen, there is a story attached to each tool, and often the story will be about people as well as the tool itself.

Because we use it most often in demonstrations, our Diamond lathe is frequently discussed. Made in Providence, Rhode Island, it was patented on March 31, 1885. It has an engineering "first" in that its tailstock has a double spindle—a lever and a screw action that adds convenience in spinning. The lever makes it possible to move the backup block quickly away from the completed work for beakers and other tall pieces; the screw would require a lot of turning to move the same distance. The lever gives quickness; the screw is used for flat pieces like coasters and plates that require very little distance to remove the finished work. The screw is used for the final tightening of all pieces in closing the backup block that holds the pewter disk in place as it is being spun. The wheel turned to close the screw and tighten the backup block allows the pewterer to feel the increasing tightness and to make it secure enough that it will not fly out while spinning, yet not so tight that it stresses the bearings of the lathe.

How I came by that lathe is a happy memory. I had been working with my teacher and mentor, Arthur Barnes, for several months, and had decided that I wanted to press on with the craft in my own shop, which was limited to woodworking. The primary tool I needed was a spinning lathe, one that possessed the special bearings that could take the thrust or lateral pressure against the face - plate and chuck over which the pewter would be spun. I asked friends to be on the lookout for a lathe—a secondhand one, as a new one was beyond my means.

Daniel Fairchild, an officer of my church and a good friend, was helping our Scout troop in its annual fund-raising Christmas tree sale beside the parish house. When I spoke to him about my interest in a spinning lathe, he exclaimed, "I wish I had known that earlier this week. We just chucked one at work." Dan was head of engineering at the Fram Corporation, where, as he explained, they had a shed with cast-off items. The president of the company wanted to put away his boat for the winter and asked that the shed be "cleaned out." "There was an old, I mean really old, spinning lathe in that shed." Dan told me. "I'll look on Monday, but I think we just missed it. Wish I had known."

On Monday he called with the good news that the men sent to clean out the shed couldn't bring themselves to discard the old lathe and had taken it apart and put it along one wall, leaving enough room for the president's boat. Dan said that there were also some metal chucks and spinning tools that belonged with it, which I could have too. He invited me to look over the items to see if I wanted them.

I was overjoyed with the lathe, chucks, and spinning tools when I saw them. Even dismantled, the lathe was clearly a very sturdy machine with great promise as the foundation piece of the shop I would someday have. Dan turned the matter over to the shop manager, Ed Morgan, also a parishioner and good friend. Ed had the lathe moved into the company shop and painted. Someone fashioned a safety guard over the pulleys and then had some of his strongest men deliver it to my house, where they managed somehow to get it down the narrow stairs to the basement.

Ed told me the story of the lathe's background. Some years earlier, they had an older craftsman on their staff who made models for them when they were working on new products. This work did not occupy all the man's time, so he was allowed to do his own work when not busy with company projects. The model-making became more complex as the old spinner reached retirement, and his tools were no longer useful. After his death, his widow had no need for the tools, and they had been stored in the shed for a number of years.

After I secured some pewter disks and began spinning, I discovered that the bearings on the headstock were overheating. I had heard that another friend and member of the parish had a sizable business in renovating industrial machinery. I spoke to Clair Hoffacker after church one Sunday and he invited me to remove the headstock from the lathe and bring it out to his company. When I took him up on the invitation some days later, I was embarrassed to find that what I had brought was minuscule compared to his

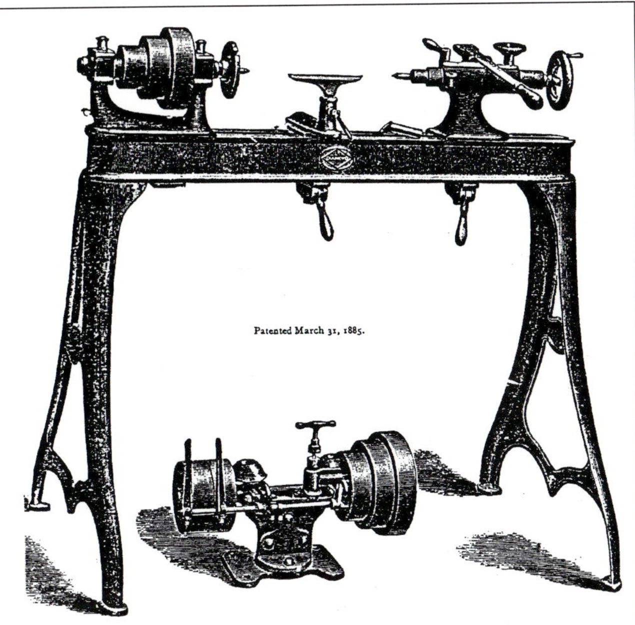

Patented March 31, 1885.

The "Diamond" Lever and Screw Feed Lathe

WITH PATENT COUNTER SHAFT.

10-inch Swing, 4-foot Bed, Patent Lever and Screw Feed Combined. Price $87.50

The lathe shown has 10-inch swing, 4-foot bed, stands 36 inches high, weighs 300 lbs., has hollow spindle, bronze boxes, patent oil cups; uses 1¾-inch belt. It is made in the most thorough manner.

Prices of Diamond Patent Lever and Screw Feed Lathes on Floor Legs:

Swing.	Bed.	Without Lever Attachment.	With Patent Lever Attachment.	With Counter Shaft.	Extra per foot.
10 in.	4 foot.	$60.00	$72.50	$87.00	$5.00
13 "	5 "	75.00	95.00	115.00	7.00
16 "	6 "	100.00	120.00	145.00	10.00

When ordered with Short or Bench Legs above prices are $10.00 less.

The "Diamond" lathe: as advertised in 1885...

... and today in our shop. The centerpiece vase chuck is attached to the lathe.

company's usual work. Huge industrial machines were brought in on a flat truck, taken off, and moved into the large plant with giant overhead cranes.

I took my headstock from the back of the station wagon and carried it into the receiving area, then went into the office. Clair appeared after I explained to his secretary who I was and why I was there. I began an apology about bringing so small a problem to so large a plant and operation, which he quickly brushed aside. He then led me to the intake area to look at my headstock. He asked an aide to call the shop foreman. While he was coming, Clair diagnosed the problem: "Your lathe has collar bearings, but no thrust bearing. You press against the face of the chuck when you 're spinning and that puts pressure here." He pointed to the inside edges of the two collar bearings.

Soon the foreman appeared, a man past middle age, smoking a pipe, jovial with me and his boss. Clair introduced him first by name and then added, "a Lutheran." Then, addressing the foreman, he said, "This is my pastor. This is the headstock to my pastor's lathe. It needs a thrust bearing right here." He pointed to a spot beside the left collar bearing. Then with a smile he added, "Your eternal salvation depends on getting this problem solved so there will be no more overheating." The foreman smiled and said, "I get your message."

Then Clair took me for a tour of his plant and explained some of the large projects under way. As we were completing the tour, we came to a cabinet with a number of hand tools in it. He said these were made available to his employees, many of whom had workshops at home. He reached into the cabinet and took out a mallet that had a head made of plastic, one face soft and the other very hard. He demonstrated the difference and said, "It has nice balance and fits the hand. Take it as a memento of your visit today." The hammer Clair gave me hangs above a workbench in easy reach, and has been used many times in situations for which no other tool in the shop would do as well.

Thirty years have elapsed since that visit. Through the years the lathe has run smoothly and without overheating. It continues to be the primary tool in our forming area. Jonathan used it for nine full days of demonstrating at the Sunapee Craftsmen's Fair for four successive years, each year having most of the forty-plus thousands of fair visitors pass our tent, many of them pausing to watch the work in progress. We put a sign on the side of the lathe facing those gathered to watch, informing them that the lathe was celebrating its 110th, 111th, and 112th and 113th year. Sometimes when we remove a chuck from the lathe, it sticks and needs a tap with a mallet to loosen it. I often use the plastic mallet given me by Clair the day I took the headstock to be repaired, finding still that it is well balanced and fits the hand.

Good fortune followed us in the matter of lathes. As I was approaching retirement, Manchester Silver, in Providence, Rhode Island, went into receivership and was selling off machinery, tools, and other items related to production. When I went to look at what was available, I met a member of the owner's family, a young man who, as a boy, had played in our backyard. His family had lived adjacent to us. He took an immediate interest in my needs, showing me what was available. It turned into the best single day of shopping in my memory. I acquired several breakdown chucks for making porringers, a valuable series of chucks for making four sizes of Paul Revere bowls, dozens of bristle brushes and cloth buffs, a set of movable type with a holder for making stamps to mark special pieces of pewter, and, best of all, a Prybyl lathe that is a muscular big brother to the Diamond lathe. Dating from the period of the First World War, this lathe was half as old and twice as strong and heavy as the Diamond. It could handle the large metal chucks like the one for the bowl of the large Paul Revere bowl weighing more than fifty pounds. The Prybyl was one of three apparently identical lathes on line at Manchester Silver, and I was grateful when my former neighbor picked the one for us that recently had been reconditioned and had the best bearings.

To own it was one thing; to get it home was another. We had a utility trailer with a reinforced axle that we used for carrying our things back and forth to the country. We had carried the Diamond lathe between our basement in Providence and the barn in New Hampshire. It had to be taken apart and loaded one piece at a time. We had even learned to put it through a back window in the basement rather than take it up or down the narrow stairs. Taking a cue from the ancients, we had learned to use round hardwood rollers to move the lathe bed, which weighed nearly six hundred pounds. The Prybyl would never go into the basement. It would be moved to a shed by our garage until it could be brought to the barn in New Hampshire, and we would have to add supports to the underpinning of the barn in whatever area we placed it.

We took the Prybyl apart and moved it in two trips with our trailer. At the factory, there were dollies that moved the heavier parts to the loading dock and then into the trailer. At home, we made a ramp of strong boards and slid the heavy parts into the utility shed behind the garage. We stored it until it was time for our move to the country. Then, the professional movers, accustomed to loading furniture, had a test of their mettle loading that heavy lathe in Providence and unloading it in New Hampshire.

The metal chucks, particularly the Paul Revere bowl chucks, were stored in our basement which was heated and dry, in order to keep them from rusting. When pewter is spun over steel chucks, a spot of rust will imprint itself in the surface of the pewter as it is spun down to the surface. If the rust has become firmly established on the steel surface and is removed with fine emery paper, blemishes will be made in the surface that will imprint on each piece of pewter spun over it. If the blemish is not deep, it can be removed in the buffing and cleanup process. If it is deep, the chuck will have to be resurfaced or discarded.

In the factory, the Prybyl had a large electric motor running on a high voltage that was not available in the country. The Diamond lathe was powered by a one-horsepower motor; the Prybyl required a two-horsepower motor. The barn was wired for only 110 volts and the Prybyl needed 220. New wiring had to be run to the barn to power the larger lathe. We had to replace the motor that came with the lathe, which meant another kind of problem. The new motor would have to fit the footprint of the old motor on the stand that rose above the lathe. It also had to fit the special pulley that drove the pair of pulleys powering the lathe. Getting it all together and working taught me a great deal about the machine before I had a chance to turn it on or spin my first piece of pewter on it.

In our shop, the Prybyl is by far the most imposing machine by its very bulk and obvious weight. It has added impressiveness: the placement of the motor and the large pulley group. On all our other lathes, the motor is behind or below the headstock. The Prybyl's motor is above, balanced over a fulcrum arrangement with the motor behind and the pulley group in front. To change speeds, a lever tilts the platform over the fulcrum and loosens the flat two-inch leather belt, making it possible to change the pulley ratios, thus altering the speed. Speeds can vary from seven hundred to four thousand revolutions per minute. When running, the large pulleys, and the fast moving belt, give an image of massive power. When a large chuck, like that used to make the largest Paul Revere bowl, or the fifteen inch charger, or the twelve-and-a-half-inch fruit bowl, is attached to the head stock and turning at two thousand to three thousand revolutions a minute, the whole spinning room feels charged with energy.

It is quite easy to draw word pictures of the lathe, bearing its heavy chuck and spinning smoothly and rapidly. It is not so easy to convey the sense of *working* with a tool, whether it is a machine or a hand tool, and especially to those who have no experience with tools and machinery. I think of

Some of our wooden chucks. Some are more than fifty years old. Most of our spinning is now done over metal chucks.

the cluster of experiences that could illustrate what I mean. I remember weaving with a two-hundred-year-old blanket loom, its wooden frame large enough to crowd a small room, which required the feet on the treadles, one hand on the beater and the other on the throw shuttle, the whole body involved. Then, the contrast with carving linoleum for a block print with a set of four small chisels whose rounded handles fit into the palm of the hand. With continued use, both the chisel and the large loom feel like extensions of the body, responding to the touch and control of the process that comes to feel more like cooperation than command.

The lathes, too, have a special "feel" as we use them. When a piece is being spun, the pewter disk is spinning and the lathe is on one side of it. On the other is the spinning tool in the craftsman's hands. The pewterer feels "united" with the machine as the piece is gradually formed at the point of meeting. It may resemble what Louis Armstrong once said about jazz: "If someone doesn't understand it, you can't tell them."

There is another story of a lathe that I purchased, used, and sold—one that was even larger than the Prybyl. One summer day in the early seventies, a traveling salesman arrived in our shop. After a brief look at our work and machinery, he came to the point of his visit. "I know a place about fifty miles from here," he said, "where there is a big 'step' lathe for sale, very old, and maybe as many as fifty metal chucks, including some really big ones. The owner has not been able to sell them and is about to sell them for scrap metal. That would be a few cents a pound. The price would be right if you're interested."

I was interested in both the chucks and the step lathe. Such a lathe gets its name from the fact that the lathe bed, between the headstock and the tailstock, has a "step" down to give clearance for a large work to be turned or spun. The Prybyl has a flat bed, with clearance allowing the craftsman to spin items up to fifteen inches in diameter. The step lathe had a clearance of just over two feet, which means that a disk up to four feet could be spun on it. It had one large chuck over which could be spun a huge copper kettle. Most of the chucks were designed to make replacement parts for antique cars, and the metal spun on the lathe had been steel and copper. The previous owner had done specialty spinning for those who were restoring old automobiles from the earliest models, and, in particular, the housing for the headlamps, a part often damaged before they came for renovation or rebuilding.

The traveling salesman gave directions, I found the place, and, though a bit overawed by the bulk and weight of the lathe, bought it on the condition that the owner would deliver it to my barn. He promised that it would arrive the following weekend. We reinforced the foundation under that section of the barn where it would be placed. When it arrived, it took eight strong men to move it into place. Again, electricity had to be run to it and we had several adjustments to make before it could be used.

The turning tools that came with the step lathe were more than twice the size of our spinning tools. Clearly the turning of steel or heavy copper sheet metal required a great deal more heft. The chucks, for all their interesting shapes, were badly rusted and of no clear use for our pewter needs. There was, however, a large wooden chuck made from laminated rock maple that looked promising. I saw in it the possibility of a salad bowl, if it were reshaped with my wood-turning tools. That accomplished, we would occasionally set up and make two or three salad bowls from our fifteen-inch disks. It took two of us to spin them, one forming what would be the outside of the bowl, and the second person using a backing stick on the inside. As the metal moved toward the chuck the backing stick would have less and less room to move. However, the backing stick helped to keep the large disk from wrinkling as it was spun. I was able to spin the salad bowl with the largest of our regular spinning tools. The ones that came with the lathe were too long, and too heavy. They found good service around the garden when a huge rock had to be pried out of the earth, or in sinking holes in which stakes were to be set.

Things sometimes have an interesting way of turning out. A representative of an antique car club visited the shop and watched us work. He asked whether his club could gather on a Sunday morning, park their vehicles, watch us work for an hour or so, and then continue on their way to a nearby eating place. We welcomed them on a bright Sunday in early summer, and when they had arrived and parked, there was strong temptation to leave the pewter shop to walk among those beautifully restored vehicles, including a Stanley Steamer that had climbed the long hill from the village three miles down the road, puffing its little bursts of steam as it came.

As so often happens, the men were more interested in the working of the machinery in the spinning process, whereas the women were more taken with the product that resulted. A few of the men gathered around the step lathe, which was in a far corner of the shop.

The step lathe was an oddity, a museum piece of sorts. Visitors who were machine-oriented would often visit it and ask me to start it so they could "see the old fellow run." Space demands made us move the many chucks to the lower level of the barn. The same growing need for space made us wonder whether it was worth keeping. When the antique car club was there, I didn't indicate that we might be willing to part with it. Two months later, we decided that we needed the space more than the lathe. We could adapt the salad bowl chuck to either the Prybyl or the Diamond lathe. The club members had signed our guest book, so it was easy to send an informal note indicating that the lathe and chucks were for sale. They sold within hours of the mail's being delivered, and several follow-up calls came after Dan Rising bought it.

Dan arrived on a Sunday afternoon, pulling a low flatbed trailer behind his heavy station wagon. He came by himself. He backed the trailer to the ramp of the front door of the barn and began to take out some equipment. "Dan, it took eight strong men to bring in that lathe." He laughed and said, "That should make it more interesting to take it out." He had engineering skills as well as some well-chosen equipment: two compact jacks that had great lifting power, and four small platforms with four rollers under each. His strategy was simple: Get the four corner feet of the lathe on the four platforms and roll it out to the trailer. After, that is, taking off the motor, headstock and tailstock to be loaded separately.

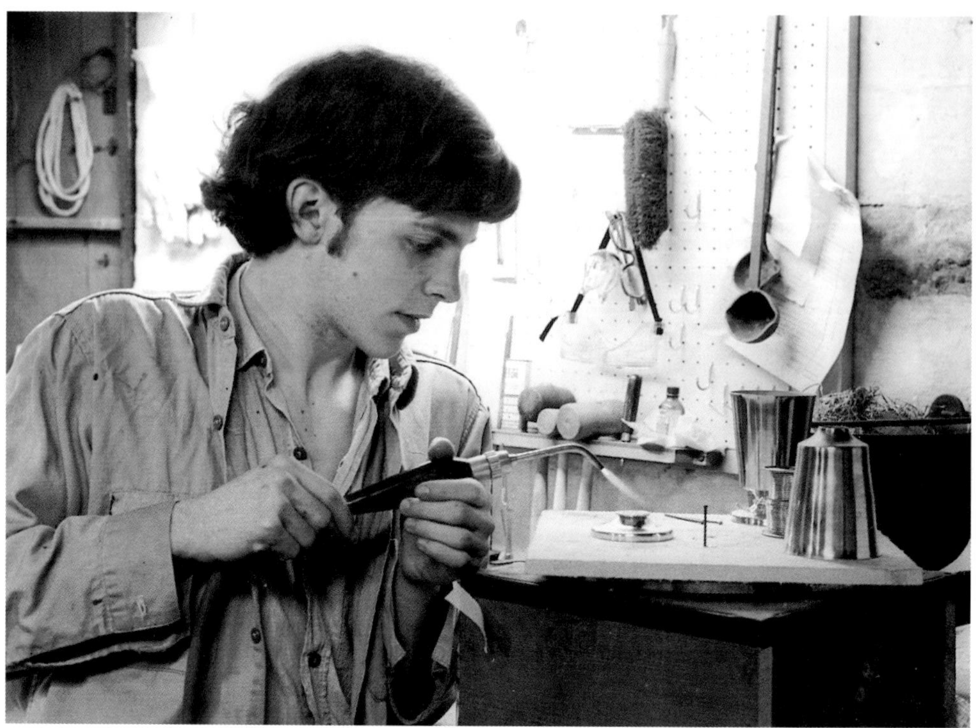

Early picture of Cyrus learning to solder.

It took some doing, but eventually the lathe was on the rollers, which swiveled in any direction. We moved it out into the nave of the barn and to the front door. There he produced two strong runners to roll it from the ramp to the bed of the trailer. He had a small, powerful winch to pull it up the incline and onto the trailer. Then it was a matter of loading the other lathe parts and the chucks. I marveled at what he had been able to do, and at the power of the trailer to hold such a load. "It's strong," Dan said, "but I'll drive slowly on the way home." Early in the evening he called to let me know that he had arrived safely.

In the barn that now houses the pewter shop, there are tools that I am convinced go back to the building of the barn nearly two hundred years ago. There are T-bar augers with strong handles and bits the size of the holes made to peg together the post-and-beam structure. In the center nave of the barn you can read the symbols, circles and the slashes that made it possible to match the joints as they put the frame together. I found in the barn the tool that could have made those circles and slashes.

This was a working farm in the 1800s, and there hangs on an outside beam of the loft the cradle scythe for cutting the hay. There is also a huge ox yoke that we can imagine on a sturdy pair of oxen, pulling the stone boat that stands against the wall of the loft. In a corner rests a no-longer-circular lime grindstone on a worn frame, used by early farmers to sharpen their axes, scythes, and other tools. If tools could talk, what a conversation might occur between that old sharpening stone and the emery wheels and belt sanders we use at the flip of a switch!

On a rafter on the first floor of the barn I found a large block plane with a blade so old we could see how it had been hammered in the forge before it was sharpened. The wood body of the plane is smooth and true, with no warping or bowing despite its years which doubtless double my three score and fourteen. I take it to a vise and tap the wedge that holds the blade in position. It comes out; I find the edge is sharp enough to work, but needing that extra touch that will make it work well. I can tell by the action of the whetstone that the metal is exceptional, very strong and hard but with a smoothness that glides on the stone. I reassemble the plane and put a pine board in the vise of my workbench to see how the plane will work. Long strokes roll up the paper-thin shavings that leave smooth the edge of the pine. I look at the old block plane and find myself wondering how many of the old drawers and cabinet doors in the house were finished with this tool.

There are layers of history in the loft of the barn. Hanging against a wall is a two-man cross-cut saw, more than five feet long - the kind of saw that would be used by two men cutting down a tree or cutting logs to lengths they desired. It shows a great deal of use and is still strong and ready for work. There is an oddity, perhaps only a hundred years old, from a period when there were all sorts of inventions that didn't quite make it into general use. This is also a saw, attached to a set of wooden wheels and arms, that would allow one person to work the saw by turning a wheel with a protruding handle. It is clearly derived from the age of locomotives, reversing the uses of wheel and bar. On the locomotive, the drive shaft turns the wheel; here the wheel turns and drives the shaft, in this case the saw. The wood is painted in designs indicating the factory wanted eye appeal as well as utility. I study the blade and the moving parts, and I find little evidence of wear. It was an interesting idea. Apparently it didn't work well enough to displace the older saw.

How many of the stories that make up the history of this old farm could be told through the tools that have aided in the creation and maintenance of the place? If the imagination turns to the future, what will become of the

Mark and I confer on the shaping of a wooden chuck.

barn and our pewter shop a century from now? If the lathes, chucks, and tools were somehow stored in the loft, could someone imagine our work with pewter, as I think of the long-ago farmer and his oxen clearing the field of stones and moving them on the stone boat I now see propped near the wall where the ox yoke hangs?

"Man is a tool using animal," wrote Carlyle. Some of the tools still stored in the loft of the barn were in regular use when Darwin was writing about evolution in the mid-1800s. There is also an evolution with tools. In the creation of our pewter shop, the tools we use span one and a half centuries. Working there, we feel a sense of rootedness in, and belonging to, traditions that are hundreds of years old, while creating forms that are new. I am a craftsman first, but I become a guide to an older time whenever a visitor points to a tool and asks, "What's this?"

APPRENTICES

For some time before our children finished their formal education and were into their careers, we hired local young people to work in the pewter shop. They learned skills and received instruction and a modest stipend. We used the word "apprentice," knowing that it was not strictly an accurate designation. There was no guild overseeing the operation of the craft, no seven years of instruction and work, no "graduation" when the master presented his apprentice to the court of the guild bearing a piece of his work and evidence that he had sufficient resources to set up his own shop. In older times and distant places, there was also, on these occasions, the party that followed. Put on by the apprentice, the party for the guild could be quite boisterous as tankards were filled, emptied, and filled again and again. Then the apprentice could strike his own "touch," which established his identity in the guild. Over time he would be allowed to work his way up—from freeman to liveryman, steward, warden, and, finally, master.

We used the term for that small fraction of the older practices that did apply. Pewter making is a historic craft; there was a master engaged in teaching newcomers the fundamentals and supervising their work. We were making numerous pieces that were replicas of the pre-Revolutionary era to the mid-nineteenth century. We had an open shop to which visitors were welcome to come and watch us at work, and it seemed part of the ethos of the history we were seeking to represent, that we would designate the young learners as apprentices. We did not expect, nor in any case so far has it happened, that one of them would continue in the craft. All, however, have had the discipline of working under careful guidance, have learned skills with their hands, knowledge of hand tools and machine work, and, perhaps most important, have learned the standards of quality required to produce acceptable work.

The first of my apprentices was Billy Potter, whom I met through his shop teacher at Moses Brown School, located just across the Brown University athletic fields from my church in Providence. There had been an article about me in the *Providence Journal* showing some of my pewter work, and the teacher called to enlist my help with one of his students. The student wanted to make a stem goblet in a combination of wood and pewter, the base being turned in wood, the cup being spun in pewter. It was his senior project and very important to him. The teacher said that he did not know anything about spinning pewter, and therefore turned to me for help. I agreed.

In the process of working with Billy, I discovered that he was facing a personal dilemma. A fine athlete, gifted with his hands, as shown by his work with wood, he was severely dyslexic and academically handicapped to the extent that he would graduate without much chance of acceptance at a college. As I worked with him on his project, which he successfully completed, I found him a very appealing young man. He was, it seemed to me, a person with a good future if only he could find a craft to which he could give his life.

Moses Brown was a traditional sports rival of Providence Country Day school, where our sons attended, and they had played each other in competitive sports and had gained respect for each other on the fields. Lacrosse was a sport in which they all excelled, and was a playtime favorite of Chris and Jonathan during the summer. We had a lacrosse goal cage with net that we placed in different spots on our New Hampshire farm, and our white Labrador got into the game helpfully by retrieving balls that missed the net and went flying beyond. Chris and Jon played one-on-one and honed their attack and defense skills. It happened later that Chris and Jon were seniors the same year, Chris at Brown University and Jon at Providence Country Day, and each played in the regional all-star game.

I asked Billy to consider spending the summer with us in New Hampshire doing pewter. He accepted and was a fine addition to the family, fitting into the pewter work, farm chores, sports, and other activities. He was gifted in his craft sense, had a natural affinity for tools and learned quickly. During the shop hours of the official "working day," he helped on our regular production items. Then came project time, during which he could design and create new pieces, asking for my guidance when he needed it. He proposed a project halfway through the summer that, given its complexity, I would have considered a third-year level in skills.

He wanted to make a pewter bottle, which meant spinning a bottom and a top, then soldering the two together around the middle. The spinning was within his reach, but fitting and soldering the middle would be difficult. He was so positive in his intent that I agreed that he could attempt it.

It was a struggle, but the kind of challenge that raised the learning curve considerably. First he found the wood to turn for the chucks over which he would spin the pewter top and bottom. They had to have dimensions that matched perfectly where the pieces would be joined. When he had finished this and spun the pieces, he worked to prepare the joint for soldering. A more durable joint would result if the edges were beveled rather than butted squarely together. They also had to fit together evenly; gaps in the joint would cause the solder to run through rather than bond the joint.

Finally, there was the soldering process, in which it was easy to destroy the piece. Too much heat would melt the pewter at the joint, instead of the solder only, which should melt and flow into the joint, bonding the sides into one. The difference in the melting point of the pewter and the solder is a matter of forty to sixty degrees, which means that if the torch were left on the joint only a second too long, the solder would melt, but so would the pewter. We used a liquid flux and wire solder. The flux would be applied, the area heated with the acetylene torch until the flux began to "boil." Then the end of the solder wire would be applied as the torch was waved on and off the surface, keeping it hot enough for the solder to flow, but not hot enough to melt the pewter. No other operation in the pewter craft requires more focus, or such steady hands, or a sense of the function of the heat in the crucial moments when the solder begins to flow.

With patience and great care, Billy brought the project to completion without losing it in the soldering process. He did have some large beads here and there around the bottle, lumps of solder that a master might have melted and brushed away. He chose, wisely, to remove them by some careful work with a file and emery paper. It was a remarkable achievement for that stage of his training and I was reminded of it later when as a student in a special arts program at Boston University, he fashioned a globe in brass by hammering and joining two hemispheres.

Billy spent two summers with us, and in the year between worked part time in our basement in Providence, spinning and finishing a number of the pieces in our regular product line. His work with us, and my knowledge of his potential as well as his academic handicap, made it possible for me to assure the university that if they could accept the problem of his dyslexia, they would have an artisan of great promise. His admission was a result of his proving himself in our apprenticeship training, and his success there was a measure of his native ability and drive to create with his hands.

In Hillsborough Centre, most of our apprentices came from the neighborhood or the town in the valley just three miles down the hill. The guilds in England and on the Continent were knit together socially. They lived in the same community, attended the same church, frequented the same pub. In their strongest years the guilds regulated standards, policed both the quality of the metal and the integrity of the workmanship, authorized the marking systems, and monitored apprenticeship requirements.

There are significant records of the guilds from the fourteenth century.

They were at the height of their power and influence in the fifteenth and sixteenth centuries. By the early eighteenth century the guilds began to lose control over the trade generally and over their individual members personally. Workers resented the interference and the policing of guild regulations. It is not surprising that the guild system never took root in colonial America. Craftsmen were scattered, individual freedom was prized, competition among them was intense, and for all of them the competition with the large volume of English imports stimulated the impetus to quality. The marketplace replaced the guild in this regard.

If there were no guilds in colonial America, it is interesting that on the contemporary scene, the American Pewter Guild was founded in 1958, its ambitions directed to stimulating concern for standards and promoting the trade. Since pewterers are so scattered, one goal of the guild has been to create a sense of community across distances. A far cry this, when compared with the earlier time when they were close enough to attend the same church and drink at the same pub.

The Shattuck family, neighbors in our small village, descended from the earliest "settled pastor," had four children whose ages paralleled the younger four of our five. Franz, Helen, Erika, and Roger all had summer jobs learning and working in the pewter shop. Roger, the youngest, started earlier and worked longer—indeed, he was with us as many years as his siblings were combined. It began when he kept visiting the shop when they were at work, and showed signs of wanting to be involved. I proposed that he come at the end of the morning and again at the end of the afternoon work periods to sweep the shop. He was paid five dollars a week for his efforts, a sum that, to his young eyes, seemed a small mountain of money.

It was not long before Roger found ways to get his hands on something besides the broom and dustpan. He was able to be helpful in other things, and gradually worked into the beginning steps of the craft earlier than anyone outside our family. With the head start, he came to such a level of competence that during his high school years he was able to make a significant contribution to our production. More than that, he achieved a level that he did not have to be told what to do daily. He saw what needed to be done and did it. In his final years with us, he was increasingly engrossed in music, playing the bass electric guitar. After-hours, and on some weekends, he used our shop's woodworking equipment to fashion the bodies of guitars. After high school he was with us during the period of application and until he was inducted into the special musical unit of his choice in the U.S. Army. Having watched him grow up, his presence was missed, not alone for the many ways he had come to contribute to our enterprise, but also for the person he was, a presence we had come to value and enjoy.

A particular memory of Roger reminds me of one whole dimension of training and apprentices. Early on, I had adopted a maxim that I used in controlling standards: "Almost is not good enough!" When an apprentice brought an item on which he or she was working and offered it for inspection, I would study it for a few moments. If it required further work, I would say "Almost," then point out what was needed before it was acceptable. The word, "almost" was the code word for our motto.

Roger had a face that often said more than he was willing to hear himself saying aloud. He had a strong enough sense of standards that he truly tried to finish a piece before he brought it for final inspection. When he fell short, I would say "Almost," and invariably I would see his jaw tighten, a look of consternation would fill his face, and he would turn back to his workstation without a word. All the body language said that he hated to hear that word, as well as the maxim that was held over all our efforts in the shop.

One day the picture changed. From the beginning, we have had an open shop, and visitors are welcome to watch the work in progress. Older people in particular would gravitate to the places where our children or the apprentices were working. They often praised the young people and expressed delight at finding them doing something like this. On such a day I came into the area where Roger was working, though he could not see my approach. Beside him stood a warm, grandmotherly type who was praising him and exclaiming about the quality of the work on our shelves. With his characteristic broad grin, Roger said with pride, "We have a motto in our work here, 'Almost is not good enough'." It was clear that difficult as that motto sometimes was to live under, Roger had made it his own.

Most apprentices in my experience have reached such a point in their learning and growth, some sooner than others, and it is a significant milestone, for in a sense that person ceases to belong to the craft; now the craft belongs to him. It is no longer the voice of another saying "Do it better," but a voice from within saying "Stay with it till you know it's right."

Chris Beard, the youngest of the three Beard brothers who spent time in the pewter shop, was, like all his family, very much at home with machinery, archery equipment, firearms, and camping gear. He was in high school when he came to us, and had a small side enterprise in fur from animals he trapped. He and his brothers had learned a lot of woods lore from their

Seth Bowley pauses to watch Chris Beard buff a fruit bowl.

father. The family's larder was filled year-round with the bounty of their sports, including venison, moose, small game, and a variety of fish.

Chris was with us during the tenure of Seth Bowley, who was one year behind Chris at the local high school. Seth had impressive skills in mechanics and both boys were at an age when the silent agenda beneath all other important matters was to get a driver's license and own a car or pickup. In both cases we watched their dreams being realized, and then the sequence of fixing up their vehicle and trading upward, a kind of adolescent puberty rite in the enterprise system they were about to enter.

They came to us, as it turned out, at a very good time for the development in the pewter shop. We were making some new and larger pieces, one of which won a significant prize and became part of the permanent collection of the Museum of Fine Arts, in Boston. It was also a time of transition in the finishing process when we were seeking a result that we believed was closer to the work of the colonial period. It was a movement from a matte or satin finish to a bright or polished one.

The combination of greater surfaces and the higher finish meant much more machine work in the buffing department. The forming would be the same no matter what the finish, but the bright finish would place large demands on the one seeking to achieve it. Every trace of a line left from the spinning process had to be removed so thoroughly that there would not be a hint of it in the completed piece. This required the use of a series of abrasive papers, each finer than the last, until all lines were removed. Then came cloth buffs with a series of compounds from tripoli to red rouge to, in some cases, lampblack. If the result was nearly perfect, the surface was mirror smooth and mirror bright.

The abrasive papers were used with the pewter turning on a lathe between center blocks of wood faced with leather. When they came off the lathe, the centers where the blocks had held them were finished by hand. For the cloth buffs, there were fast and slow buffing wheels, the fast one having more power.

Both Chris and Seth had a streak of perfectionism in their nature; both brought mechanical skills to the task of adapting the machinery we had to the greater demands we were facing in the work. Chris preferred to be above the piece he held to the buff, so he lowered the wheel and sat on a stool above it. Seth addressed the wheel standing straight, with the wheel nearly chest high. Both brought an intensity and focus to their finished work that was a joy to watch. When New Hampshire PBS station Channel 11 did a program on my work, the cameraman, Steve Salniker, saw the boys at work and wanted them in the story. With excellent camera work he caught the intensity of Chris bent over the fruit bowl he was buffing on the fast buff, as well as the focus of Seth, teamed with me, applying the backing stick as I formed the large fruit bowl on the Prybyl, the heaviest of our lathes. In both cases, there was total absorption in the task at hand, the best of several qualities that help make a fine craftsman.

Chris went from our pewter shop to a demanding job at Sylvania, the major company in our community, and was in its training program while still a senior in high school. He proved himself there very quickly, and was given positions of significant responsibility. Seth was recruited by General Motors to learn and practice auto mechanics, and has advanced in his skills as he applied them in a series of different settings. Both boys had, I was sure, all the basic preparatory skills and attitudes needed to succeed. Happily, Seth had a younger brother, Jake, who joined forces with us during Seth's final year, working out-of-doors much of his first summer, and then moved into the training program, assuming ever more complex and demanding tasks. With his powerful build and quiet manner, Jake brought a number of interests and skills, and enlarged them as he worked in yard, garden, fields, woods, and pewter shop. He became proficient with trimmers and brush cutters, small and large tractors, and the big garden cultivator used to plow in spring and loosen the soil after late-summer rains. He became comfortable with lathes and buffing wheels, and mastered the intricacies of grinding the parting lines off castings, and bringing the candle stalks, or porringer or tankard handles, to a finish ready to be soldered to base, bowl, or can.

Bowls, plates, platters, and chargers require cleanup on the lathe with emery papers, then a series of buffing operations. Jake mastered the sequence of skills to take a piece from its forming to its finish. When we demonstrated at the Sunapee Craftsmen's Fair, Jonathan and I demonstrated spinning and casting, while Jake did finishing work, demonstrating the range of procedures needed to finish a piece formed by the spinning process or casting. After watching me cast spoons from a very old mold, he asked if he could fill in for me when I took a break. After I watched him awhile, I felt comfortable leaving the demonstration in his hands during my breather.

There have been other apprentices. Some of them are mentioned in different parts of our story. Looking back at the experiences with them over the years, I find joy in remembering the young people, in thinking about how they grew and of what they have gone on to do and become. I remember comments by thoughtful visitors. I think of a professor from the Midwest who taught social sciences, watching two apprentices at work for a time and then saying to me that he thought it a tragedy in our modern society that there is not more sharing and passing-on of skills between the generations. It's as if we set partitions between the age groups. That's why youth culture is a matter of learning from peers. It's why traditions are not carried on the way they were in the past. My impulse was to agree, but I had to make a different point that was important to me. I see it not only as a matter of what is not passed down from older to younger, but also what is lost to the older of what they can learn from the young. The tragedy, if that is not too strong a word, is in both directions. If I have shared or taught craft skills, and in some cases life skills, I have also learned from the young, especially my children, much that enriches my life. Burke wrote, "The arrogance of age must submit to be taught by youth." That is stronger language than I would use, but it expresses a truth to ponder. Teaching apprentices has always proved a learning process for me.

THE SHARON ARTS CENTER

My relationship with the Sharon Arts Center began when the center was part of the League of New Hampshire Craftsmen, and continued after the center withdrew from the league. Located near Peterborough, New Hampshire, an upscale and handsome town with a number of cultural attractions, the center has a varied program.

Much more than a "store" where the work of league members and other craftsmen was handsomely displayed, the center is well named—it's truly an "arts center." There are ongoing classes in a number of media, a reading room with a library on the arts and crafts, and a sizable gallery with excellent exhibits, drawing viewers from throughout the region. The center has a professional staff, aided by many volunteers, which makes possible the diverse scope of its program.

There has been a number of directors of the shop over the years. During the tenure of one of the most creative in my experience, the director decided that it would be good training for the volunteers to have them visit our pewter shop and see the work in progress. There is enough mystery about the craft and few individuals have ever seen pewter being formed or finished. In successive years, we entertained the volunteers from the center who came, watched us work, and had a picnic lunch on our terrace. I have no way of knowing how much the outing aided them in their work of presenting our pewter to their customers, but it created a nice personal bond and made my visits to the center more enjoyable.

In the early 1980s, the center invited me to take part in a special event. Demonstrations and sales would be held on the grounds of the center for one day. Lauren and I decided that we would participate. It was not possible to transport and set up a lathe to demonstrate spinning; we were left, then, with casting as the only option. There were problems to be solved before we could agree. The "plumber's furnace" made quite a lot of noise. The pot of molten pewter presented a number of dangers, and required a placement that would keep viewers at a safe distance.

We set up on the periphery close to a building, our two tables between us and the flow of viewer traffic. The ends were sealed off with ropes. Lauren set up one table with our product. I set up the other with the working tools for casting and placed the furnace beside my chair. The tools I used were a bronze spoon mold held together by a hinged handle and clamp, several smaller silicone rubber molds, a hard rubber mold for porringer han-

Lauren in our early shop, before we winterized the pewter area of the barn.

dles, an open-faced plaster of Paris mold for a heart, and a variety of C-clamps and duck-bill clamps.

The open heart mold is the simplest to use and has the most immediate audience appeal. People seldom if ever see molten metal, especially in a close-up situation where the ladle goes into the pot, lifts the metal, and pours it into an open mold. They can watch it change colors, then contract enough that there will be a small wrinkling at the center, and solidify as it cools. Poured at 500-plus degrees Fahrenheit, the metal is shiny bright; as it cools and hardens, it turns gray. The contraction of the metal as it cools causes a dimple or small crater at the spot where the last of the molten metal turns solid. As soon as the heart is solid, we turn over the mold and tap gently to make the newly formed heart fall out. The metal is still about 400 degrees, and this is a danger time for the demonstrator. For some, the fact that the metal is solid makes them assume that it is cool enough to touch. Actually, it can burn someone badly if touched. I learned early to keep the operation on my side of the table, and to issue a verbal warning as I drop the new heart from the mold: "Don't touch, it's very hot!" Children, especially, are eager to touch the new creation, but adults have the impulse as well.

Experience has taught me to keep a piece of lexan, or some other material that cannot be burned by 400-plus degrees of heat, on my side of the table, onto which I let the pewter fall when it comes out of the mold. As soon as it has cooled enough to touch, it can be handed to viewers who want to inspect it. Young people especially need to hold and handle something they have seen, before they feel that the knowledge of it belongs to them.

The day went smoothly until midafternoon, when I had an accident that resulted in part because I was so concerned about the safety of others that I had a lapse in protecting myself. I was using a silicone rubber mold to cast a small Celtic cross and holding the mold and the metal plate backing to it in a metal duck-bill clamp, so named for its broad, flat, clamping jaws. The handles required a firm grip. They were rounded and short enough that my little finger and the one next to it were off the end of the handle.

The sprue, or intake opening for the metal, was small and the mold itself did not require a lot of metal to fill. On one pouring, too much metal left the ladle, spilled over and down the silicone in such a way that it found the inside curve of the handle, and ran over my two fingers at the end of the handle. It happened quickly. I flinched a bit, but did not drop the mold or the ladle in the other hand, which still had molten metal in it. I put the ladle back into the pot and changed hands with the mold, trying to keep my composure. I kept on talking to the dozen or more individuals who were watching the demonstration and who did not realize what had happened.

Lauren did realize. She asked out of the side of her mouth, "Burn yourself?" "Get the Solarcaine," I answered in a quiet voice. As I removed the mold from the clamp and then removed the metal plate, those watching could see the nicely formed Celtic cross. The demonstration completed, I turned away and then looked at my hand. It had a burn across the two fingers about one-eighth of an inch wide and was turning pure white. Lauren handed me the Solarcaine. I applied it to my hand and waited as the pain began to abate. I found a white cotton glove and continued with the next round of the demonstration, using another kind of mold. One or two of the onlookers had, by this time, figured out what had happened and asked if I was all right. I thanked them for their concern and said that I had had a "learning experience."

It turned out to be a learning experience in another way that changed my manner of viewing the rewards, or lack of them, in doing demonstrations. At the end of the day, Lauren had sold ninety dollar's worth of product and the arrangement called for a one-third commission to the center, a typical and fair practice. Still, it seemed a lot of work for the two of us for sixty dollars. There was, however, a hidden reward, a factor that escapes immediate calculation in any craft demonstration.

Late in the day a woman looked at our product and found nothing she wanted. She looked across to where I was working and saw a squat candleholder that I had made quickly out of damaged pieces of pewter disks in our shop. In my demonstration I would need to have a candle for "lampblacking" the colonial spoon mold. I wanted to have a short, thick candle that would burn down slowly. We had no such candleholder in our shop, so I made one hurriedly a day or two before the demonstration. It was roughed out and not buffed. She liked the design and asked Lauren whether it was for sale. Lauren asked me, knowing what the answer would be. "Sorry. It was too crudely made and not finished. I wouldn't want it in circulation as an item of my work."

The potential customer asked whether I would be willing to make one in that design for her. Answer, yes. "Price?" I told her. "Make me two," she said. She gave her name and telephone number. When she came to the shop a week later to pick up the candleholder, she looked at our other work, including a number of larger pieces that we had not taken to the center demonstration, and placed a substantial order that began the building of a significant collection of our pewter. She came from the southern part of the state and would never have known of our work without the demonstration at the Sharon Arts Center.

Apart from the business relationship with the center, which has always been modest in the amounts of pewter sold, we value the association. We attend its art exhibits and visit the shop from time to time for the inspiration of seeing the high quality of the craft items. The changing exhibits in the gallery are of a consistently high standard. And the people are friendly. Occasionally I meet one of the volunteers who will remember coming for a picnic and watching us work. The center enriches the region by its presence. It was at the center that I gained a fresh insight about my work, but that is another story.

A STYLE OF MY OWN

It was a shock—call it a shock of recognition, in this case, the recognition of my style as a pewterer. The visual memory is still quite vivid. I was at the

The charger was the first large piece that I designed. Here it is flanked by colonial style porringers and a candlestick.

Sharon Arts Center, in the main crafts display room of the shop that was, in those days, related to the League of New Hampshire Craftsmen. I was there to see an exhibit in which I had been asked to participate. At their request, I had supplied a dozen or more pieces of my work, ranging from coasters to chargers, including porringers, candlesticks, chambersticks, bowls, plates, basins, goblets, and vases.

The exhibition contained the work of two other pewterers, and was arranged on three low platforms placed in a line in the center of the room. The platforms were four feet square and the arrangement of the work was accented by pedestals of varying heights on which individual pieces were placed. There was no mixing of our work; each platform was devoted to a single craftsman.

As I stood looking at the exhibit, I was impressed by the taste and creativity of the designer's placement of the individual pieces. The same quality was achieved on all three pewter displays. Overhead spotlights enhanced the visual effects. I stood for some time looking at the exhibit and at its parts in particular pieces, my own and the work of the other pewter-

Gifts taken by leaders of the United Church of Christ to leaders behind the "Iron Curtain" (1978).

ers. Suddenly it struck me. If someone had taken any single piece of my pewter and placed it on either of the other platforms, it would have looked out of place. Clearly, it would not have belonged there. I looked at the other work and the same would have been true for them. Each style was so distinctive that a mix would have created a sense of confusion.

This was the shock of recognition. For the first time I saw my work in a context that revealed something about my way of working. I realized that I did not just make pewter. In the practice of the craft, a style had evolved that was clearly my own. There it was, and seeing it for the first time in such a setting, it was obvious and irrefutable. What was not as clear was where the style had come from and what influences had shaped it. I had never planned to have one or another style. I had not thought about the matter in a general way, or even as an abstract consideration. I made things one at a time, without some greater context in mind. Perhaps I just "grew" a style by practice, by an instinct for line or simplicity.

Where did my style come from? What influenced it? How did it develop? I find it easier to list a number of components than to assign the importance of any of them singly. My mentor, Arthur Barnes, was important, though his influence was more significant in such areas as care in workmanship and in techniques of constructing a variety of forms than in the style of particular pieces. During my first year under his tutelage, I made a copy of one of his footed goblets and produced six of them. He chose that piece because it required several skills, all fundamental to pewter work, and doing six repetitions would reinforce the lessons. Nearly three decades later, those goblets are prized possessions in our home and we use them for special feast days such as Thanksgiving and Christmas. They became important enough that as the family grew through the marriages of our children, additional goblets of the same design were added to the collection. Still, closing my eyes and remembering all of Arthur's work that I have seen, our styles are significantly different, and it would be impossible to show that my style derives from his.

The help I received from the metal spinners at the Gorham Company as they made silver plates, trays, and the like made me more aware of their traditional designs. When they acquired the rights to do pewter replicas of the work of Lester Vaughn, a contemporary Taunton pewterer whose work was being collected soon after his death, I studied Vaughn's designs. Though I never patterned any work after particular pieces he made, I admired a certain cleanness of form achieved by uncluttered lines that characterizes his work.

There was a powerful precedent in colonial pewter for being aware of designs in silver. William Will (working dates 1764–1798), the most celebrated of early American pewterers, worked in Philadelphia, a sophisticated and style-conscious city. There are three distinct stylistic periods in Will's production: the Queen Anne, rococo, and neoclassical, and his evolution reflects the change occurring in the styles of silver while he worked.

I own two pre-Revolutionary porringers that I used as models for replicas: a Gershom Jones (working dates 1774–1809) and a Richard Lee (working dates 1788–1820). There are several basic styles of porringers, but it is not a form that invites innovation so much as replication. The discipline in making them involves creation of a handle that can be one of a half-dozen styles, then attaching it to a bowl that can be one of three or four basic styles. Proportions are critical. Montgomery has it right when he makes the judgment, "Conception and proportion give an object nobility and distinction." (*A History of American Pewter*, A Winterthur Book, New York: Praeger, 1973, p. 44)

Friends gave me a nine-and-a-half-inch plate by Roswell Gleason (working dates 1821–1871) with a gift note that said "For the other RG in American pewter." Having the gift and becoming aware of the similar initials prompted me to look at Gleason's work. There was much to admire and some things to avoid. I replicated the plate in somewhat heavier metal, and later created a near-replica of his chamberstick. These became standard parts of our production. When asked to make a presentation plate for the University of New Hampshire to celebrate its centennial, the Gleason plate, with the centennial logo, made a fine gift. Again, if Gleason's general work were on exhibit beside mine, it would be difficult to see distinctive similarities.

The first significant design creation of my own was a charger made from a fifteen-inch pewter disk. Chargers need size and 15 " was the maximum-diameter disk that could be worked on the Diamond lathe, the only lathe I owned at the time. For a charger, the four most important decisions for the design are: the diameter of the whole; the width of the rim; the shape of the booge, that is, the curved side rising from the base to the rim; and the edge of the rim, which can be single or double thickness and ornamented with lines. If all the proportions are right, the eye is comfortable with the result in a glance. If one measurement is off, the eye will keep coming back to that part of the design every time it is viewed. But how to get the proportions just right?

To make the chuck, or spinning form over which the charger would be spun, I started with a fifteen-inch circle of mahogany wood one and a half inches thick, drilled and threaded in the center and fitted to the headstock, or power end, of the lathe. The chuck when finished would give the shape and proportions of the charger when spun. I could see the design take shape as the wood-turning tools formed the chuck. But beware. If too much wood is removed, there is no way to put it back. The whole process must begin all over again. Mahogany is expensive. Time is money. Therefore, be careful.

I took a circular piece of white cardboard the diameter of the charger I wanted and tried to visualize how wide the rim should be to create a pleasing proportion in the design. I transferred the result to the wood and began cutting away the wood just outside my line. I could always take more off if necessary. I worked the wooden chuck down gradually, stopping as needed to study what was happening with the form taking shape.

I was tempted to fantasize. Did Michelangelo see the Moses in the marble as he worked on that great sculpture? Or did he keep going back to the working drawings to check measurements? Too grand a thought for the scope of the task at hand, even if the problem is the same for both. Take off just as much as required and no more lest you spoil the work. Get the shape of the booge and the height of the rim just so. Then shape the rim so that it will have a gentle lift toward the edges. Rough-sand the wood to take out tool marks. Take it off the lathe and look at it from all angles. Is it ready for a prototype to be spun over the chuck? No. Take away a little more wood at the top of the booge. Now a bit more sanding and then the first charger can be formed. The spinning will take some time. Then we will know. So by stages the design found its way from the head through the hands to the materials being worked. When it was completed, the head and heart said, "Yes, this is it." Is that the genesis of style?

Now, a quarter of a century later, the mahogany chuck is on the shelf, still ready to be put on a lathe to spin yet another charger. The many times the metal has been formed over it have firmed and smoothed the surface until it is like velvet to the touch. It is a thing of beauty in itself. The chargers formed over it have traveled far, and some have had special uses. At retirement, a much-loved teacher of surgery of the hands was honored by twenty-one of his students. Durer's "praying hands" were etched in a charger's center as a tribute to him, and around the rim were inscribed the names of his students who were practicing the surgery he had taught them. Another was engraved with a design of Mexican bats, done in the style of an Indian ceremonial painting, and presented to a world authority on bats. Still another met a far different fate, meeting its doom when a gourmet chef put it into a hot oven to keep some stuffed mushrooms warm until they could be served to his guests.

On a memorable Thanksgiving Day I carved a turkey on a charger that had the numerals for the year it was made, 1971, stamped just below the touchmark. It was that year, or the year before, that I had offered a charger for the show at the Sunapee Craftsmen's Fair of the League of New Hampshire Craftsmen. It was chosen as the centerpiece of the metals exhibition and a staff member who assisted the European designer of the show reported that he had held it at arm's length and said, "This manages to combine a feeling of the traditional and the contemporary."

I stand before the shelves where our pewter is offered. I see suggestions of the old and the new, the past and the present. From the evidence before me, I have much the same feeling that I had long ago at the Sharon Arts Center. There is a unity of some kind in the style, even though there are many variations and no deadening sameness. The pieces never seem at war with each other. None looks out of place. Yet, strangely, each seems to draw some attention to itself for what it is. Clearly, each has a simplicity of line and a coherence in proportions that give integrity to the total form.

Where does it come from? I don't know. Perhaps no one knows. I have a theory regarding my own sensibility. Thousands of impressions of work that was created over many centuries and by countless artisans have been seen and responded to, and have created a vast reservoir of data. This unconscious or subconscious mass is not a "ready-reference file," for I cannot summon it at will to the conscious mind. But because they were seen, recorded, responded to, and considered, they have nourished a wide spectrum of potential creativity. Something in each artisan is, I believe, influenced by the way he responded to each datum when it was experienced. What emerges from that vast realm of the unconscious may very well be the result of the countless responses made over time in discerning what was found to be most memorable and pleasing, and thus forming his personal aesthetic sense.

Learning and Growing

ABBEY PEWTER AND THE LONDON GUILD

I was surprised to receive a letter from Charles Hull, the curator of the London Guild, asking if they might catalog my work as part of a project seeking out individual pewterers around the world. I responded that my pewtering was a summer-vacation activity in which our children and I engaged, and that I doubted that we were a large enough enterprise to interest them. I did, however, send a list of our products and the prices, newspaper articles, and several photographs of our work. The return letter indicated that they were still interested. Indeed, it seems our situation resembled some of the family firms around London in the seventeenth and eighteenth centuries. They requested pictures of as many of our pieces as we could send, and especially those of our own design. So began a series of events and relationships that were to have a future we could hardly have imagined.

In 1979, some months after our first exchange of letters, our tankard was designed and sixteen were produced. When photographs were taken, a set was sent to Charles Hull, curator of the Worshipful Company of Pewterers (WCOP), the formal name of the London Guild. In strict usage, our tankard would have been called a mug, or an "unlidded" tankard, the word "tankard" generally being reserved for lidded drinking vessels. When I heard from Charles, he did not engage in a tutorial on nomenclature but adopted my usage. His letter also included two invitations.

His comment about the tankard lifted my spirits. "To return to your own work" he wrote, " I very much like the straightforward simplicity and elegance of your latest tankard and hope you will be able to continue developing further interesting pieces in the future, as I believe this is what the industry—certainly in England—desperately needs."

His requests opened two doors. As curator of the WCOP he had been asked by Batsford, a reputable publishing house, to write a definitive book on the pewter craft. He foresaw one difficulty ahead: getting a written description of the pewter-spinning process, "as so much of the technique is developed from 'feel' and individual sensibility to the material," as he put it.

First of our unlidded tankard line. Praised by the curator of the London Guild.

He was, he said, anxious to obtain "experienced comment from craftsmen in order to make the instructions as practical as possible." Would I be willing to help? He outlined a variety of areas where assistance was needed.

The other opened door was an invitation, expressed in the hope that I might one day find the time to "visit us in London as I think you would find our extensive collection of antique British pewter of interest." The invitation could not have been more timely. He had written on May 23, 1981. I was planning to be in England from June 9 to July 1, as international guest preacher at the historic Bunyan Church in Bedford. I replied at once, sending the telephone number of the manse in Bedford, and indicated that I should be delighted to visit the Guildhall, see the collection, and converse about his book project.

Charles Hull, I was to learn, is descended from a distinguished line of pewterers. His family were practicing pewterers as early as 1451, antedating by twenty-two years the granting of the first Royal Charter to the guild by Edward IV in 1473. His company, Hull Pewter, continues in a leadership position. In 1982, they produced a two-handled covered cup in Queen Anne style, believed to be the first pewter ever to be cast under vacuum, using silicone rubber molds. He had, at that date, been experimenting in the techniques of the craft for more than twenty years. He was a member of the Court of the Worshipful Company of Pewterers as well as curator, the former being a reminder of the special history the guild had in maintaining standards for the craft.

The guild movement grew in importance from the twelfth century, as workers grouped together, often living in a close community. Their formal guild structure was well established in several countries by the fourteenth century. They had control over the trade and the lives of their members. In Germany, guilds date from: Nuremburg, 1285; Augsburg, 1324; Hamburg, 1375. In Sweden guild rules date from 1485. In France: Paris, 1268; Strasbourg, 1363; and Dijon, 1478. In London, the fellowship of pewterers was strong enough to gain official recognition by 1348. Edward III granted them royal privilege in 1363, and in 1473 Edward IV granted the charter that gave the London Guild the power to control the trade throughout the country.

The height of the guilds' power throughout Europe was during the fifteenth and sixteenth centuries. Their function was primarily to check the quality of the metal used by members, to authorize the various marking systems, and to regulate and monitor wages, prices, hours of work, and the organization of apprenticeships. There was some control or influ-

Charles Hull with a partner of Abbey Pewter.

ence in private lives, influencing whom the members married, what church they attended, and which taverns they frequented. They were, clearly, close-knit in both business and social matters.

The power of the guilds faded in the eighteenth century. Owners and workers resented the interference in their work by the courts of the guilds, and gradually paid less attention to the rules. The French Revolution sounded the death knell of guilds in France, and the Low Countries and Germany followed suit. The guild system was never introduced into America, doubtless the result of the entrepreneurial spirit and the ethos of freedom.

I had read enough about the guilds in Europe, and in particular about the London Guild, to be particularly excited about the prospect of visiting, especially as I would have the curator as guide. Once settled in the manse in Bedford, I soon heard from Charles Hull and we planned a day together. He would meet Susan and me at Abbey Pewter in midmorning, introduce us to one of the small but very high-quality pewter firms in London, then take us to the Guildhall, where, as he said, they would "lay on a luncheon" for us in the formal dining room. It was a memorable day.

We arrived at Abbey Pewter, where we met Charles Hull and Jack Murrell, a longtime teacher in metal craft and engineering subjects who was collaborating with Charles on the pewtering book. Before we went in, Charles told me that Channer and Webster, the partners in Abbey Pewter, would be featured in the book they were writing and that the pictures would be taken here to illustrate the casting process.

I was surprised to find that Abbey Pewter, for all its well-deserved reputation for traditional pewter of the highest quality, occupied a space no larger than the barn space we used for our production in Hillsborough Centre. I marveled at the compactness of the operation. Every nook and cranny was used; the furnace and cleanup lathe and the worktable for soldering were efficiently arranged to require the fewest steps but still have elbow room for the work required in production.

It was impossible to be there without a sense of history. Casting is the oldest method for the production of pewter, and the kinds of metal molds being used there were traditional—and durable enough to last hundreds of years if given proper care. The production under way was a tulip mug, or baluster. It required three sets of molds: one for the handle and two for the body of the mug. The body would be cast in two parts, cleaned up on a lathe, joined by soldering, then cleaned up again. The handle would be cast, cleaned up, fitted to the curve of the mug, and then soldered on.

One of the partners was casting, the other taking the rough castings to the lathe and skimming them to remove surface imperfections. As the morning wore on, he had a number of halves stacked beside the soldering table. He began to solder them together, and this gave us a chance to see the forming operation through to completion.

I had had some experience in casting into simple silicone rubber molds and with a bronze spoon mold. However, the casting of the bottom and top of the mug was new and exciting. The gunmetal molds were made in several parts that fit together and were locked in place by metal pins. To keep the inflow of molten pewter from blocking the exit of the air, the mold was tilted to the side; the pouring proceeded as the mold was slowly brought to an upright position. A surplus of pewter was used to fill the cavity in the sprue, providing additional pewter to fill any shortage caused by shrinkage as the metal cooled.

When the casting had time to cool enough to become solid, the pins were taken out and a knocker—a round, hardwood block, looking like a short, oversized policeman's stick—was struck against the sides of the molds at odd angles to loosen and release the castings. They then would be inspected for imperfections. If any were found, the piece went back into the melting pot. There were very few rejects while I was watching. The men wore thick gloves to handle the hot molds. I was impressed by how quickly the work went, and was caught up in the rhythm in the sequence of motions used, as the workbench soon had a stack of the parts now ready to be finished and soldered.

The work in cleaning up the castings was more familiar. The lathe used had forms that centered the pieces so that the surface imperfections could be skimmed away. Abrasive papers smoothed the pieces inside and out. Special care was taken in preparing the joint, which needed to be well fitted for the soldering process.

The torch for the soldering had a small, intense blue flame that came to a point like a pencil. The focus of the heat allowed the pinpointing of the seam with a concentration of heat that added efficiency and danger. If the torch were to be left in one place a second too long, the pewter would be melted and the piece ruined. I was impressed by the sureness of control of the heat and the stick solder used to seal the joint. There was very little excess to be cleaned up after this operation.

There is a distinct difference in the look and feel of pewter that is cast, rather than spun on a lathe. The cast pewter looks, and is, heavier. The London pewterers chose to stay with their molds and older technology after the rise of spinning in the early 1800s, whereas Sheffield pewterers embraced the spinning and used it for both pewter and silver plate. Today, in Britain generally and in the United States, spinning is the predominant method. In the London area, and in Germany, the use of molds is more common.

For nearly two hours we watched and questioned the craftsmen about their procedures and techniques. I proposed to the partners, Channer and Webster, that I buy some of their wares for resale in my shop, so that my customers could see the differences between the cast pewter of tradition, and our spun pewter. They agreed and gave me their catalog to use when ordering from America. We later ordered six of their products, and after a time reduced that to three: a mustard pot, a bud vase, and a tulip mug, these being the most popular with our customers.

At length we took our leave and headed to the Guildhall. We paused at the doorway, posed for pictures in front of the guild sign, then went in. If there is religious awe in arriving at a holy place of pilgrimage, there was for

At the London Guild. (Left to right) Raymond and Susan Gibson, Peggy and Jack Murrell, and Charles Hull.

me a special feeling about this place, for centuries a center in the pewter trade and now holding a collection spanning that history. The setting was reminiscent of a great hall of a medieval English manor house, with all the manorial ambience.

We gave our attention to the remarkable collection of pewter, then had lunch in the spacious dining room, where we were the only party present. Looking across the empty tables, Charles Hull said that their most recent formal occasion had been a dinner in honor of "your President Reagan's ambassador to our country."

As much as the spirited discussion at the luncheon, my memories, now two decades old, are still visually powerful. I can see the walls of the guild's meeting room, with oak paneling on which, in column after column around the room, are carved the names of the Worshipful Masters and their dates from the earliest days of the guild. I can see the needlepoint on the backs of the many chairs in the dining room. The needlepoint design is a rendering of the intricate gold medallion worn by the Worshipful Master when presiding at guild meetings. I recognized the design immediately, for Hull Pewter had done a casting of the medallion, using modern silicone molds in a spin-casting machine, and Charles had sent one to me. I can see the large glass cases holding the priceless collection of pewter, and while I cannot remember particular pieces, the cumulative effect, plus the knowledge of the age of the collection, is awe-inspiring.

The courtesy of Charles Hull and Jack Murrell to Susan and me on that day in London was to prove the beginning of a warm friendship. I watched from afar with interest as they put their book together, then suffered with them as the publisher pared away large chunks of their research and writing. Nevertheless, when it appeared, the book was handsome and very useful in its depth and range. We entertained Jack Murrell and his wife, Peggy, in Providence, and kept in touch through the years by Christmas letters. In 1984 I tried, without success, to get an American edition of the book by encouraging Anchor Books to deal with Batsford.

One legacy of the trip was a challenge Charles Hull addressed to me personally. He spoke of being a "complete pewterer." He encouraged me to attempt all aspects of the craft and to seek to master each one. His venturing into casting under vacuum set an example of one who was willing to test the frontiers of the science of production and the possibilities of the trade. I have remembered his challenge as I have gone beyond the lathe and spinning processes into casting in bronze molds, in working with plaster, clay, and silicone molds, and in spin-casting. Hand- forming by hammering I have not developed, though I admire such work by my mentor, Arthur Barnes, and marvel at some of the pieces done by his mentor, Frances Felton. The challenge is always there in any case, but it is strengthened when personalized by my memory of Charles Hull's friendly comments that day at the London Guild.

When we left them, we went on to Saint Paul's Cathedral, where workmen were busily engaged in preparing for the upcoming wedding of Prince Charles and Diana Spencer. It was apparently a great attraction to the schools, as we could scarcely move for the press and flow of the young scholars visiting. Charles Hull had told me of the guild's gift to the royal couple, and the challenge of producing it. They had taken a great bronze mold from their collection that had been used to cast a large charger for one of Prince Charles's forebears some hundreds of years earlier, and put it into use for this new occasion.

The art of heating such a large mold and the prospect of getting a good casting were challenges they enjoyed. The first few attempts produced, as they expected, only partial results. There wouldn't be a complete charger. As molten pewter is poured into the mold it begins to cool and turns pasty before becoming solid. As it becomes pasty it ceases to flow. To be successful it must fill the entire mold before it turns pasty, then solid. As the great, heavy mold was used, it became increasingly hot throughout. At a certain point, pewter would flow into the whole cavity and then solidify. Then, and not until then, a complete charger would be the result. Once that temperature was reached, charger after charger could be poured. Charles Hull said that when they had a good one, they made extras, in the event that the engraver made a mistake. They had met the challenge and felt good about the results with the centuries-old mold that had been so long out of use.

We remembered the story of that wedding gift when, back in New Hampshire, we rose very early on the royal wedding day and watched the ceremony from Saint Paul's Cathedral beamed to the world by satellite. A happier time. We now remember that day with sadness, knowing what happened in a marriage so brightly begun, and the tragedy that ended Princess Diana's life.

However, the other London memories are undimmed, and I am grateful for gracious friends we made, the warmth and kindness they extended to us, and continued sharing over the years. The visit to Abbey Pewter prompted me to stock and sell several of its lines since, so that visitors to our shop have been able to see excellent pewter made in the older method of casting from bronze molds. In our showroom we keep a ready copy of *The Techniques of Pewtersmithing* by Charles Hull and Jack Murrell. For those interested, we enjoy opening it to the pictures it contains of our pewter, and to the generous comments about the quality of contemporary American pewter.

CASTING PRAYERS

Members of the Hillsborough Historical Society came by the pewter shop to ask if I would take part in a fund-raising event to support the care and maintenance of the Franklin Pierce Homestead. Pierce, president from 1852 to 1856, though not always treated kindly by the historians, is New Hampshire's most distinguished personage, and his homestead is the focus of much of the activity of the local historical society. They were planning an open house with a small fair, historical booths, and demonstrations of some early crafts. There would be a great deal of publicity and then Governor Sununu had agreed to attend. They thought that several thousand people might come.

The lathes and buffing machinery could not be moved and would not make a particularly fitting demonstration. However, the one portable part of the craft, and the most appropriate for the occasion, was the small furnace, with the large melting pot, ladle, and spoon mold. The historical period was correct, and the exhibition could be contained in a small area. I knew from two similar occasions in Rhode Island that casting is a popular attraction. People like to see molten metal poured into a mold and to watch as the mold is opened and the newly cast object is revealed.

At an earlier demonstration, at a fair to raise money for a Rhode Island historical building, a boy edged his bicycle into the front of a dozen or so onlookers, saw the pouring of metal into a mold for a porringer handle, and narrowed his eyes with intensity and expectancy. I watched his face as I opened the mold and took out the handle. He looked for a second at the handle, took a deep breath, and then left hurriedly. I wondered at his sudden departure, but understood it a few minutes later when I saw a half-dozen boys his age coming on their bikes. He had rounded up his friends to see what he had seen. They crowded in as close as my safety barrier would allow and their eyes were riveted to the process as I poured the molten metal. I gave it thirty seconds to cool, then opened the mold and lifted out the gleaming porringer handle with my small pliers. Two or three of the boys said in unison, "Cool!" I repeated the word back to them with an inflection that said, "Cool?" They looked at the metal and at each other and then burst out laughing.

When the casting process is going well, it looks simple. But that is deceptive. Dozens of things can go wrong and in any casting session at least one or two will. Casting spoons is particularly difficult because the metal has to stay molten while it runs down the full length of the spoon's handle and it must spread evenly outward into the broader expanse of the spoon's bowl. The mold needs a surface that the metal will move over without sticking. Impurities in the metal will leave small pits or holes. The temperature of the metal is critical and cooling must be uniform.

A collection of spoons.

The afternoon before we were to demonstrate at the Franklin Pierce Homestead, I asked our apprentice, Willie Guinn, to set up for casting practice just outside the front of the barn. A clear, still day, as was forecast for the following day, made the outdoor casting acceptable. While we did, on occasion, cast indoors, we felt safer outdoors, or in our special forge area, a shed attached to the barn with a dirt floor and cross ventilation.

As I took the rat-tail spoon mold from its special storage area, I remembered the process leading to its purchase. I had asked a friend who dealt in antiques and traveled a lot to be on the lookout for an early spoon mold in good condition. Scars or scratches on the inside of the mold would produce those same blemishes on the casting. If the halves of the mold did not fit together properly, metal would escape and casting would be impossible.

Just over a year later I received a call on a Sunday evening. My friend was in Pennsylvania at a show and sale and had found a rat-tail spoon mold in good condition that dated from around 1790. "Are you sitting down?" he asked. "Why?" "I am going to tell you the price being asked." I sat down and he told me. A quick calculation indicated that with normal use, I would have to live to the age of 105 to sell enough of the spoons I would expect to cast before the cost of the mold was amortized. "Buy it," I said. "What's a pewter shop without a spoon mold?"

A new spoon just out of the mold.

When Willie had the setup completed, I lighted the propane "plumber's furnace" and placed the large melting pot over it. We put in the pewter ingots and waited for it to reach the desired temperature for pouring. For small castings the desired temperature is around 300 degrees Celsius, or 570 degrees Fahrenheit. Larger castings, like plates or chargers, need temperatures ranging upward to 400 degrees Celsius, or 750 degrees Fahrenheit. One of the tricks of the trade in earlier times when they did not have thermometers that could measure such high temperatures, was to use a dry cedar shingle. It would be thrust into the molten mix and held for two or three seconds and then withdrawn. If it came out very light tan, the mix was not hot enough. If it came out charred and burst into flame, the mix was too hot. If it came out a rich, in-between brown, the metal was perfect for pouring. This would work for small castings, but it would not be helpful for the large, high-temperature casting. I had never owned a metal thermometer at that point, and had relied on the cedar-shingle method to test my metal.

When I was satisfied with the temperature, I began to pour the metal into the mold which was held in a near-vertical position by specially designed handles. The handles allowed the mold to be managed while hot, gave leverage to clamp the mold firmly together, and opened to remove the spoon. The process is called "gravity casting" for obvious reasons. There would be a steady, continuous pour of the metal into the sprue hole and it would flow down and fill the bottom, forming the handle first and then the bowl of the spoon. The flow must be quick and unimpeded; and premature cooling would solidify the metal and block the flow. The result would be a deformed suggestion of the piece you were anticipating when the mold was opened.

We expected to have half a dozen misses, or partial spoons, as the mold itself was heated to the temperature needed. Some people heat their molds in an oven, but with a spoon mold, I have found it best to heat the mold with several trial castings, as it gets me into the rhythm of casting. Still, we were not prepared for what followed. After a dozen castings we were still getting partial spoons, some resembling a surrealistic Dali painting—interesting, but not a spoon. They were returned to the melting pot, where they quickly disappeared into the mix.

I let the mold cool and cleaned the inside of it, thinking that there was something about the surface that was interfering with the flow of the metal. Then I held the clean surfaces over a lighted candle and "lampblacked" the entire inner surfaces, a traditional practice from colonial, and even earlier, times. The soot was like velvet and would give a minimum of resistance to flow.

We started over and proceeded through the six or seven expected failures, then watched for the first good one, a complete spoon. None came. We kept working, and while some results were better than others, none was good enough to save. With the shining new metal, each flaw seemed to announce its presence and draw attention to itself. A recalcitrance in the metal? A rebuff to us? What was happening? Whatever it was, it had never happened this way before.

As failure followed failure, I was aware that Willie was becoming very tense. He was an excellent apprentice, with good hands and a quick mind. He had responded well to the requirements of an exacting craft; indeed, he seemed to welcome them. I intuited what he was thinking, and actually was beginning to think the same thought myself. Finally, he took a deep breath and said, "It's going to be very embarrassing tomorrow if it goes like this!" I couldn't have said it better. We had passed thirty without getting an acceptable spoon.

We were approaching quitting time. As I turned off the furnace I said, with a mixture of conviction and playful bravado, "Willie, you just say your prayers for us tonight. We are going down there tomorrow and cast spoons!" I looked at his eyes and he was not smiling. He had seen repeated reasons to worry about tomorrow. He was enough of a perfectionist to find failure hard to handle. There was no visible reason for either of us to be optimistic. He helped me put the equipment away and as he left, I called after, "Remember to say your prayers. We are going to have a good day."

The next morning was hot, clear, and dry. Very little air was stirring and the forecast was for temperatures in the nineties. We were assigned a spot beside the Homestead, in front of the carriage barn, and with no shade from a sun that was bent on setting some sort of record. As a safety measure, we placed our low worktable as a barrier between us and the visitors. Our stools were placed on each side of the furnace. Willie would "top off" the metal in the pot when it needed additions, and help in the mold release by taking the spoons if they did not separate quickly. I would pour the metal and manage the casting while fielding questions from onlookers. There was a fairgoers' mood; laughter and good spirits flowed by us in the stream of visitors.

I cannot recall how I felt as we reached numbers five and six and the mold was approaching its required heat. Willie and I had not looked at each other after the first fragment of a spoon appeared. However, number five was better than four, and six was better than five. They were still imperfect though, and Willie put them back into the melting pot. Then, number seven was perfect: fully formed, with no visible blemishes. Willie placed it on the metal tray on the work table. Our eyes met but neither of us spoke. Numbers eight, nine, and ten were flawless. We were in a rhythm now. The crowds were building and the onlookers, feeling the pressure of those behind, still held their places to see the cycle through a second time. When the numbers allowed, people would stay longer, ask questions, and express their pleasure at seeing the process for the first time in their lives.

By midafternoon the heat was truly oppressive, made more so by our proximity to the furnace and that unrelenting sun. Our pile of cast spoons was high and growing. We liked it that way. Governor Sununu approached and stopped to watch. He demonstrated his engineering background by asking technical questions. Happily, I knew the answers. When he was gone and the crowds began to dwindle, we slowed the pace and eventually I turned off the furnace. As I did so, I poured one final time. As Willie took the finished spoon out of the mold, I said to him in a voice no one else would hear, "Those must have been some powerful prayers you said last night." As he placed the spoon on the large pile representing our day's work, he looked at them with an expression of quiet satisfaction, and the playful edges of a smile lighted his face. He was too private a person to reveal whether he had invited some special help from the Almighty. We were both tired, pleased with the day, and willing to let the mystery of it be our benediction.

SUNAPEE II

In his *The Two Paths*, Ruskin wrote, "Fine art is that in which the hand, the head, and the heart of man go together." Any visit to a good craft fair provides a showcase for that collaboration: skills, intelligence, and feeling resulting in the endless marvels of human creativity.

Each time I return to the Sunapee Craftsmen's Fair, I have variations of the same experience. First there is the overall impression: the mass of tents, the swarm of people, the concentration of booths snugly fitted together, and an incredible variety of crafted offerings. Second is the experience of standing still, looking at a single exhibit and seeing the handiwork of a single artisan, the year's work reflecting many years of development and practice of his or her craft. Here are the results of a continuing interior collaboration, skills of hands, powers of thoughtful probing, and decisions among competing options, the execution and results that communicate spirit and quality of feeling. Here, on this sloping hillside, under these tents, is gathered an aggregate of personal craft experience that, if measured in years and projected through time, would reach backward to, and beyond, the era of ancient Greece and Rome.

The Sunapee Craftsmen's Fair is sponsored by the League of New Hampshire Craftsmen Foundation and calls itself "the oldest crafts fair in the nation." The 1997 fair was the sixty-fourth in a series that has grown steadily from modest beginnings. The league had its genesis in the mid-1920s, when craft classes in Wolfeboro under the sponsorship of the Rotary Club's A. Cooper Ballentine began collaboration with Mrs. J. Randolph Coolidge, leader of a craft shop in Center Sandwich. They formed a cooperative committee to promote a handicraft movement, then sought and secured guidance from Royal Bailey Farnum, then director of the Rhode Island School of Design, and Allen Eaton, of the Russell Sage Foundation.

These advisers gave both inspiration and guidelines that were important for the organization being formed.

The founding committee secured support from Gov. John Winant, who established the New Hampshire Commission of Arts and Crafts, the first such state support of crafts. The seven-member working group formulated a report to the governor, later shared responsibility for the founding of the league in February 1932, and served as its first council members. In a review of the early history of the league, Betty Steele wrote:

The first report to Governor Winant, in September 1931, outlined values of hand versus machine work with emphasis on individuality of expression, and stressed the need for developing competent community leadership, locating good instructors, and employing a properly trained and compensated director. In it the following statement of philosophy was made:

> To raise New Hampshire crafts and craftsmanship to the highest aesthetic level.
>
> To provide gainful occupation for men, women and youth of the state in home industries, native handicrafts and the arts.
>
> To promote this philosophy adequately through carefully devised procedures . . . and through the development of confidence and State pride in local ability and creative power.

It is of special interest to see that at this early, and pre-mass production era, Farnum had warned, "The moment ideals of art are relinquished for the sake of quantity production or seeming more rapid sales, danger lies ahead and the strength of the League's work will begin to weaken." (Betty Steele, *The League — Its First Forty Years.)*

The Craftsmen's Fair today continues a legacy reaching back to its beginning. There is an emphasis on quality of result and the integrity of the craft's production. A jury process seeks to safeguard the standards of the work on display, and booth monitors from year to year set standards for the way the work is presented to the fairgoers. The various committees are made up of league members; thus, both meanings of "league" are present; an association, and a level of performance.

I doubt that anyone can visit the fair and look at every booth, even if a full day or more is committed to the task. I cannot focus after the first hour or so, at least to the extent necessary really to see what I am looking at. I notice how many others have, as the day goes on, a glazed expression. My interest level among all the offerings is higher in media where I have actual experience. Weaving, woodwork, and pewter get quick and knowing attention. Painting and sculpture are areas of some experience and continuing interest. Ceramics and leather are realms of mystery, and basketry a marvel of unity between design and material. Part of me would like to attempt them one and all; a wiser, inner voice reminds me that it takes a whole life to master just one craft.

When pewterers demonstrate, I have watched for pleasure and to learn as much as possible. No two pewterers do the craft the same way. We do not watch in order to copy, but to fill our own data bank of possibilities. Given a new situation when I am venturing into untried techniques, a blend of several different possibilities drawn from the data bank of memory may evolve as my solution to the problem at hand. If it works well, there is a new weapon in the arsenal.

The first pewterer I watched at Sunapee was Lindsey Shuford, a quiet, steady, pleasant man who demonstrated the making of cordial cups, quick and easy to complete while visitors watched. He used a three-inch pewter disk, and formed and finished the piece on the lathe. He did not comment as he worked, but would respond to questions with clear, concise answers. Pewter was not a primary occupation; he had a regular job with the phone or power company in his Massachusetts town. He took a kindly interest in my development, and in retirement moved to the Carolinas, selling me a South Bend metal lathe he did not want to take with him.

One of the most colorful demonstrators I can recall was Fred Pulsifer, a pewterer with a distinctive style in his technique and in his presentation of himself and his work. Of medium build, weathered from outdoor work, he was seldom seen without a corncob pipe in his mouth. He clearly enjoyed demonstrating and, unlike Shuford, would talk about what and how he was working to achieve a particular result. His machinery had not been new for a long time, was adapted to special uses he had designed, and was treated to the kind of care some antique-car buffs give their aging vehicles to keep them running as smoothly as when they came from the factory.

Fred had fashioned a set of tools and jigs to create special effects in his designs. His work was normally begun on the lathe, which meant that pieces formed would be circular. He could form a bowl on the lathe, then take a jig he had designed and roll the edges inward at four points to create a scalloped effect. The marvel of that operation was his capacity to make each of the "roll-ins" identical in shape and precisely spaced to produce a bowl that was perfectly symmetrical. His concentration was evident as he aligned the jig, steadied the bowl, and rolled in the edge. Talk would stop, and sometimes the pipe would go out. When finished, he would hold the piece at different angles, studying the light on the curved surfaces. If it pleased him, he would hand the piece to someone watching him work, and light his pipe before going on to the next operation.

After Fred became aware that I was learning the craft, he was generous in sharing his knowledge and would take me step by step through a set of procedures, alerting me to the possibilities of mishaps at various stages. I saw Fred answer questions from those watching who didn't know enough to form a proper question. He reminded me of the German-American theologian, Paul Tillich, under whom I had studied at Union and Columbia. A student would ask what everyone in the class would think a "dumb" question. Tillich would listen carefully, find something in the question that he could rephrase into a "good" question, and answer it to the edification of everyone in the room, never leaving the original questioner feeling "put down." Pulsifer would do that, standing by his lathe, puffing on his pipe, teaching those watching something about pewter making and, too, the appeal of a generous spirit.

In his later years, Fred and his wife wintered in the Southeast, traveling from one craft fair to another. Fred had rigged out a caravan that contained travel space for them, and the back had doors that opened outward, creating a mobile workshop. His wife, who did the selling of his production and the bookkeeping, was vital to the traveling operation, as she was at Sunapee where she managed the booth where his product was sold. "How can you travel with living quarters and workshop, plus the product for sale, all in one vehicle?" I asked Fred during an intermission in his demonstration.

"The living quarters are tight," he said. "The workshop is simple with the minimum of tools needed to do small pieces, enough to let people see the metal being worked. For product, we carry a little to sell, and for the rest, we take orders." He smiled as he continued, "I'm usually a year or more behind in filling my orders."

"How do you keep people waiting for that long? Do they prepay?"

"No. I don't take any money down. They are told that I keep my orders on a list and when their name comes up, they will receive a postcard telling them that they are near the top of the list. If they still want the order, they should send a check and mailing address, and they will get their pewter."

"Don't you lose a lot of your orders a year later?" I asked.

"No, not many," he answered. "Maybe ten percent. But people know the rules when they order. We lose them then if we are going to lose them. I think they value a piece more by having to wait for it."

At the Sunapee Fair there is an annual juried show that exhibits the best work of the various crafts and features work in all media. Awards are given in separate media and each year there is an award for Best in Show, a much coveted honor. It was, as I recall, the year before his death from a heart attack, that Fred won Best in Show for a water pitcher, done in a contemporary design, the handle coming vertical from the base and the body of the pitcher "leaning" toward the pouring spout. It was a striking and imaginative piece, well crafted by his seasoned skills and careful workmanship. It was a popular selection because it was fine work, and because the craftsman had won both the admiration and the affection of the league membership.

THE CHALICE

I had just finished the first Jefferson Cup and begun another when I was aware of a presence behind me. That was not unusual; ours is an open shop and visitors have always been welcome. I turned to greet a tall, elderly man who was looking back and forth from me to the work on the lathe.

"Go on with your work," he said, "I want to watch you."

"Have you seen pewter being spun before?" I asked.

A broad smile lighted his face. "I was a spinner at the Towle Company for over twenty years."

I had seen ads in the *New Yorker* magazine showing items made by the Towle Company and had enjoyed a caption under each ad; "Pewter is not a precious metal, if by precious you mean expensive."

He laughed, and said that he had seen a recent article about my work in the *Concord Monitor* and decided to pay a visit. He wanted to see my work and had brought some of his own to show me.

"I should give you my tool and let you show me," I said.

We had a spirited exchange for the next hour. He asked how I had learned and I told him about my mentor and tutor, and about my informal instruction from the spinners at the Gorham Company in Providence, Rhode Island. The talk was special, in part because it was rare. In the craft for thirty years, I have met and talked to fewer than a dozen working pewterers, and watched only half of them at work. Each has a different

Chalice given by the United Church of Christ to church leaders in Japan, the Philippines, Chile, Ghana, and Zimbabwe.

style. This visitor, Merlin Smith, was interested in my technique and made comments about his own when he saw something that he did another way. After watching me work and examining the work on my shelves, we went out to his car. He opened the trunk and took out several pieces for me to examine. He was, indeed, a fine craftsman.

Then Merlin surprised me by picking up a metal chuck and offering it to me. "I want you to have this." he said. He turned it over and added, "I think it will fit your lathe. It is one inch, eight." (This means that it would fit a spindle that was one inch in diameter, and had eight threads per inch.) It would fit one of my adapters, and was a welcome gift.

During all this time, Merlin's wife had been waiting in the car. She said that she had come along for the ride and to keep Merlin company. I invited her into the shop to see our work and found her both interested and knowledgeable. She picked up a chamberstick and commented about its "nice proportions." Looking at its handle and stalk, both of which were soldered on, she said, "Merlin can do about anything except solder." One of his arms was, I had noticed, withered and stiff. I had wondered how he was able to spin. It would be even more difficult to solder with the disability.

I took the chamberstick from her and wrapped it up with the comment that in honor of their visit, I wanted her to have this memento. Then, as I walked them back to their car, Merlin invited me to visit them.

"I'm gradually closing down my home shop," he said. "I have promised my machinery to a nice young fellow who wants to learn. I have a lot of chucks, and some of them might be of interest to you. I would like to think of some of them being a part of your operation." I asked for directions and promised that I would call when I had some time, and would certainly enjoy seeing his shop.

Though I could not know it then, the visit from Merlin was to mark the turning point in a design problem that had stymied me for much too long. Some of my pieces are replicas or variations of historic porringers, plates, chambersticks, and bowls. Others are of my design. A shelf in the shop is devoted to designs in progress. On that shelf was a chalice, or part of one. For over two years I had sketched and worked at a prototype, far longer than for any other piece I ever attempted. Part of it seemed right, but it would not come together as a total design. When completed, it would be made of three parts: a base, a midsection, and a bowl. Each would be made separately, the base and bowl spun on the lathe, and the center section, or stem, would be cast. Then they would be soldered together.

I was happy with the base and midsection. But the bowl was never right. Several drawings looked promising but when the chuck was made and the pewter spun over it, the result didn't satisfy. Our daughter, Lauren, spending a summer on vacation from the Parsons School of Design, encouraged me and made suggestions. One bowl was pronounced "almost." But

At the General Assembly of the United Church of Christ, the Chalice is presented by Paul Sherry to Noah Dzobo, moderator of the Evangelical Presbyterian Church in Ghana.

the motto used with our apprentices had been from the beginning, "Almost is not good enough!" I had to be governed by that same standard.

It was two weeks before I managed to return Merlin's visit. He lived in a small house beside a lake, with a smaller workshop attached. It was a marvel of organization and had the feel of a place that had been much used and a source of great pleasure. As he opened cupboards and moved among the shelves, he selected chucks that were duplicates or ones he was ready to part with.

We looked at his work and talked about techniques of the craft. He was a seasoned professional and had discovered ways to create special results by adaptations and "tricks" of the trade. Every spinner, he was sure, has a few tricks unique to his way of working. Merlin had a wry sense of humor, and commented about one or two failures so dramatic that he had kept them to show. As in my own case, each piece had its story, doubtless improved upon and refined with each retelling.

As I was nearing the time of departure, Merlin surprised me with his last offering. He picked a chuck from a lower shelf and handed it to me.

"I want you to have this. This is for the bowl of my chalice."

"Merlin, I didn't know you had made a chalice."

"Yes. I did some years ago. I don't have one around anymore. If ever I did want to make one again, would you let me come to your shop to spin it?"

"I'd be proud to have you spinning in my shop," I told him.

On the drive home I kept wondering if his bowl might match my work. He had shown me a drawing of his design, and the base—a simple, straight cone broadening toward the bottom—was completely different from mine. But his bowl design struck me as compatible with my beginning pieces. I wouldn't know until I attached his chuck to the lathe, spun the bowl, and took it to the shelf to see whether the pieces would work together in a total design. I felt a strange sense of anticipation tinged with wonder.

When I arrived home, I was informed that supper was ready. I ate quickly, telling Lauren and Susan briefly about the day. However, I didn't mention the chuck for the chalice. I wanted to be alone in the barn as I spun the first one. I left the table and hurried to try it. I put the chuck on the lathe and started the motor. It was perfectly centered, and the spinning went smoothly. I trimmed it to the proper height and cleaned it with a succession of abrasive papers, each finer in grit as the bowl became brighter.

My hands were steady in the forming process. But as I took the bowl off the lathe and went toward the shelf for the matchup, there was something in my hands that, while they were not exactly trembling, felt full of mystery and expectancy. I placed the bowl on the base and stood back. I felt myself taking a deep and thankful breath. Just then I became aware that Lauren was standing behind me. We were both quiet for a moment and then she asked, "Did you get the chuck for that from Merlin Smith?"

"Yes."

"Dad, this is too good to be an accident."

"I'm glad you think it's right, Lauren."

"It's more than right, Dad. It's a perfect match."

Two years later, in 1985, the national leaders of my denomination, the United Church of Christ, presented chalices that I had made as ceremonial gifts to church leaders from Japan and Chile, symbolizing the establishment of fraternal relationships. I wrote Merlin and enclosed the news story of the event, and heard from him that he was so happy to know of it.

Merlin died before the third chalice was presented, in 1987, to Bishop

Erme R. Camba, of the Federation of Protestant Churches in the Philippines. President Avery Post said, in making the presentation, "We are in full solidarity in the mission of God, and we are partners in that mission. With thanksgiving I give you this chalice." I wrote to Merlin's wife, who answered that Merlin had received great pleasure from his part in the creation of the chalice.

In 1991, the new president of the denomination, Paul Sherry, presented still another of our chalices, this time to another faith group on another continent. This was presented at a plenary session of the General Synod, to Noah Dzobo, the moderator of the Evangelical Presbyterian Church of Ghana.

The New Hampshire Conference of the United Church of Christ entered into a special fraternal relationship with the United Church of Zimbabwe in 1996, and at their annual meeting presented a chalice to the head of that group.

When I look at the shelf in the corner of our shop where the chalice is normally kept in its velvet-lined, walnut box, I sometimes think "long" thoughts. The words of the Creed about "the communion of the saints" makes me imagine the Christians in Japan, Chile, the Philippines, Ghana, and Zimbabwe, and to wonder what has happened in the bonds of fellowship across such distances and across the denominational lines that have been partly bridged in symbol and, I hope, in fact, by these presentations.

I also think "nearer" thoughts of individuals and parishes where the chalice has gone: Baptist, in Fall River, Massachusetts; Methodist, in Marlborough, Massachusetts; Episcopal, in Arlington, Massachusetts; Lutheran, in Minnesota; United Church of Christ, in Long Island, New York; and the Roman Catholic Church in my own community. The last was given in memory of a child who died while quite young, and I remember the priest, Father Bob, telling me how pleased he was to have the special chalice with the child's name engraved on it. In all these churches, with their variety of traditions, the communion is the central rite. It remembers and reenacts the central event in our faith on which eternal hope depends.

Though it is not a matter as grave and as religiously profound, sometimes I find myself thinking of another kind of "communion": of craftsmen and creation, of the sharing of skills and the joy of forming something that, until it was created, never before existed. I remember my teacher, Arthur, and my friend, Merlin, and the way their knowledge, skill and friendship enriched my life and work.

The "communion" is not with mentors and other guides alone, not merely with the older, but also with the younger—our children and the apprentices. At times when they have fashioned something so well, or have created something so truly their own, I could see the joy they felt in belonging to the company of creators. Perhaps they will never use the word "communion" and, indeed, may find new words for the experiences they have had. Whatever the words, it is the reality that matters. The longer we pursue a craft, and the deeper we go into it, the less we are able to express in words what we are finding very real in life.

THE BUNKY MYTHOLOGY

Bunky was a foundling puppy in need of food, shelter, and a family. A white Lab with a small mix of something else in his inheritance, he showed signs of having lived less than a safe and happy life in his first months. As he became secure in his new situation, began to believe that the good things happening to him would not be withdrawn, or the affection of our large family turned off, he responded with an unfailing love that lasted to the end of his life.

Each member of the family developed special ways of relating to him. No game found him relegated to the sidelines. When it was lacrosse, his retriever instincts were invaluable when a shot on goal missed and went flying into the tall grass beyond the stone walls of the yard. He found the ball and brought it back to the players. He took a lifelong joy in making a quick circle of the pond at the water's edge, watching the frogs ahead of him diving into the safety of deeper water. Lauren made a judgment once that "Bunky is the Elmer's Glue that holds us all together."

My own "Bunky thing" was to create a special language. To some, it sounded as if I were speaking in tongues, though it had some resemblance to the sound and cadence of a variety of European languages. It became a source for numerous stories. I also spoke to him in plain English when appropriate, and he developed a sizable vocabulary.

One midsummer day a group appeared in the pewter shop during a break in their schedule at a nearby college, where they were part of a special conference. Bunky had met them coming in and picked up a stick he had been retrieving. One of the group obliged, tossed it away, and watched as Bunky sped off and brought it back. The group wandered about the pewter shop from one workstation to another, watching the work in

Bunky was a special part of our family.

He was remembered by customers who asked for him after his death.

progress, and then to the shelves where our pewter was available for purchase.

Working at my lathe with my back to the group, I picked up a rather spirited series of exchanges, and recognized a number of buzzwords from the educational psychology discipline. One voice with a note of authority rose above the others and used the term "sequential signal system" in relation to learning. He liked the phrase and used it several times.

As they were about to leave, I turned off my lathe and went to the front of the barn to pick up Bunky's retrieving stick. "I'd like to show you something," I said. Everyone watched as I looked at Bunky and said, "Sit! Stay," then threw the stick into the parking lot. "Go!" Bunky was off at the word and brought it back to me. And, as I had expected, the voice I had been hearing declared, "That's a perfect example of the sequential signal system. The dog doesn't understand a single word, but he knows the sequence and follows it."

"Do you mind if I test your assumption about what Bunky knows?" I asked. "I think he recognizes words,"

"Go ahead," said the visitor. The others were now watching with interest.

Speaking in a perfectly level voice that did not accentuate any word, I began talking to Bunky. "It would please me if you would sit and plan to stay in your place." At the sound of the word "sit," Bunky sat down and stayed rooted to the spot. Then I continued, "Bunky, I believe this group would be interested if you would go get the stick." At the word "go" he was off. The group erupted in laughter.

"Let's try it another way," I said, using a three-word sequence and altering the third command. They watched as I said "Sit" and "Stay." Then in the same tone, and pointing to the stick I had thrown, I said "Don't!" Three times I repeated it, but Bunky remained rooted and watching me. Then I said simply, "I guess you won't move unless I use the word 'go.'"

He was off the instant he heard the word, to the renewed chorus of laughter.

One evening we had gathered in the barn after dinner and were having a table tennis tournament when a family drove into our parking lot and proceeded to the barn. They were interested in seeing our pewter operation. Staying in a nearby camp-site, they would be available the next day, so I invited them to come back when we were working. As I walked with them to their car, I bent over and spoke to Bunky in our playful, private language, unaware that they overheard.

The next day the family returned: parents, two sons, and two daughters. I taught the young people to engage in some of Bunky's games. They mixed the play with watching us at our various workstations, forming, cleaning up, and buffing. As I was working at the lathe and the father stood watching, he said in a rather quizzical manner, "Last night we had a big discussion about what language that was you spoke to your dog. Some thought it was Italian, but we weren't sure." I went on with the spinning tool, shaping the pewter. "No, it was not Italian," I said. As I finished the stroke and curled down the pewter to the chuck, I said, "I was speaking Retriever." I said it in a matter-of-fact voice that was meant to suggest that this was ordinary.

Then, as I turned from the lathe, Bunky came hurrying back into the barn, having retrieved a small piece of wood for one of the sons. The boy, however, was now looking up into the rafters where the bats were hanging during the daylight hours, and did not notice Bunky. Bunky dropped the wood, looked expectantly at the boy, then glanced at me as if to say, "What shall I do with this fellow?" Holding out my hand, I spoke several syllables to Bunky in our private language. Quickly, he picked up the piece of wood and brought it to me. I tossed it for him and as I turned back to my work on the lathe, I said matter of factly, "That's Retriever talk," and resumed my spinning.

Some weeks later, when being visited by a longtime Dominican friend, Father Mark Heath, O.P., I told him the story, following it with some observations of a playful theological nature: "I believe there is a myth growing somewhere in the Midwest," I said, and the myth goes something like this. 'In New Hampshire there is a strange pewterer, parson, philosopher who talks to his dog in the dog's language. I heard him do it; I saw him do it. Very clearly the dog understood because he responded exactly as he was directed.' This myth not only grows but it is carried forward by other people who say that while they have not been in New England and they have not seen the pewterer or the dog, they have seen the man who did see the pewterer talking to his dog in the dog's language. So, the myth grows in the Midwest."

Mark, in a playful way, perhaps mimicking Tillich, said in a mock-German accent, "Vas ist the purpose of such a myth? If a myth is to endure in history, it must have some benevolent purpose. Vat do you see as the purpose of this myth?" Responding in a mock-Bultmannian accent, I answered, "But don't you see? The ancient problem for the orders of nature is always in part the estrangement and alienation between the creatures. Here is an existential overcoming of part of that estrangement."

We play games with the games we play and are tempted to let the pyramid grow higher. Telling this story later to a more literal-minded clergyman, I added, "If you travel in the Midwest or some other places where the myth might have reached and hear the story while it is still 'oral tradition,' you might find yourself ready to engage in the process of demythologizing. If you begin to demythologize the story, be careful. There are dangers of hurt feelings. Bunky and I were talking about this whole development recently and he assured me, in the strongest possible Retrieverese, that it would hurt his feelings terribly to have our communication treated as a fiction."

THE COLLECTOR

Mabel Miller began visiting the pewter shop in the mid-1970s. I soon discerned that she was not the usual customer. She asked good questions and took a lot of time. Though she knew our various pieces, she would go to the price list posted on the beam at the corner of the shop and study it at length, sometimes with a piece of pewter in her hand. I knew that frugality was not her intent, for when she decided on a piece, price was never an issue.

Then one day she carried an item from the shelves to where I was working at the lathe and said, "I can't find this one on the price list."

"It's not there," I said. "It started out as a larger piece and something happened to the metal. I trimmed away the damaged part and then salvaged the remaining metal with this improvised design."

"Is that why you didn't put your touch on the bottom?" she asked.

"No, that's an oversight."

"I'd like to buy it," she said, "if you will put your touch on it."

I took it to the flat-topped stake, placed it carefully, centered the touch above it, struck one quick hammerblow, and it was done. As I was wrapping the piece, I commented that she, of all our customers, gave the pewter we made the most careful scrutiny. Her answer was very direct: "I'm collecting 'early Gibson,' and I especially like one-of-a-kind pieces!"

It was not long after this exchange that Mabel told me she was on the committee to arrange meetings of the New England branch of the Pewter Collectors Club of America. She proposed that they visit our shop and see us at work at their next meeting in three months. "We meet somewhere for a program, usually a talk or a visit to a museum with a pewter collection, and then we have a luncheon at some good restaurant where we hold a business meeting." Mabel was confident that it would be a successful program, that the members of the club would be charmed by the old barn, the historic village, and watching me spin something on the lathe.

I had been juried by the League of New Hampshire Craftsmen and had given their shops a little of my work. There was a good response from friends, neighbors, and visitors to what we were making. Still, the thought of having twenty or twenty-five individuals who collected pewter—and belonged to a pewter collecting club—in the shop at once, was daunting. At the same time I liked the challenge and the wider exposure it would give our work.

When the day arrived, the spring weather was bright, clear, and mild. The members of the club were friendly, warm in their response to our work, and asked questions to which, happily, I knew the answers. They were enthusiastic in watching the spinning of a vase over a breakdown chuck, and then seeing the chuck come apart like a Chinese puzzle as it was removed from inside the vase.

I had hoped to get through the day without having to demonstrate soldering, a part of the craft that works best, for me at least, in privacy, when I can devote full attention to the task. But I knew that I would have to suggest, if not show them, something of how it worked. I did a setup of a large porringer bowl with the cast handle held in place by wire clamps, with the solder and torch in their ready position.

After the spinning demonstration, one of the visitors, in a voice that was heard by most, said, "I see you are set up for soldering on a handle to the large porringer. I have a terrible time with my soldering and am looking forward to seeing how you do it." All the men, and a few of the women, gathered in a tight circle around me as I sat on a high stool, adjusted the clamps, brushed some flux into the joint, and lighted the acetylene torch. As I moved it carefully into the area to be heated, I said, "There is about forty to sixty degrees difference between the melting point of the solder and the melting point of the pewter. That can be less than a second with the torch. So you'll excuse me if I don't talk. It takes 110 percent of my attention."

The heat spread over the area to be soldered. I held the torch away for a few seconds and applied a bit of flux. I brought the torch back and, as the flux began to boil, applied the solder from a stick held in one hand as I kept the torch moving with the other. The problem is always whether the solder will run into the joint, or away from it. If it runs away, you can sometimes coax it back. If not, you will have hours of cleanup to do with files, emery paper, and buffing wheels. Fortunately, the solder flowed into the joint and most of it disappeared as it should. What little remained at the edges of the joint was teased away with the torch and the flux-filled brush; I relaxed and turned off the torch, wondering whether they could tell how relieved I was that it had gone well.

The visitors were probably relieved for me. They were warm in their praise and first one and then another told horror stories in which they had made a mess of the solder, or had gone through the pewter they were working on and ruined the piece entirely. In some of those disasters, it was valuable old pewter that was damaged or ruined.

Later, near the end of the 1970s, we designed an unlidded tankard, a piece that is usually called a mug, especially in England. It was to receive high praise from Charles Hull, then curator of the London Guild, or Worshipful Company of Pewterers, who said it had "straightforward, elegant simplicity."

The creation of the tankard was not quick or easy. As our product line was growing, there had been stirrings in the shop to include a tankard. Both Lauren and Jonathan were in college and witness to the beer culture of their peers. Lauren became our leader by involving all of us in a project of what turned into a one-of-a-kind tankard of spectacular proportions. The size may have been determined by making the handle first.

Lauren worked on a model in wood that was then used in sand casting to make the handle in pewter. We were new to sand casting, and the resulting rough casting required a tremendous amount of work with the belt sander, as well as handwork with files. While that was in progress, I was enlisted to spin a body for the tankard. A search through our chucks found one that came with the "step lathe" I had purchased and had been used only in making our salad bowl. This chuck was in poor condition, and had been exposed to weather enough that it was covered with a thick layer of rust. It did fit one of our adapters to the Diamond lathe and was cleaned up with a sequence of varying grit of emery paper. Spinning the body involved a large disk but was straightforward. When the body was done and the handle finished, the soldering remained. The heavy handle would be slower to heat than the wall of the tankard, so the work with the torch required care. The heat was focused on the handle near the joint, and when the flux boiled, the solder flowed into the joint.

Lauren's brothers made numerous suggestions about it's being a "man-sized" tankard, and more appropriate for them than for her. She, however, had pushed the project and done the lion's share of the work. It was proudly hers, and remains so.

Enough was learned in making the big tankard that the following one was planned with more attention to scale and with an eye to production. Whatever we created should be accompanied with the molds and chucks designed for continued use. We took great care in seeking a good match between handle and body, and the most desirable size for the whole.

Lauren worked tirelessly on the handle design and, as it turned out, on the production of the first sixteen. Experiments were done with plaster molds, sand casting, and with silicone molds. Whatever the mold, the casting that was produced needed a lot of handwork. While similar in appearance, there were small variations in each one. When we returned to Providence, I took a carefully made model, formed with much handwork, to a mold maker and had a bronze mold made. That supplied our needs for a number of years, until we updated the technology and made them by spincasting.

The body of the tankard was spun over a metal chuck, from the top down, and a fold was turned down to give it double thickness at the bottom. Then the top was cut out, a recessed bottom soldered in, the piece buffed, and the handle soldered on. Once the chuck, handle mold, and various jigs had been made and adjusted for production, it was all very straightforward work.

For some reason we selected the number eight for the first run of the new tankard. In spite of the difficulty of making the handles, the enthusiasm mounted among us all as we neared completion. We decided that we would make them in a numbered edition and keep a "tankard book" with the name and address of every purchaser.

When the eight were completed, they were placed in a line on the top shelf in the selling area. Before anyone appeared to purchase one, the children came to me with a very strong suggestion. It was their position that this line of tankards would be a major item in our continuing production. Therefore, these first eight should remain in the family. The numbers should be in the order of their birth: Number six would be given to Susan, and numbers seven and eight should be mine; number seven would be for me, and eight for my guest when there was one. The idea had appeal, and their very positive feelings about family, tradition, and the future line of tankards sealed the decision.

With that decision, however, we did not remove the tankards from the shelf. We wanted customers to see the new product. At this point Mabel Miller appeared and immediately fell in love with them. "I'll take them all!"

she said, without asking the price. Lauren explained that these were for show, that they were staying in the family. She also mentioned that this was the first piece that we were numbering. Mabel said, "Lauren, write my order for numbers nine through sixteen."

It was the end of August. Jonathan would be leaving for Hobart College, Lauren would return to Parsons in New York, and we would move back to Providence on Tuesday after Labor Day. It appeared that the Miller order would have to wait until the following summer. However, after Jonathan had left, a weather system moved into our area and the forecast was for storms and rain for three or four days leading into the Labor Day weekend. Lauren issued a challenge: "Dad, let's make the Miller tankards. You cast the handles and spin the bodies. I'll finish the handles and do most of the buffing, and we'll get them done. It's bad weather and we can make the most of it."

The weather that blew in was not like the summer storms that we could watch come up from Monadnock, lightning flashing in jagged streaks, marching toward us like a determined celestial infantry. Nor was it like the spring storms that appeared all at once with large drops of rain and wind cutting crisscross patterns on the surface of the pond, as if some large heavenly broom were sweeping first this way and then that. In spring storms, lightning would seem to strike on a different side of the barn with each new flash, but never far away. Crackling in the electrical wires would make you flinch if you were working at a lathe, and an occasional flash would cause the lights to go out, until some circuit breaker down the line reconnected and they would come on again. In such storms, Bunky, our white Lab, would find me. Even at the lathe he would stand behind me, lean against my legs, his whole body quivering, with low moans escaping at the heavy thunder.

The rain that came this time was soft and steady, sure of itself and ready to stay for a few days, with fog patches rising at the edge of the woods—a graying of the light that made the whole day like a gathering twilight. Not fearsome, nor violent, it repaired the dryness of summer and replenished the pond. We could see trout rising and wondered if there was a hatch out, or whether the fish were welcoming the healing rain.

It was good weather for work. With all the lights on in the barn, no temptations to venture outside, and a goal of eight tankards in three days, our spirits rose as we saw the bodies and the handles of the tankards taking shape. Lauren was always a bright presence in the work, but never better than when she was facing a challenge.

The casting of the handles went steadily and required much handwork. Lauren did it cheerfully. The procedures involved work with files of various cutting capacity, sanding with a fine-grit, narrow belt on the upright sander, all this followed by a series of buffing operations beginning with grade C Lea Compound, then buffing with Tripoli.

I made the tankard bodies without mishap, cutting out the tops and soldering in the recessed bottoms. I stamped the bottoms with our touchmark, and put in the sequence of numbers from nine to sixteen. The edges of top and bottom were rounded and the bodies were prepared for buffing while on the lathe, using a series of 320, 400, and 600 wet and dry emery paper. Then Lauren buffed them to a bright finish.

There is a sad irony and injustice in an otherwise happy story. The touchmark was one used from our early days. It marked the tankards GIBSON & SONS. The touchmark was replaced later with one saying simply, GIBSON PEWTER. It should have been replaced much earlier, and I regret that it was not. The injustice was heightened in this case because Lauren played such a major role in the tankard's design and creation.

As each was finished and ready to receive its handle, I shaped and fitted each handle at the top to match the curve of the tankard body, and flattened it a bit at the bottom where it would be joined. Then it was placed on a special holder made of plaster of Paris, resting on the top of a turntable, so it could be rotated and the torch applied from any direction. At every stage in the creation of a piece, there is jeopardy and the possibility of ruining the work. However, with tankards, the final soldering on of the handle is the point that requires the greatest concentration.

The handle is solid and slower to heat to the melting point of the solder. The body of the tankard is thin, approximately sixty-thousandths of an inch thick, and it heats very quickly. It can overheat and melt out. That leaves a ruined tankard body, for a hole cannot be repaired. The work with Lauren's big tankard had been instructive. Focus is needed to keep the torch on the handle more than on the body, and to bring them both to the right temperature at the same time. Then the flux begins to boil and the solder is applied, flowing quickly and evenly into the joint. Needless to say, when number sixteen was completed without mishap, there was more than enough joy to brighten a rainy day.

When it appeared that we would be able to complete the tankards, Lauren called Mabel and asked whether she would be home on the weekend. Mabel sensed what the question meant and asked, "Lauren, have you done the tankards?" "We're working on them and believe we will have them by Sunday." Mabel conferred briefly with her husband Leo, then invited Susan, Lauren, and me to a buffet supper on Sunday at which "we will christen the tankards," as Mabel put it.

When they were done, we called Mabel and the party was confirmed. Mabel came by and picked up the tankards, as Leo had plans to hang them in a special spot and wanted that done before the party. We turned our attention to moving back to Providence, which required a series of tasks that we had not addressed in the rain and in our preoccupation with the tankards.

On Sunday the sun returned and it was a beautiful day. The Millers lived in a brick house between Hillsborough and Deering, a lovely, much admired brick house with four corner chimneys. It was built in the same era as our brick house, which had been added to the older wooden ell behind it, in 1815. We went at four-thirty and were entertained first in the kitchen and then on the terrace behind the house. Leo had put hooks under a high mantel to hang the tankards. It would be a fine addition to a large kitchen furnished with antiques selected and arranged in perfect taste. Leo took five of the tankards and placed them in the freezer compartment of the refrigerator. As he made other preparations for our buffet on the terrace, Mabel asked me to follow her.

We climbed the stairs and turned into a large room. "We show this room only to trusted friends," she said, "and do not want its contents known outside that group." On shelves and in cabinets, there was the largest private collection of antique pewter I had ever seen. She introduced me to a large section of it which was from France from the 1700s and 1800s. It was too much to take in! I was amazed not only by the size and value of the collection, but also at seeing Mabel in a new light as a collector.

Later she took Susan and Lauren for a tour of the house, stopping in at the pewter room with them as well. The party on the terrace was preceded by Leo's asking each of us to select one of several brands of beer, most of them imported. We were given a cold bottle of our choice and then he delivered from the freezer a "frosted" tankard to each of us. We poured the beer and raised the tankards in a happy round of toasts. I can remember no other occasion in which our work was commissioned to its intended use with such style and ceremony.

SETS OF PEWTER

Quite early in the practice of the craft I made a set of ten-inch plates for our family, which we used daily for many years. I had made half a dozen footed goblets with the guidance of my mentor, Arthur Barnes, and would later add four more for our set. Then adding a set of six-inch bread and butter plates, we had the rudiments of a set of pewter for our use. Various serving bowls were added as well as a compote made in Arthur's shop. A friend and professional photographer, Jim Fraser, came to New Hampshire for a day's shooting that he hoped to market with *Yankee* magazine. He included one excellent color photo of our dining room, the table set entirely with pewter, the mantel filled with a mixture of English pewter, pieces by Arthur Barnes, and one or two from my early work. An enlargement of that picture, suitably framed, has hung in the shop through the years so that customers could see what is possible. It became an incentive to some to begin collections of their own.

As the pewter items grew in number, Susan devoted one section of the kitchen cupboards to the family collection. The kitchen and dining room were part of the original house and probably dated from the 1770's. There was a hutch from the late 1700s in the kitchen, containing many eighteenth-century chinaware pieces mixed with later ones.

It is interesting to imagine the original farming folk who lived here, and to wonder how much woodenware, pewter, porcelain, and glassware they owned. The rise of pewter had displaced woodenware, just as china and porcelain displaced pewter with the rise of the China trade in the early 1800s. In the house were a large wooden salad bowl, a long wooden trencher, and wooden butter molds handed down from earlier times.

It did not occur to us that we were reversing these earlier periods of history, were latter-day recidivists, going now from glassware back to pewter. Actually we were not replacing the glassware, just adding some pewter, taking pleasure in the historical images it provided. One special moment came with the first Thanksgiving on which a pewter charger was used for serving a turkey cooked in the Quaker Social kitchen woodstove. From this beginning of our own "garnish" of pewter, I could not have foreseen the later ones made for friends and customers.

Friends Ed and Joan Steckler showed interest in our work and ordered a set of stem goblets and plates. Ed was a dealer in antiques and his ware was mixed with the family things in their beautiful home on Providence's historic Governor Street. It was in their dining room that I first saw a display of our work in a private setting. Plates were standing on the back edge along a shelf, and stem goblets were in front. It was a striking combination and warmed my heart.

The first full set of pewter was made for Susan Adams and Tony Campagna, ordered soon after they became engaged. We worked together on the design. Tony wanted the footed goblets to be a bit taller than our usual design because he liked wine with his dinner and didn't want to be refilling his goblet. Susan was a dear friend of our family, having spent a summer with us in New Hampshire as a mother's helper. She was like family, and our children responded to her bright and cheerful spirit.

Susan and Tony asked whether they could announce to their friends that they preferred pewter to silver, and that their design was registered at Gibson Pewter. That practice would be repeated with other couples later. Theirs was the first full set designed and made as one project, including plates, tumblers, footed goblets, soup-salad-cereal bowls, and serving dishes.

After their wedding, they had planned to spend their honeymoon on a camping trip to Nova Scotia. Somewhere in Maine they stopped at an antique store and discovered the "perfect hutch" for their pewter. They considered the price and counted their resources. They could continue their planned itinerary or they could buy the hutch. They opted for the latter and camped slowly homeward, stopping at our shop in Hillsborough Centre to pick up the last of their set, and to tell us about the hutch they would have in their home.

A few years later, after they had moved to the Midwest and were on their way to a family reunion in Maine, they stopped for a visit. Tony told me an interesting story about insuring their pewter. They were entertaining their insurance agent for dinner. He noticed the pewter on the table and in the hutch and said to Tony, "We didn't list this on your homeowner's policy. I'd like to do an inventory with you after dinner and file that with the policy." Tony said they did that, and although the pewter was only a few years old, the agent insisted in placing a value three times the original cost. It was a "one-of-a-kind" set done by a New England pewterer, and would continue to escalate in value as it aged. With a smile, Tony added, "I have nothing in my stock portfolio appreciating that fast, and I'm eating off the pewter!"

I don't recall how this next customer found me, perhaps from a story in the *Providence Journal.* A Navy petty officer stationed at Newport, Rhode Island, called and made an appointment to come to the "winter" shop in my basement in Providence. He spent some time looking at our work and then made a proposal: "I would like to have you make a full set of twelve place settings over the space of this year," he said. "I am completing my career in the Navy a year from now. We have secured a property in the Black Hills of the Dakotas, really back in the woods. I plan to build a long, rustic, cabinlike home there, and we want to stock it with pewter for regular use." I asked him how large his family was. "We have three children," he told me. "I want twelve place settings for family with company, and I'd like to have each child inherit four place settings when we are gone." Clearly he had done a lot of thinking about his future.

The financial arrangements were interesting. He had a year to go on his enlistment. He wanted twelve place settings. We laid out a setting of the proposed pieces, priced the cost per setting, and arranged for him to send me a monthly check throughout the year. I explained that I would not make it one set at a time, but twelve of each piece until the set was done. It was agreed. The checks arrived on schedule each month. Halfway through the year he came by to see the work in progress and liked what he saw. One month before the time of his discharge, he called and asked whether he could add to the order. He wanted to get a charger, keep it secret, and present it separately to his wife when they came to pick up the pewter.

It was a touching scene. They were on the eve of a new and totally different life, almost equidistant between the oceans that had been his home during the twenty-some long years of his enlistment. When the set was turned over to them, and as they were beginning to take their leave, I went into a corner and brought out the charger, wrapped in tissue paper. He presented it to his wife. When she unwrapped it, her eyes filled with tears of joy. I held the charger as they held each other. That may have been the dividing moment between their old and new life together as they headed out to the Dakota hills to make a new home.

Clair Hoffacker, always genial and inclined to do thoughtful things for his friends, ordered eight place settings of pewter designed to match the style of a nine-and-a-half inch dinner plate, a replica of a Roswell Gleason plate made sometime between 1820 and 1870, his working dates in Dorchester, Massachusetts. I have written elsewhere of Clair's help with the headstock of the Diamond spinning lathe.

In the space of a few years, I had officiated at the wedding of his two daughters, one in the family home and the other from a town house on Beacon Hill in Boston. Both were lovely and gracious affairs with much warmth of family feeling. Following one of these happy occasions, Clair and I were talking about various drinks we had found off the beaten track, enjoyed, and considered special. I told him about a fine Scotch to

A punch bowl design, as requested to resemble the Jefferson cups it would be used with.

which I had been introduced as I was being entertained at the home of a solicitor in Dunlop, Scotland, during a pulpit exchange in Glasgow. It was named Laphroaig and was made, as I recalled, on the Isle of Islay. To my surprise and joy, he had a bottle of that brand delivered sometime later with a note saying he had bought it on a business trip to Scotland the week before.

Kay Croak, a customer who became a friend and enthusiast for our pewter, collected a lot of it over several years, and gave many pieces to friends. Her daughter, MaryBeth, often accompanied her mother and showed interest in our work. When she became engaged, she asked me to make a set for her. I enjoyed the collaboration as we designed her set, and was pleased by her affirmation of our craftsmanship when she was interviewed by Ann Hoder, writing about us for the *Concord Monitor:*

> Gibson recently wrapped the final pieces to a wedding gift he took six weeks to create–an eight-person dinner set, each setting including three plates, a bowl and a goblet, with candlesticks, a prize-winning fruit bowl, a large Paul Revere bowl and a platter completing the set. Each hand-

> formed piece is unique, a quality which attracts people like MaryBeth who will be married Saturday.
>
> "Since I met him (10 years ago) I knew I didn't want china, or silver," she said.
>
> Gibson said he knows of no other U.S. pewterer who makes complete sets. There is mass-produced work on the market, but MaryBeth said that she had no doubt she wanted Gibson's work.
>
> "It's the weight, the simplicity, the care that goes into each piece," she said.
>
> The pewter Gibson creates is simple, yet exquisite. His pewter vessels have elegance without ostentation; they are treasures to be used. — (*Concord Monitor*, June 11, 1992)

While still in his teens, Robert Reynolds began coming to our shop with his family. From the beginning it was clear that Rob was with them because he wanted to be, and that he had set himself the goal of becoming a collector. He had his own money, his own ideas about what he wanted, and was not an impulse buyer. He took his time, asked good questions, and became the kind of discerning customer a craftsman respects and enjoys.

Then Rob began appearing by himself, and we found ourselves talking about life as well as pewter. He was bright and had a good disposition, and I found increasing enjoyment in his visits. He began to bring Jennifer Leary, and as they moved toward marriage, we had long planning sessions about the design of the pewter they wanted. They were not in a hurry about the wedding, and they took their time considering the options in the designs we discussed. We set up place settings from our work in all the possible combinations. I did one or two prototypes of possible variations. They finally decided on their basic set, after which family and friends added special pieces like salad and serving bowls. Later, I received a picture taken of the head table at their wedding dinner, and was pleased to see our stem goblets being used in the toasts to the happy couple. It was a reminder of how much more we had come to share than the pewter.

Sometimes the friendship can dwarf the pewter, even when there is a lot of the latter. So it has been with the Robert Stocktons, who own the largest set of Gibson pewter made to date, and whose collection continues to grow. Robert and Karen Stockton, with their children, Sarah, Chris, and Heather, began visiting our shop on an annual basis in 1982. Their home is in upstate New York, but they spend a summer vacation each year near Lake

Sunapee, New Hampshire. Their arrival for visits to Hillsborough Centre always created a rush of welcome and greetings, catching up on things, looking at new products, and long conversations about work, life, the society, and our hopes and dreams for ourselves and our children. This is a deep and deepening friendship.

In the first years, the young Stocktons would stay in the pewter shop for a quick look around and then ask permission to head for the pond, where they often competed in catching frogs. Robert and Karen would look at our pewter, watch work in progress for a time, then Karen would find Susan, usually at work in her flowers. Often I would turn off whatever machinery I was using and Robert and I would find a stone wall where we could sit, look off to the hills, and talk about all manner of concerns of life and world. With a keen mind, and deeply caring, his interests varied from family to community, from national life to the way nations treated other nations and their own people. Through it all ran a thread of equity and compassion. I was not surprised when his peers in the legal community voted him among the top one percent of all lawyers in the nation.

Robert became hooked on the sport of fly-fishing, an interest of mine in younger years when there were trips to Vermont and northern Maine. My fishing in recent years has been limited to stocking our pond with rainbow trout. I share them willingly with the great blue heron that comes to fish the southern end of the pond and unwillingly with the marauding otters who occasionally invade and clean out all the trout. Robert's visits brought tales of faraway, exotic fishing waters I had dreamed of but never managed to fish.

We watched the Stockton children grow into fine young adults, just as we watched their family collection of our pewter become the largest anywhere. We collaborated on the designs of special things, including a punch bowl made to resemble a giant Jefferson Cup, gently flared from the bottom, with a large number of Jefferson Cups to go with it.

In the early 1990s they spent several hours photographing their collection of our work arranged for use on their dining room table, sideboard, and stately cupboard, holding chargers, various Paul Revere bowls, and other pieces. They have continued adding to their collection, and have given the "Fruit Bowl" as gifts to a number of colleagues. In 1995, '96, and '97 they came to the Craftsmen's Fair to cheer us on in our demonstrations. While that was special, I missed the ability to turn off a lathe and share with them our current views on the things we care about. The friendship deepens with the years and we rejoice that so much human meaning and sharing has grown out of the "pewter connection."

VISITORS

A sizable book could be written about the visitors who have come to the pewter shop over the years. From near and far, young and old, novices and the knowledgeable, curious browsers and serious collectors, all have found us. We are on a hilltop three miles from town, and many miles from the nearest mall, so those who come have some degree of interest in pewter. But their interests vary remarkably. There are stories, and stories to spare.

Early in the week some summers ago, a man in his late thirties came in who did not go to the shelves to look at the pewter. Rather, he approached the lathe where I was spinning a bowl. While most people can get caught up in watching the spinning process and are fascinated by it, as a general rule there is some degree of gender difference. Women focus on the product displayed, men gravitate toward the machinery, especially if some operation is under way. This visitor watched and asked lots of questions, mostly technical, though the questions indicated that he was seeing the process for the first time. I asked where he was from and what he did —Southern California and NASA. He was part of a group of space scientists attending a conference at New England College. That's in Henniker, New Hampshire, "the only Henniker on earth," about nine or ten miles to the east of us. When Henniker marked its bicentennial several years ago, Lord and Lady Henniker came from England to help celebrate. The scientist had used the afternoon break for some back roading to look at the countryside and happened upon our pewter sign. He decided on the spot to look in.

It was a throwback in time, a manufacturing anachronism that fascinated him. His delight in what he was seeing, and his probing questions about all aspects of the craft, prompted a spirited exchange. Time passed quickly. He left with only a brief look at the finished pewter on the shelves, mainly asking about techniques used in making this or that piece. At dinner he told the other members of his NASA group what he had seen and they agreed that they would all come watch the following afternoon. At dinner that night I reported that we had had a NASA scientist, and that it was a most stimulating encounter.

After he left, I recalled having gone through the space program part of the General Electric Company in Pittsfield, Massachusetts, some twenty years before. Work was being done on the guidance package for the Polaris missile. This part of the GE plant was the factory of the future. Technicians wore special suits, and areas were kept assiduously clean of dust. I realized that my NASA visitor had fallen back a hundred years or more in time. What he had seen in my shop was the "cutting edge" of pewter-making at the time of transition from casting in brass or bronze molds to spinning on a lathe, and that transition occurred in the early 1800s. Hands in those days were used with tools. Today hands are used to run machines or, more likely, to work on the keyboard of a computer-driven machine.

That week was memorable. Members of the NASA group came each afternoon and there are stories within the story. A woman member of the group became very taken with my large chalice. Her interest was so evident that I thought she might buy it on Thursday afternoon, as their conference ended at noon on Friday. Though she went back to it several times, she left without it. It was the most expensive piece in our shop, but I doubted that money was the barrier.

Then, at eleven o'clock on Friday she arrived in a rush, asking me to wrap it quickly, saying that their plane would be leaving in an hour and a half. As I wrapped the chalice for travel, I confessed my curiosity: "Why? You have a clergy friend? Want it for your church?" She laughed. Then she said simply, "I like it. I think it's beautiful. I am not particularly religious and don't attend a church. But I'm drawn to it." Then with a warm smile she said, "Perhaps living with this lovely thing will make me more religious. Who knows?" She hurried away to catch a plane that would take her back to that future-obsessed world of space probes and lunar landings. A number of pieces of our pewter went with the men in the group, presents they purchased to take home to their wives.

It was a rainy afternoon and I expected no one. The great sliding doors at the front of the barn were closed to a narrow slit, enough to indicate that they could be opened, but not enough to let in the blowing rain. I heard the doors slide on their hanging rollers and then saw three men. The director of a nearby internationally known summer camp had two guests, a cultural minister from China and his translator assistant. The camp arranged an annual tour to China for selected campers, and this visit was connected with that exchange. They gathered around the lathe where I was forming centerpiece vases, one of the most popular pieces we make and most interesting to observe being made.

The cultural minister watched intently and asked questions through his assistant. I answered in short statements, waiting as he translated, watching the face of the visitor to see if he understood. He nodded vigorously as he heard the replies. He went to the shelves and looked at all the pieces we had for sale. The assistant came back and asked if they could purchase one like the one they had seen being made, and would I be willing to stand with his superior holding the vase? I agreed, and we stood close, each holding a hand under the vase he had bought, both of us smiling for the camera.

While it was unusual to invite a customer into our house, I considered this occasion special and asked the camp director if his guest would like to see "the house." "We didn't dare ask, but we would love to see it," he replied. Susan was away, and I conducted the tour through the downstairs portion of the house. On the screened-in porch, I paused and lifted off the top of the well, showing him the water some ten or twelve feet below, water that was always five or six feet deep. Then I took him directly into the kitchen to the Athol pump and began to pump up some water. When it ran clean and cool, I drank briefly from the copper cup, pumped some more and offered him a drink. After drinking some, he smiled and said, "Good, good, good."

I showed the wood-range kitchen stove, then took them through the dining room into the living room and explained the Franklin-front fireplace, the Shaker chair, and some other things. Then on to my study, with its small Franklin-type stove, my desk, computer corner, and book shelves. Next, we went through a hall and back into the dining room. The assistant asked if they could take a picture in that room, pointing to an old tavern chair in a corner where his boss wanted to be photographed.

They had had a quick exchange that I wondered about but of course could not understand. I gave permission. The room where we were standing dated from the 1770s, had Indian shutters, paneling around the Franklin stove, and floor-to-ceiling cabinets on one wall with a counter-height, deep shelf between the cupboards above and below. The chair he had chosen was in the corner beside that large cupboard. I was convinced that something was special about this request and watched as the assistant positioned himself to take the picture. As I looked over his shoulder when he framed the shot, it became clear. On the shelf behind the chair were two Chinese Cantonese ginger jars.

As the Cold War began to thaw, a group of Russians attending a conference at New England College were to be entertained by a neighbor in the village. She asked if she could bring them by the pewter shop to see us working. We welcomed them one afternoon and they were quite interested in the various processes we were engaged in. They spoke to each other in excited tones—something they saw must have reminded them of something from home. Like other visitors, they were most fascinated by the spinning process, in which they watched the metal being formed from a flat disk into the shape of the form on the lathe while it was spinning at about two thousand revolutions per minute. Their knowledge of English varied from a little to practically none. I did not try to explain to them that some years before, the leaders of my denomination had taken a number of my pewter pieces to Russia to give to church leaders with whom they would be meeting. We managed, often by talking with our hands, to explain the craft they were watching. Later in the visit they communicated their interest in our pond, clearly visible from the back of the barn. It looked to them, as it did to us, as relief from the heat.

It was a warm summer day and we spoke of swimming. They brightened but their schedule did not allow it that day. They were free however, the following morning and would be having lunch with our neighbor. It was arranged that they could come early and take a swim. They were for the most part large men with lots of energy. They were like giant children splashing and playing in the water. One or two, in coming through the meadow to the pond, had noticed that the wild strawberries were ripe. They interrupted their swim and went in search of the small berries, moving on all fours from one cluster to another. The sight was memorable. The spirit was wonderful, and the thought must surely have occurred to most of us that much of the pain and conflict between our countries could have been avoided had there been many exchanges and sharing like this in years past. Could we, I wondered, learn such a lesson in a way that might avoid future conflicts?

Photographers visiting the shop to see the pewter or to see it being formed often watch awhile and then ask, "May I take pictures?" I learned from an early experience not to tell them there was not enough light. An attractive woman had once asked permission and I had looked around, and made a judgment from my own limited experience and equipment: "Not enough light."

"That is my problem," she replied, "I'd like to try."

"Sure, go ahead," I told her.

She returned in a few minutes with a camera that was larger than any I owned, and a bag that contained several lenses and other accessories.

She had been fascinated by one aspect of the spinning process that she wanted to capture on film. When I trim a piece after forming it into a desired shape, the cutting tool will often shave off a continuous strand of metal that curls upward through the air almost to the level of my face. This was what she wanted to catch in a picture; it would freeze the motion of the

The pewter curls upward as it is trimmed.

pewter shaving flying in the air. When I understood what she wanted, I had a challenge to meet.

No one practices making the strands rise so high, or at all. You are simply trimming the excess metal away, and where it goes doesn't matter. You can influence the action somewhat by the steadiness of the cut, the speed of the lathe, and the thickness the tool is cutting by the pressure you put on it. It is certainly not an exact science. And it is not a skill that anyone would practice. Making a strand of pewter rise—while dramatic—is irrelevant to the job. In fact, you might prefer that it took a low arc and fell curling at your feet rather than flying upward where it can fall into the turning machine and have to be unwound or removed by a slow and time-consuming process. I had caused one strand to fly upward without trying, and now must try to duplicate the act.

Happily, on three of the next four trimmings, I managed to get the strand to curl upward, reaching the level of my face, and heard the repeated clicks of her camera trying to "stop" it in motion. She was pleased and expected some intriguing results. I was glad that I had been able to make the metal fly upward.

After she finished shooting, I found that she taught photography at a women's college in Connecticut. I offered an exchange of work: "If you are pleased with the pictures, send me a couple and I will send you a piece of my pewter."

"Sounds good to me," she agreed. So we left it.

Some weeks later I received a packet with three or four 8 x 10 black-and-white pictures. I was amazed. She had not only stopped the flying, curling pewter rising almost to my height, but she had also captured the intensity of my focus on the trimming process. The light from the window across from the lathe—that I had thought not enough—had worked to her advantage. It shone on the flying metal, on the lathe, my hands and face, and otherwise was almost "Rembrandt" lighting. I included the picture in the next few occasions when I had a public display of my work, and eventually had a postcard printed with it to use for notes to friends and customers. It is a prized part of our photo collection.

Once, when three of our children were working in the pewter shop for the summer to earn money for their school expenses, there was a visitor whom I have remembered with a wide range of feelings and questions that will doubtless never be answered. We were at our different work stations. I had given them lofty titles to go with their various specialties: Jonathan, vice president for intermediate processes; Chris, vice president for buffing;

Christopher brings a basin for consultation on the buffing process.

Lauren, vice president for making hammered pieces and for customer relations. Jon worked at the "red lathe," a smaller lathe used for cleaning up the pewter and removing the tool marks made in the spinning process. Chris worked with the various buffing wheels and bristle brushes finishing the pieces. Lauren did hand- rubbing, hammered bracelets and napkin rings, and met customers who visited the shop. I worked at the initial forming of the product on the larger spinning lathes, usually working at a wonderful old Diamond lathe that I have mentioned before. The "vice presidents" had individual tasks, but there was lots of sharing and conferring about pieces going through the process toward completion.

I remember the visitor watching me for a time and then going to watch the others one by one. It was not unusual for visitors to take special interest in the young people at work, and some who were repeat visitors would form special attachments to one or the other, especially Lauren, who not only was warm and outgoing, but also dealt with them more than her brothers, as she helped them select items and then wrapped them. Lauren had a gift for remembering names and little things about people that impressed them and won their hearts.

This man stayed longer than most visitors. He would watch the young people, then come back to me and watch me. He seemed to notice particularly when as one or another of them came for a conference about some problem: "Dad, what do I do about this?" We would talk and they would head back to their work.

After a time the visitor said he wanted to make a proposal. He was, he said, a filmmaker in Canada. He did not do full movies but, rather, short subjects that were used as fillers in the movie houses between feature films. They were usually nature shorts or human-interest subjects. "I would like to do a film of all of you working," he said. "The barn is picturesque, the craft unusual, and I believe it would make an excellent short movie." It was mid-August and we would be going back to Providence in two weeks. It would have to be next summer. He was still very interested and wanted some assurance that we might plan on doing it. I agreed.

But I sensed that there was something more than a simple movie to be shot. The quiet intensity of his voice and a look in his eyes made me feel he was thinking of other things, though I could not be sure. Perhaps he was merely thinking ahead to where he was going later. But a kind of intuition I sometime have about people made me wonder. We talked about how much equipment he would need to bring, and how long it might take to do the film. Not much equipment. Not a long process. "The shooting can go quickly," he said, "and we would do a lot. The editing and writing is what takes the time, and I would do that back in Canada."

He went from one to another of the work stations, came and watched me for a last time, then said he would be going along. I turned off the motor of my lathe and walked with him to his car. There was still a feeling that was seeking some kind of expression. As we reached his car and he turned to say good-bye, I asked, "Is there any special reason you want to do this film with us?" He looked at me a long moment, and his eyes seemed also to be looking at something far away. Then he answered. "I was raised in an orphanage," he said. "I never knew my father. . . . What I have seen here today ...I would like to, at least try, to get onto film."

We shook hands, and I believe the handshake said more than any words we could have added. He drove away and I went back to the barn. Above the sound of the work in progress was the talk and laughter of the three "vice presidents." I made the rounds looking at their work, then went back to my lathe. I thought of the visitor. I could not imagine what it was like for him never to have known his father. Even less could I imagine my own life without our children. I looked across the lathe into the orchard beyond, and up the gentle slope to the stone wall. I picked up my forming tool and turned on the lathe, but could not see the spinning disk for the tears welling in my eyes.

PEWTER, PLACE, AND TIME

We enjoy the visits of a pair of wild ducks to our pond, and watch with interest as they swim about, occasionally diving out of sight to feed. This becomes for me a metaphor for a recurring experience as we work with pewter. As we live and work, the surface is the present we "live on," but we often "dive" into the underlying past, where the history we feed on instructs, inspires, and nourishes our pursuit of the craft.

I sometimes think of this as I mow the fields of our hilltop New England farm. The stone walls that border the fields are there because land use required some separation into parcels, and because stone had to be cleared before the land could be worked. I admire the settlers who moved so much stone to make those walls, and I notice some, the size of which must have been a challenge. They had no mechanized equipment, no backhoes or pay loaders, just oxen and rugged flat sleds, called stone boats, and strong poles to leverage the stone onto the sled, and into place on the walls. They moved a lot of stone. Peter Sauer's study of the stone walls of typical Green Mountain foothills in Vermont indicates that the aggregate volume of the stone moved to make the walls of four townships would have equaled the volume of stone in the Great Pyramid. (*Orion*, Winter 1992.)

I helped build wire fences while growing up on a farm in Kentucky. We dug holes, planted posts and aligned them, tamped the dirt firmly around them, and stretched woven or barbed wire along them. The flat, gently rolling terrain was free of stone. Underground there were thick layers of limestone that we saw as outcroppings–where streams had cut valleys across the plain. The fences we built sixty years ago may be there today. They could have been easily removed, and would have required some maintenance. The stone walls bordering the fields I now mow were built more than two hundred years ago, and, like the Great Pyramid, could well be there for centuries to come.

As my pewter skills developed, various pieces drew me into the exploration of earlier times. One of our earliest pieces was a porringer, a replica of a Gershom Jones and Samuel Hamlin piece. They were pre-Revolutionary pewterers in Providence, Rhode Island, who had married sisters, were associated for a time in business, and used the same handle mold for their large porringers. I acquired a Gershom Jones porringer that was later stolen when our house was robbed. We replaced it later with a Hamlin porringer of similar size. I fashioned a form in clear maple wood over which I could spin the bowl. A Providence friend in the jewelry business made a vulcanized rubber mold in which I could cast the handles. The soldering remained and, while a test for a beginner, could be done if the worker were in "a state of grace," a term we have used over the years for procedures of some difficulty.

As I handled the porringers made by Jones and by Hamlin, there was a reminder that they did not solder on their handles. They were "burned on," a process I have often described to visitors in our shop, because we get an expression from their process that the visitors will know, but will not know where the expression came from.

When Jones or Hamlin made a porringer, he first made the bowl, then fitted the handle mold directly onto the bowl and poured the molten pewter into it. The pewter flowed down to the bowl and melted the surface enough to bond the two. To keep the rush of molten pewter from melting a hole through the side of the bowl, he, like other pewterers of his time, would fill a small linen bag with wet sand and press it firmly into place inside the bowl fitting it snugly against the inside surface where the handle was to be poured on the outside. The molten pewter would not melt through the wall, but it would soften the metal enough that the linen would be "printed" on the inside of the bowl, in the shape of the handle base that joined on the outside. The linen sock of wet sand was called a tinker's dam. Pewterers and tinsmiths were sometimes called tinkers; the sock was a "dam" that stopped the molten metal from melting a hole and flowing through it. While it stopped the metal from burning through, it was itself charred enough to be worthless after a few applications–thus the expression, "I don't give a tinker's dam." Collectors look for this linen mark inside a porringer as a sign of its age. I would often show this mark to visitors as I told the story.

The colonial pewterers had no acetylene torch, with its steady, controlled flame. When they used solder, they used soldering irons for some tasks, a very chancey business, as anyone knows who has used them. There was an evolution in which the pewterer used a blowpipe and a candle flame, later a whale-oil lamp, then a gas flame in the 1850s and later. Like the use of stone boats, these were cumbersome and slow, but in pewter joining, whether by solder or by burning on, the results are excellent, like the stone walls we still admire.

My conversations with pewter collectors have made it very clear that history was important to their interest–not history in general, so much as the specific history of place, time, and person attached to each piece. And this was indicated by the "touch" or "maker's mark" stamped on the piece of pewter. The serious collector gathers more than old pewter. Each piece is enhanced in meaning by knowledge of the person who made it and the area and period from which it came. Kerfoot early began to create tables of comparative rarity for pieces surviving from colonial times, that being one guide in establishing the value of a piece.

I gathered what knowledge I have of pewter history more by the case method than by systematic study. A single piece may prompt me to read about its maker and then be drawn into a further look at the period in which he worked. This is especially true when I have chosen to make replicas of the work of an earlier period. Why I chose a particular piece or the maker involved is very often a story in itself.

On a busy Sunday in 1968, I officiated at the baptism of the grandchild of Dr. Rudolph Pearson and his wife, Betty. After the baptism, Betty gave me a handsomely wrapped present. "Open it later," she said as I started to loosen the ribbon. When I finally opened it, I found a note that said, "From the other R.G. in American Pewter. With affection, Betty and Rudy." Inside was a nine-and-a-half-inch pewter plate made by Roswell Gleason sometime during his working period, 1821–1871. It was in good condition and had a clear touchmark. I thought it was doubly thoughtful of them to give me a pewter piece so early in my own efforts in the craft, especially a piece made by a famous pewterer with the same initials as mine.

It was a handsome plate, typical of its era, and before long I had made a chuck over which I spun a similar one. Then I scribed a line just inside the bottom of the booge, the curved section from the rim of the plate to its flat bottom. Not long after, an antique dealer brought in for repairs a chamberstick with the Gleason touchmark. Its ring handle needed to be resoldered. While it was in the shop, Cyrus, our oldest son, made a drawing of it from careful measurements, which we filed against the time when we might add that item, or some variation of it, to our production.

Gleason, I learned, worked at a time of transition from production by individual craftsmen to industrial-style production. The changes altered the relationship between the craftsmen and the quality of work. The new situation placed great emphasis on quantity, sometimes at the expense of quality. In later years Gleason had as many as 120 employees. Pewter making was now a part of the industrial revolution. Variations of the assembly line replaced the older craft practice in which the pewterer made the whole piece. Gleason experimented widely in metals and styles, with some outcomes more fortunate than others. He was one of the three largest producers of Brittania metal, the other two being Reed and Barton of Taunton, Massachusetts, and the Boardmans of Hartford, Connecticut. After the 1850s, much of the production was silver-plated ware. Gleason was in Dorchester where he was a leading citizen.

Collectors have regarded some of his earlier work very highly, and have dismissed the later work as an illustration of the way craftsmanship can be diminished in mass production. It was not a matter of pewter only. A tide of industrialization radically changed the country. It replaced the old order of personal pride in individual performance, the core idea of the guild-taught order. The new order featured organization, and sought speed of production and quantity. We can speculate about whether the individual workers were willing to accept the decline in quality because the product was identified with the factory, not with an individual craftsman.

A century later, after World War II, the rise of the craft movement signaled that some were willing to devote their lives to reclaiming what had been lost. They were part of a larger counterculture movement that insisted, among other things, that the meaning of individual, personal existence could not be mass produced. When individuals pick up and praise our chamberstick made in the Gleason style, I wonder whether they ever sense that this is in some way a testimony to another time and to qualities we have worked to reclaim. Like every craftsman, I often have to make decisions that will affect the quality of the product. At such times I have a lesson from the era of the "other R.G. in American pewter."

Our pewter is displayed in an arrangement that allows us to keep on view at least one example of each piece we make. Across the north end of our shop, the shelves are nearly twelve feet long, and above them is a beam that is part of the post-and-beam structure of the barn. From this beam is hung our display of porringers, and here we have a number of each design. They are a source of interest and questions; these porringers are also the only pieces that do not have a modern equivalent. "What were they used for?" is the usual question, though some ask simply, "What are they?"

"Porringers," I tell them, "were in a sense the colonial 'dinner plate.' Food was cooked in a large iron kettle hanging in the fireplace, containing the soups and stews that were the staple of colonial cookery. It was ladled into the porringer, and was hot enough that the handle was important for holding it. It was used for porridge at breakfast, and for soups and stews at the other meals."

"But what was the little one for?" The question is asked of a porringer that is two and five- eighths inches across the bowl and a half-inch deep. There are a dozen possible responses, none definitive. Most of the answers relate to the makers, and the principal makers of these small porringers were the Richard Lees, father and son. The father, born January 1, 1747, in Scituate, Rhode Island, was the oldest boy in a family of sixteen children. The son was born May 6, 1775, in Rehoboth, Massachusetts. Their story is one of personal and business travail, at least the father's story is that. We know very little about the son, except that he made a lot of the small porringers and that his father spent the final years of his life selling his son's brass and pewter wares.

Today we know that these little porringers are made of good metal, are of interesting designs, are very early, are in several variations in design and size, and are much sought after by collectors. In the 1970s I saw one offered at auction. The bidding began at $1,000 and reached $1,850.

What were they used for? The theories vary and no one knows for sure. Were they children's toys? A bit fragile, and too expensive for that. Were they for wine tasting, or for hard spirits? The elder Lee was a fundamentalist Baptist who did some lay preaching, so it is not likely that he would have catered to that trade. A more likely explanation is that one was kept near the fireplace, or kitchen stove when there was one, and used to feed the baby, test the stew, or measure condiments into the stewpot. A case has been made that they were measures.

This latter idea of the measuring use is given thoughtful elucidation by Richard L. Bowen Jr. (vol. 10, No. 2 December, 1990, pp. 26ff, Bulletin no. 101, The Pewter Collectors Club of America), who noted that the small porringers were in a variety of sizes that correspond to modern stainless-steel measuring cups of 4 ounce, 2 ounce, and 1 ounce capacity, and that they could have nested together on a shelf. "When for measuring flour, sugar and other solids," it says in the bulletin, "the porringer was used as a scoop in a larger container. The wide mouth was ideal for this purpose where it would be filled to the brim and leveled off." (p. 42) Using it as a scoop would put stress on the handle, and Bowen notes that Lee's handles had added material for strengthening the base of the handle. Bowen concludes his monograph with these words: "The modern kitchen measures probably are descendants of the early-nineteenth-century small pewter porringers used in kitchens and as measures for dispensing medicines." (p. 42)

Alice Morse Earle, in her book *Home Life in Colonial Days,* mentions that wills and inventories listed porringers of all sizes, and notes that they are almost universal on such lists: "Some families had a dozen. I have found fifteen in one old New England farmhouse." (New York: Macmillan, 1899, p. 87) When these were not in use, she says, many housekeepers kept them hanging on hooks on the edge of a shelf, where they "formed a pretty and cheerful decoration. The poet Swift writes:

> The porringers that in a row
> Hung high and made a glittering show. (Ibid, p. 86)

The Richard Lees have been a corrective for me personally in my tendency to imagine, or form mental pictures of, the colonial pewterers at work. I have tended to make them into variations of a Norman Rockwell painting of the village smithy at work, with all his tools in the picture and an admiring neighbor or youngster watching. I have studied the engravings that illustrate the eighteenth-century French treatise *L'Art du Potier d'Etain,* by M. Salmon, a pewterer from Chartres. The workers portrayed are in large, airy, well-appointed, shops, with the machinery of the era clearly shown. Perhaps these pictures could resemble the work in some early American shops, par-

In our shop, the porringers are "hung high"—in a row.

ticularly the more successful family businesses that turned into dynasties like the Boardmans and Danforths. It interests me that Laughlin, in his three-volume *Pewter in America,* chose the French engravings to illustrate shops, and just tools and molds from the American scene.

But the Lees do not fit into such a picture. The elder Lee wrote a personal history that centered more on his spiritual struggles than on his vocation as a pewterer, a trade he came to relatively late in life. He says that he was put to work at five years of age. He moved about and lived in five different townships before he enlisted in the army in 1775. He served several tours of duty, then later complained that it had broken his health, which never recovered after the service in the Revolutionary army. The second period of life, his postwar years, were a continuation of wandering and living in different towns and working at different trades: tanning hides, selling real estate, keeping store, making hardware buttons, trading in wild land. Sometime about 1788 he mentions pewter. Laughlin quotes from his writing,

> My next object was pewtering with my son." He says this in such a way as to lead us to believe that he had never had any previous training for this type of work. How did Lee secure the knowledge and experience to enable him to become a pewterer? And back in the woods, far from any pewter-making center, where did he acquire his molds and how did he pay for them? (vol. I, p. 122)

Richard Lee continued to move around, and misfortune followed. His tools were seized to pay what he termed "unjust debts," and brought scandalously low prices. He eventually returned to Springfield, Vermont, married for a third time, and spent the next years working for his son, peddling pewter and brass. Laughlin writes of him,

> Pursued by misfortune which seemed to keep right at his heels no matter how fast he traveled, Richard Lee was one of those individuals who cannot settle down. The end of the rainbow was always just on the other side of the hill. In spite of ill health he had no lack of energy, for, in addition to his many vocations listed above, he was at times an itinerant preacher, an herb doctor, and a maker of children's books.

When I look at the small porringers we make, not replicas but in the size and style to suggest Lee's work, I think of him as a person and as a craftsman. Knowing that small porringers comprised the preponderance of his work, I am reminded of a comment about him read many years ago, that his was a troubled life, and the small porringer was of a size and scope he was able to handle. But that must be balanced against a judgment I find in the first edition of Kerfoot's *American Pewter,* in which Kerfoot gives none of the facts about Lee's life but praises his work. He has examined four pieces of Lee's work: a basin, a small plate, a ladle, and a porringer. About them, Kerfoot writes, "All four pieces are of the finest metal; are of excellent design and proportions, and bespeak for their maker the possession of taste and a touch of independence. I have known no other instance where, out of four specimens found by one maker, four distinct types of article were represented." (First edition, 1924, p. 83)

The small porringers suggest a family story that took place far from the pewter shop. In August 1970, our family was crossing the Atlantic on the *Statendam* on the way to a safari around Europe. I had been granted an Underwood Fellowship from the Danforth Foundation for a study that would take us through ten countries. We would tow a caravan behind a station wagon and camp along the way.

There was great excitement as we boarded the handsome ocean liner, found our quarters, and had a brief champagne farewell party in our cabin with friends who had come to see us off. They waved to us from the dock as the ship moved away, pointed downstream in the Hudson and headed for sea. We used the time before dinner to explore the ship and go through our

Skimming an apple bowl with a tool given by the pewterer in Delfshaven, Holland.

introduction to the safety procedures in case of emergency.

At dinner, our family of seven nearly filled a table set for eight. The dining room was festive and high spirits were evident everywhere. The wine steward came to our table to assist in our selection. Jonathan, then ten, sitting at my left, became excited and could hardly wait to get my attention. When the order was taken and the wine steward left, Jonathan said, "Dad, did you see? He has a little porringer just like ours." I had noticed it too, hanging on a chain about his neck and reaching almost to his waist. "Watch how he uses it," I replied. When he returned, the bottle was opened with a levered corkscrew, and after the steward poured a bit of wine into the small porringer and sampled it, he pronounced it good and filled our glasses. All eyes were on him during the small ceremony. Back home, we had been making the small porringer for only a few months, and it had never occurred to any of us that we would see a porringer used this way or in such a setting.

We disembarked in Rotterdam in the midst of a dock strike and had a busy time gathering our sixteen pieces of luggage, mostly duffel bags and large canvas bags with handles and shoulder straps. There were seven of us, and each had been allowed one each of these. We also had two large suitcases. We had to move this from ship side, past the striking dockworkers, to the street, where we required two taxis to take us to our lodging. The hotel manager looked at our growing pile of baggage and asked, "Emigrating?" We explained that we would be traveling for five months in a caravan and had our winter clothing and some camping gear.

While in Rotterdam we had our first direct plunge into the history of pewter. We visited the shop of a working pewterer in nearby Delfshaven; he had molds dating to the 1400s. It was open to the public and he sold his work. The afternoon we were there, he was casting small porringer bodies onto which he would solder two handles. He did not speak English and I did not speak Dutch, but I had some pictures of my work and we talked with our hands as the demonstration went on.

He had a melting pot with perhaps thirty pounds of molten pewter, and his mold, the two sides hinged together with handles for opening and closing. Standing beside his melting pot was a five-gallon pail containing a reddish brown solution that was heated. In the casting-process, he would dip the hot mold into the solution with the handles apart and the mold somewhat open. As it came out, the heat immediately dried the mold and left a thin residue on the mold surfaces. That would aid in the parting process after a piece was cast. He closed the mold and picked up his ladle, skimmed back the surface oxidation on the molten pewter, filled the ladle, and poured it into the sprue, the mouth of the mold. We waited a minute or two until the pewter had gone down in temperature through the pasty range and had solidified. He then opened the mold and removed and examined the bowl. He found it acceptable and put it on a workbench beside a small lathe used for skimming. The cycle took about four minutes, and as we watched, the pile grew. When there was an imperfection in the casting, the porringer went back into the melting pot.

After building his pile of castings to a dozen, he put aside his ladle, picked up one of the bowls, and fitted it into a special soft wood chuck on his lathe. He turned on the lathe, picked up a small skimming tool made of thin spring steel, and proceeded to skim the inside surface of the bowl as the lathe turned at about one thousand revolutions per minute. I had never seen this process and was excited by it and by the result. What would have taken me several minutes using both wet and dry emery paper, he had done in seconds with the skimming tool. He saw that I was interested, and asked, by gestures, if I did this. When I said no, he prepared the next piece for skimming and offered me the tool. I smiled and gestured my hesitation, saying that I would ruin the piece. He insisted. I took the thin piece of spring steel and tried to skim the turning bowl as he had done. The tool vibrated wildly in my hand and, instead of skimming it clean and smooth as it was supposed to do, put in a series of marks around the bowl that ruined it. The pewterer smiled as he removed it and put it back into the melting pot. Then he put another piece in place and pointed to me to try again. I was reluctant, fearing the same result. He took the tool and showed me how to hold it in my grip in such a way that there would be a bend, or spring, in the metal, to stabilize it as it skimmed the pewter. I tried again and–to my surprise and relief–executed the action without mishap.

After we had studied the racks along a wall that held molds of many descriptions and from different centuries, we purchased a porringer like the ones we saw being made. As we were prepared to leave, he gave me the skimming tool that I had used. There were smiles all around as I responded to his generosity by giving him one of the pictures of my work. I wrote on the back a greeting and thanks for our visit and his gift.

I have used that skimming tool for years and have fashioned a variety of similar tools for skimming in special curves and corners of pieces being finished, whether they have been cast or spun on the lathe. In part of my mind I associate that tool with the shop where I first saw it used, and when

I think of the shop in Delfshaven, two things stand out with clarity. One is the memory of a friendly craftsman, confident in what he was doing, probably a descendant of pewterers who had worked in that shop for generations. I had another feeling, standing in front of the wall where all the molds were displayed. One of the largest of the molds was for a charger, a piece about fifteen inches in diameter. The mold, in bronze or brass, had the date 1425 cast in the center surface of the top half and must have weighed more than a hundred pounds. I realized that I was standing in the presence of the primary tools of the trade for many centuries, and that these dozens of molds had been used over the centuries in this shop by generation after generation of craftsmen. I cannot imagine standing in one place that could put me any closer to the history of the craft in its actual practice. That charger mold had been made before my own country had been discovered and settled, before the colonists had begun their tug-of-war with the British about establishing their own pewter production. It may have been fitting to make this connection, for down the street from that pewter shop was the historic site where the Pilgrims gathered as they planned their move to the New World.

REPAIRING PEWTER

In repairing pewter, and particularly old pewter, novices will often rush in where the experienced will hesitate. With every good intention to improve a piece, they inflict damage that is irreparable. A lot of knowledge is required to diagnose what is needed, and even more hands-on experience to accomplish the repairs. It's a catch-22 situation. How does someone get the experience to acquire the knowledge?

Ideally, an apprentice learned by standing beside a master who had both knowledge and skills. In an older time, when there were guilds, a journeyman was with the master craftsman for several years and would be able to watch, and perhaps help, in making repairs, long before he took on the total responsibility for his craft. In those days, before the guilds began to dissolve, there was a much wider use of pewter and many more repairs to be made, giving frequent opportunity to learn and practice.

Anyone who has made repairs to old pewter will have memories of successes that are a joy to revisit, along with horror stories he would rather not relate (or even remember). I think of a day in the early 1970s that still has

Christopher removes a scratch from the bottom of a bowl.

an almost magical quality in the recollection of it. In my lexicon of repair stories, this is the one I like most to remember and to share.

On an early summer day, Dan Hingston, a friend and neighbor, a professional dealer in antiques, stopped by the shop with a quart, domed-top tankard in hand. He placed it on my workbench and with a characteristic smile said, "It needs some friendly attention and help. See what you think can be done for it, and I'll check with you later." Dan had bought the tankard and other items on a recent trip to the British Isles, which he visited regularly, carrying items both ways. Quick, bright, and of enormous energy, he was most knowledgeable about antiques in general, and pewter in particular.

After Dan left, I sat looking at the tankard. It did indeed need some friendly help. The dome-shaped lid was dented and twisted askew; the pin for the hinge to the top was missing and had been replaced by a rusty steel screw. There were dents here and there in the body of the piece but, happily, no breaks, folds, or holes. The entire surface was so covered with oxidation, scale and corrosion that almost none of it looked like pewter.

Still, something about it spoke of a former estate and dignity that misuse and lack of care had not been able to destroy. Its proportions were right, in the sense of classic design. I held it in my hands, bonding with it, turning it to the light first this way and then that. Feeling is important. My hands sometimes "see" things that my eyes miss. Help? Yes! I wanted to restore it. I held it at arm's length and tried to imagine it new, nearly two hundred years ago. What did the pewter shop look like where it was first offered for sale? Who had owned it? Where had it lived? How far had it traveled?

Now it was in my hands. What would I do with it? I had learned a lesson about diagnosis in a very different and unlikely setting, but one that has worked well over the years. I had been privileged, during the 1950s, to hear a lecture by Karl Menninger to the senior staff at the Riggs Psychiatric Foundation in Stockbridge, Massachusetts, on the "perils of diagnosis." It had a strong central point: "Don't do it!" In a quiet voice full of authority, this giant in psychiatry gave the other giants in psychiatry a simple admonition. "In diagnosis," he told them, "you select a few technical words, and you lose the human being who depends on you for healing. You stop seeing the person and see the paranoid, or the schizophrenic. The person is your client. Keep relating to the person and treatment is possible because you will see ever-changing realities you would miss if you were thinking of your diagnosis."

In my adaptation of the "Menninger principle" to repairing pewter, I stay in an open, dynamic relationship with what is occurring, and may change procedures as I see something new happening with the work. I do not construct a plan of approach; I start working and keep thinking about what I am finding as the work proceeds. My knowledge grows by the engagement; my sense of reality of the piece is enhanced. So now to work.

I removed the long, rusted, steel screw that had been inserted where the pin had originally been in the hinge to the top. I took measurements of the domed lid, which was misshapen from several dents. I would use the measurements to turn a hard wood mold that would allow me to remove the dents with a paper or rubber mallet.

Next I prepared a bath of lye deep enough to cover both the tankard and lid, and submerged them. Then I turned my attention to making the wood mold.

The lye solution required some caution. I used a plastic bucket holding five gallons of warm water. Into this I slowly dissolved more than half a can of lye, stirring until all was in solution. I was careful to check the handle of the tankard for holes, which might let lye into a hollow center left from the process of slush casting. A hollow handle could trap the acid and later damage a tablecloth or a tabletop. Throughout the process I wore rubber gloves and protected my eyes with goggles.

For metal that has not been cleaned for a long time, the lye solution is always a good first step. It will loosen whatever clings to the metal without damaging the patina. It can be a slow process, sometimes requiring a series of baths with intervals in which one brings the piece out of the solution, holds it under a running stream of warm water, and brushes it with a soft brush. These brushings allow a look at what is coming off and what is yet to be removed.

I worked on the wooden mold for the lid and returned to the acid bath from time to time to check the process. The lye was making slow but steady progress in showing what the metal would look like when it was clean. Certain areas cleared ahead of others. The corners and decorative lines would be last to give up the accumulated matter that had hardened in place. A soft toothbrush is helpful in these places, and patience is a craftsman's best ally.

The novice, when given the task of cleaning such a piece, may be tempted to hurry to the buffing wheel, where a wide selection of compounds can be enlisted to remove a little or a lot of the offending surface buildup. Only one advice is normative: "Don't!" Laughlin quotes with approval the dictum by Kerfoot, "Once buffed is always buffed." It is possible to destroy a century or two of patina in a few minutes on the buffing wheel. It is impossible to "unbuff" a piece.

The third time I took the tankard out of the lye solution and brushed it under a gentle stream of water, I began to be excited by what I was seeing. The metal was of high grade, of good color, and free of even small pits. When I was sure I had rinsed and brushed off all the lye, I covered the surface with a cleaning polish, let it dry, and then rubbed it with a soft cloth. I found some areas that needed further work by the lye, but I discovered areas that had a quality of luster I had seldom seen. Before putting it back into the lye, I measured the hole for the pin in the hinge to the top.

While it had its final bath, I looked about the shop for something I could use for the pin. It occurred to me that the handle of our cast colonial rat-tail spoon was nearly round. Among some that had been cast but not finished, I selected one that had problems in its bowl but possessed a sound handle. Happily, the micrometer indicated that a little work with a file and emery paper would make it fit nicely.

After a break for lunch, I returned to an afternoon mixed with careful work and an occasional reverie. With it finally out of the lye baths, cleaned and brushed gently, I now could work on the body and lid. Small dents were removed, flattened areas rounded, and the lid restored to its original shape with help of the wooden mold and some rubber and paper mallets. As I handled the tankard and its top, I found my imagination working on pictures of how this piece had been originally formed, fitted, soldered, and finished. The mental images were aided by memories of pictures, old woodcuts and lithographs, and sketches in my collection on the history of the craft. And more than that.

I had a sense of kinship something like that Robert Frost describes in his poem *The Tuft of Flowers,* in which he comes to turn the grass that has been scythed earlier by another. Frost discovers, with the aid of a butterfly, a tuft of flowers that the man with the scythe chose not to cut. He writes about his response as he feels

> a spirit kindred to my own:
> so that henceforth I worked no more alone.

The poem ends:

> "Men work together," I told him from the heart,
> "Whether they work together or apart."

The best part came at the end. When all the cleaning and shaping was done, I could now work to bring out the luster I had noticed earlier. I had fitted the pin made from the section of the spoon handle, and could assemble the tankard whenever I was ready to. But first I wanted to use cleaner and polish and see what would happen to the metal. At each cycle, a longer period was devoted to simply rubbing the pewter with a soft cloth. First apply the polish to the separate pieces, then rub and rub. What was happening was incentive enough to keep on.

I was sitting before a large window in the soft light of late afternoon. Occasionally my eyes were drawn to a trout breaking the surface of the pond behind the shop. But they would be drawn back to the metal to which, with each cycle, the rubbing brought a greater luster. How account for it? A theory grew in my mind to near certainty. The piece was well over a century old, perhaps closer to two centuries. Lead would have been used in the mix. Sometimes lead had a small component of silver that, in those days, would not have been removed: a small amount, but enough to account for that soft, glowing sheen.

At last I assembled the tankard, and hammered the ends of the pin holding the lid in place, to keep it from slipping out. Then I rubbed the whole tankard one last time and placed it on a shelf. I was back in the shop working after dinner when Dan Hingston, passing by, saw the lights of the pewter shop and stopped. As he entered the work area he said, "Did you get a chance to look at—Oh my! my! I can't believe what I'm seeing! I can't believe such a difference could be achieved!"

The value of the tankard was much enhanced. The dignity of its former estate had been restored. It had been accomplished without losing any of its many, many years. Indeed, its age was integral to its restored beauty.

THE HINDU TRANCE

From the early years of our pewter shop, people have come singly, in families, and in groups to visit and watch us at work. There was a summer conference center several miles south of us operated by a mainline Protestant denomination at which its leadership and ministers and some laity gathered. Each summer some of their participants would find us, and one year when they were holding a conference on lifestyle, a sizable group asked to come and see our work in operation.

I chose to demonstrate pewter spinning by making a centerpiece vase, a process that is more dramatic and interesting to the viewer than any single piece we form on the lathe. It is our demonstration item of choice. Years later, a writer for *Yankee* magazine would comment, "If the finished product tricks the eye, the spinning process used to make it boggles the mind. Watching Ray at the lathe turning a flat pewter disk into a small round-bottomed vase is like seeing an apple slowly push its way through a car door. Metal isn't supposed to move like that."

The centerpiece vase has a tulip-shaped bottom that curves in gracefully at the top. We start with a seven-inch flat pewter disk, sixty-thousandths of an inch thick, and form it over the steel chuck. For those watching the spinning process for the first time, it is fascinating to see the flat disk form around the chuck spinning more than two thousand revolutions per minute. Many who have watched us spin pewter have used the analogy of throwing a pot, or forming clay as it revolves on a turntable. In our case, we form something that is turning, but our hands are not touching the material directly. We hold, and control, a highly polished metal tool that strokes the metal, moving it a little with each pass, gradually forming it onto or around the turning chuck.

On the day this group came, they watched with genuine excitement as the metal began to move, forming around the bulb, or bottom, of the vase. It became more dramatic as the spinning metal was "necked down" to the top of the chuck. Watching, the visitor sees a chuck totally encased within its metal vase. It is, to all appearances, trapped inside.

As I was bringing the metal down to the neck, a voice behind me said, in surprised concern, "How are you going to get that off?" Others murmured, too. I was expecting the question, having answered it many times. Only, this time I chose to be playful. I finished the strokes of the forming tool and turned to the group. In a serious tone, I said, "First I will go into a deep Hindu trance. Then I will expand the molecules of the pewter and contract the molecules of the steel chuck. I will take it off and then return both to their proper molecular structure. Then I will come out of the trance."

I turned my back on their puzzled expressions and hesitant smiles—one or two looking at each other with a "Did I hear correctly?" expression. After they had time to register what I had said, I continued, "One thing is important. I can't do this if there is an unbeliever in the shop. It just won't work. So if any of you don't believe me, I will have to ask you to leave the barn while I do it."

No one moved. I turned to the work, trimmed the top of the vase as the lathe turned at a reduced speed, and began to apply a series of wet and dry abrasive papers to smooth the surface of the piece. Then it was time to remove the vase-enclosed chuck from the headstock of the lathe. I did so and carried it to the workbench. There I placed it in a vise, tightening the vise around the part of the chuck that was not enclosed in the pewter.

All eyes were watching and there was silence as I bent over the piece, placed my hands on each side of the vase, closed my eyes, and vocalized a steady Ommmmmmmmm. I lifted and the vase came upward with my hands as the chuck separated into two parts. What was left in the vise was a center stalk. In my hands I held the vase, inside of which were nine carefully machined pieces that could now be removed one by one and assembled around the stalk to rebuild the chuck to its full size for spinning another vase. It was like a Chinese puzzle coming together before their eyes. They began to laugh and make comments about the trick I had played on them.

Later in the week, when one of the conference people came back to the shop, he told me that I had become a staple in their consultations. "Whenever the question has arisen this week about how you do this or that," he said, "someone has answered, 'First, you go into a deep Hindu trance.'"

The chuck I used for the demonstration has its own history. It had been machined from steel sometime after the First World War, and was now a half-century old. The invention of these "sectional" or "breakdown" chucks, as they are called, has never been assigned to a particular pewterer, or even to an exact period. It belongs to the transition from casting to spinning as the principal method of production. That transition occurred by the mid-eighteenth to early-nineteenth century, following upon the water-power and steam engines that made the industrial revolution possible.

The breakdown, or sectional, chuck was an important reason that spinning pewter was able to compete with, and often replace, casting as the method of production. In casting, the molds locked the pewterer into one changeless, permanent piece. Not only that; it was impossible to cast a vase in one piece, as I had spun the vase, for you couldn't get the solid "inside part" out after the casting. Holloware was therefore made with multiple molds, and the pieces were then soldered together. A breakdown chuck could be assembled, put on the lathe, and the piece completely formed around it; the chuck was then removed piece by piece. It was efficient and cost effective. Those who continued casting did so out of the conviction that their results were of superior strength, a case that could be made against spinners who thinned their metal in the spinning process.

Jonathan as a beginner—washing emery paper for reuse.

Having once told the "Hindu story" to the conference group, it became a staple in demonstrations. When someone saw the metal forming around the chuck and asked the obvious question, "How are you going to get that off?" I would say, "I'll tell you a story." Sometimes people who knew the story brought friends who didn't, and would ask me to "tell the Hindu trance story." My children, and later the apprentices, did not always relish hearing the story repeated yet another time, and I would see them silently mouthing words with me, a gentle mocking expression on their face.

Perhaps our frequent choice of the centerpiece vase for demonstrations is the reason it became, and continues to be, the most popular of our wares. It is also a fine design and makes a lovely gift. At the Sunapee Craftsmen's Fair, when Jonathan and I demonstrate, I do the casting while Jonathan is the spinner. He has used the centerpiece vase to good effect and to the obvious pleasure of the forty-five thousand or so visitors who come to that fair in any given year, many of whom pause to watch us work.

THE PARTNERSHIP

> I am getting more depressed about New York every day. If the filth and crime does not upset your stomach, the advent of a blistering summer will. We're going to stick it out as long as we have to in order to build up enough savings to move. In the meantime, we are beginning to study our options.

In this letter written on April 23, 1990, Jonathan voiced a discontent with life in New York that had been growing in the preceding months. He also said that he would like to "log some hours" with me in the pewter shop during his vacation. In his correspondence during the late 1980s, his unhappiness in the city was often coupled with thoughts of the country, of Hillsborough, and of the possibility of working in pewter.

Jonathan was born in 1960, and was seven years old when I began working with pewter. He was part of the development of our summer cottage industry as pewter became an increasingly important occupation for family members at home in Hillsborough Centre. Being the youngest, he had more years—and wider experience—than his brothers in making pewter, though none of them had extensive experience in the primary role of spinning or casting. His sister, Lauren, had nearly the same number of years, though her participation was devoted more to managing the shop, meeting visitors and customers, hand-finishing our pieces, and hammering bracelets and fashion accessories of her own design.

When the prospect of Jonathan's entering the pewter operation emerged, a host of possibilities and problems presented themselves. The thought of having Jonathan and Camille nearby was a happy one. The life we enjoyed in this beautiful little hilltop village would be far richer if shared with family. Whenever we anticipated the visit of any of our children's families, our spirits rose as the time approached. Family reunions on such holidays as the Fourth of July, Thanksgiving, and Christmas, were the highlights of any year.

Could the pewter enterprise support the venture? I spent numerous evenings poring over records of our financial experiences, finding in every session reasons to doubt that it could produce a "living wage" for Jonathan. With me, it had always been a creative endeavor, engaged in for the joy of the craft and the relationships that had grown from it. It had provided some help for the education of our children, contributing to their school bills and teaching them to work creatively. I had never worked in the pewter shop except in summers, and even then reserved time for the farm and the garden. During the fall, winter, and spring, I was professionally engaged in church and parish life and college teaching in Providence. In retirement, these seasons were spent in writing books. The barn had not been winterized in any way. Jonathan had wondered about creating a new and more efficient facility, perhaps somewhere else on the farm. In one of my letters to him, I described how I saw myself in relation to the craft and raised questions based on this experience:

> About myself. I will only be working from the late Spring to the early Fall. I have a strong *identity formation* that includes me, the barn, the lovely grounds around, the lane leading west over the hill into our woods, the view of the pond, Cy's sculptures, Susan's flowers, the garden, etc. While I believe that our present customers come for the pewter, it is clear to me that these other factors are meaningful parts of their experience too.
>
> I don't think pewter, even Gibson pewter, has to be sold only in this way. But it is meaningful to me and to the customers, and there are satisfactions in these relationships that are more than making a sale. Admittedly, it takes time away from production, though it does promote sales. If pewter were my only livelihood, would I do it this way? Probably not. But if it came down to doing nothing but production, with all that that implies, and I had to do it year-round, I don't know how long I would be able to enjoy working within the lifestyle or even working with the metal.

When I studied the financial statements for the preceding years and analyzed the costs of operation and production time in relation to profits, my doubts grew about the possibilities Jonathan had in mind. If we were to go to a larger, year-round operation, there would be substantial capital costs for winterizing the barn and adding some needed machinery. I worked on numerous models in which mass marketing was used and the possibility of an expanding work-force was introduced to enhance production. But the balance sheets always ended in negative numbers. Letters to Jonathan shared my findings and spelled out these discouraging prospects.

After Jonathan was graduated from Hobart College, he moved to New York, where he wanted, as he describes it, "to work in the world's most competitive job market." He loved the work, the competitive grind of the commercial real estate business. He says now, looking back on the experience, "Slowly, however, city life lost its appeal, and living in midtown proved to be quite a test. Camille and I did not want to have kids in the city and we both wanted to work for ourselves." He admits that he "dreamed of running a business which offered more rewards than money. Sometime in the late 80s," he said, "I began thinking about the creative possibilities of being a full—or part-time pewterer."

There were special moments when things seemed powerfully clear. "I remember standing on a roof-top one hot day in July in mid town Manhattan with a group of coworkers," Jonathan recalls. " We were taking a lunch break and hoping for a cool breeze. As I looked down onto 6th Avenue and over across 38th Street, at the masses of people, the traffic moving slowly, horns blowing, the whole mess—I knew then and there that I was not going to spend the rest of my life living in a big city."

As 1990 passed, Jonathan began to formulate a plan for transition that would include a combination of real estate and pewter. He would begin with a major portion of his effort devoted to real estate, expecting to use his well-honed commercial real estate experience and to cross the bridge to residential real estate sales, while working in the margins of his time reclaiming and enhancing his pewter skills.

On July 20, 1991, Jonathan and Camille packed their U-Haul and moved from New York City to New Hampshire. They stayed in our house until they moved into a cottage owned by a neighbor whose property joined our own to the south. It was a charming antique Cape, dating from the late 1700s, with wide pine floors, Indian shutters, fireplaces in the living room and study, three bedrooms, two baths, and a kitchen, with a screened-in porch and a view of meadow and hills. Part of the rent could be worked out in care of the grounds and mowing the meadow. The owners, a retired doctor and his wife, lived in the "barn" that had been transformed into a latter-day rustic mansion. The lawns and plantings around these houses on the Mary Gay

Jonathan solders a handle to an unlidded tankard.

Farm of thirty-nine acres were lovely and required a great deal of care.

Jonathan worked with a local real estate agency and "moonlighted" in the pewter shop when he could. Camille continued special contract work for Simplicity Pattern Co. and sewed for local clients as well. Making the necessary connections and passing the local real estate qualifying exams, Jonathan became an independent broker late in 1992, which gave him control of his schedule and freed him for greater time commitments in the pewter shop.

Our experience in the winter of 1991 convinced us that drastic changes had to be made if we were to be able to work in the pewter shop between November and April. Our attempts at temporary plastic partitions and propane heating created what Jon called "our near-death experience." There just wasn't enough oxygen for us and the heater. During the summer of 1992, we began thinking through what changes we would make, and how we would redesign the shop for efficiency and the best use of the space we would insulate. A heating specialist conferred and decreed the requisite "R" factors: 30 below the floors, 20 in the walls, and 40 above the ceiling. "It will cost quite a lot up front," he said, "but it will save you money in the long run."

As we thought about the adaptations of the barn space to our needs, we found ourselves thinking about the integrity of the building. It had been there about two hundred years and had been subject to rearrangements of space usage, and some partitions had been installed or taken down over the years. The stanchions had been removed when it was no longer used as a dairy barn. But the integrity of the post-and-beam structure was still intact. We decided that whatever we did with the space, we would not "hide" the posts and beams. Another important decision had to do with windows. We would be inside much of the year during the daylight hours. It was important to have as much of that daylight as possible for two reasons. It was the best light for seeing the pewter, whether we were working it, finishing it, or packing it. Also, we were addicted to the beauty of the surroundings—the apple trees, stone walls, meadows, animals and birds—so that we did not want to lose that sense of space or what was in that space. Windows with insulated glass capable of meeting the R20 decreed by the heating engineer would be quite expensive. We would bear that gladly.

There were four "rooms," or separate spaces created initially by the existing post-and-beam structure, and utilized by our design for the winterized shop. Three of them have doors opening to the center nave of the barn; the fourth has a wide window looking from the nave into the forming area. Each of the doors is made of layered wood and has a clear glass window about shoulder high. As you walk down the center section of the barn, it is possible to see into each of the areas. From the front of the barn, the first section has a door leading into the selling area The second section, the spinning or forming area, may be seen through a wide window. It contains all of the lathes, chucks or spinning forms, and forming tools. The third section is administrative, with desk, phone, and catalogs; the major books from our pewter library on the history and practice of the craft; and the wrapping, boxing, and mailing operation. It has a door from the nave of the barn on one side and a wide window toward the meadow on the other. The fourth section is entered by a door from the central nave and contains the buffing, casting, and soldering operations. It has wide windows with excellent views on the west and south walls, keeping the room alive with light needed for the finishing process.

All four rooms of the shop are heated by a high-tech kerosene stove so small that it is hardly noticeable. Fuel is pumped to it from a large tank in the basement of the barn; it vents out of doors so that none of the combus-

The partners in the newly winterized shop.

tion fumes get into the shop—no "near-death" experiences here. It is controlled electronically and can be programmed for a night temperature and a daytime heating level. Highly efficient in its combustion, it is relatively inexpensive, enough so that some of our customers have taken away with them heating ideas as well as our pewter.

Our builder, Dan Paul, of Daystar Builders, was sensitive to our concerns and had craftsmen who were quick but careful. One carpenter, given the task of constructing the barn-length, insulated wall that separates the four sections from the main nave fitted the rough-sawn pine boards into the post-and-beam frame as carefully as if he were working with finished pine doing cabinet-work in a kitchen. He worked with a care that enabled me to feel free, as we talked one day during his coffee break, to tell him about a near mystical experience I had had in the barn some years before.

The barn was being reroofed. The workmen had stripped away the old asphalt roofing and repaired the roof boards before putting down the new roofing. There were gaps between the boards that would let in rain, so they had covered the whole roof with a transparent plastic before leaving for the day. I came up from Providence to check on their progress and arrived after they were gone. It was twilight, and the sun was going down behind the woods. I opened the door and went into the still barn and looked up. The barn was empty above the first floor. The post-and-beam structure was caught in an eerie light from the cracks between the roof boards. It could have been a cathedral! In fact, I had a flashback, and remembered going into the famous Le Corbusier church at Ronchamps in southern France in the early evening with our son Mark, and walking around with the reflected light coming in at the tall, silolike tower and spreading downward. It was a powerful experience that I have never forgotten. Now, I stood in the barn in a silence that was almost like sound, as if the light through those narrow slits, giving definition to the beams and bracing angles at the corners, were a kind of mute music. The harmony in the proportions, and the absolute fitness of function in each piece that made the whole, gave a quiet sense of the utter rightness of it all.

As I spoke about the experience, I was looking up to where the roofing boards met at the ridgepole of the barn, remembering what I had seen. Now, as I looked back at the young carpenter, his eyes were bright with recognition of what I had described, his head nodding in understanding.

During the winter of 1992–93, the newly winterized shop was warm, the air was fresh, the surrounding snowscape beautiful, and the production was interrupted only by cleaning up outside after the occasional snowstorm. Jonathan had made steady progress in extending and enhancing his skills from the time he moved to New Hampshire. He now made dramatic advances in the two key areas of spinning and soldering, and pioneered in product development that would be his alone. A hammered sculpture, bracelets, and an extensive line of earrings came first, then several cast pieces, and, later still, some replicas of historic mugs and tankards.

I tried to remember the things that had been most helpful to me while working with my teacher and mentor, Arthur Barnes, and to share these with Jonathan. I discovered that there was a large gray area in my memory. I could not distinguish with clarity just what had been Arthur's teaching and what was a result of my learning by doing. I had moved ahead by experience in the work itself, but relied on Arthur as a ready presence when problems arose and I needed guidance. Jonathan and I did the same without discussing or planning the way we would work together. When he needed help, he asked for it. When I noticed some practice that might better be done another way, I offered a suggestion. It was eventually verbalized by Jonathan to a TV reporter who was interviewing him in the midst of some pieces we had made. She asked what he felt about the work and the craft. In describing the things he liked about the work, he concluded, ". . .and if I have any problems, my teacher is close at hand."

As we neared the end of winter in 1993, it was clear that expansion was ahead and that Jonathan would be devoting more and more time to the pewter shop. On May 10, a legal document was completed and signed that created a partnership. We had been working and thinking as partners, but up to now the legal and tax identity made me the owner and Jonathan an employee, with wages, withholding, and seemingly endless paperwork. The partnership simplified much of that and allowed flexibility in work patterns and compensation. Our shop was winterized, production would certainly double, and the question became one of marketing. We could create ever-new designs, produce more and more product; but could we sell it? The year 1993 taught us a tough but valuable lesson that helped define the direction and shape of our future.

The University of New Hampshire program, in its Office of Economic Initiatives, in connection with the New Hampshire Small Business Center, worked with a similar group in Maine to sponsor a Northern New England Products Trade Show. It was directed at small businesses wanting help and exposure to larger marketing opportunities. Reading the glowing reports of successes in the previous year, we decided to explore the world of wholesale merchandising, and signed up for the program in 1993. It involved three training sessions to be held at the International Trade Resource Center at Pease International Tradeport (formerly the Pease Air Force Base) in Portsmouth, New Hampshire. We would then design a booth and participate in a three-day megashow at the Cumberland County Civic Center in Portland, Maine.

We attended three seminars during January and February, traveling to Portsmouth, leaving early, and returning in time for a late supper. Each seminar focused on a special aspect of trade shows: developing pricing and credit policies; designing and building an effective display; and selling techniques—the do's and don'ts of trade shows.

We enlisted the help of woodworking friends to construct pedestals. We created some large pictures of the pewter shop for wall hangings, built tables and shelves that would display our product, and had a video playing a six-minute segment from *New Hampshire Crossroads*, a TV profile of our shop that showed the process of spinning pewter. We made our reservations at the Holiday Inn by the Bay, and took our best hopes and optimistic demeanors into the three days of meeting prospective buyers.

Every craft show becomes an exercise in amazement: the wonder that so much can be arranged in a space that is usually ten by ten feet; the disbelief that the frenzied beehive of activity and the chaotic effort in setting up can produce such an ordered and attractive result; that a very large space can be subdivided into so many small spaces and manage to create a distinct or unique setting for the product displayed. Pass a partition and see a new world!

Our booth was set up on time. I got a picture of it before the crowds came. People said it was lovely. They also said that the pewter was lovely. But nobody placed an order. Three days went by, with hundreds of buyers passing. That was the story. We were passed by.

We learned for sure what we had suspected, and what I had voiced at the training sessions in Portsmouth. Our craft is very labor-intensive, and that raises the price. If the price we must receive is doubled by the retailer, it will be prohibitive. We had spent the major part of three months in the process of learning what would not work for us. We would have to do direct marketing, or find special outlets where price would not prove an obstacle. We would have to gain more direct contacts by participation in quality craft fairs and by seeking higher visibility for our work.

One anomaly emerged from this experience. No one questioned the quality of our work, the fitness of the designs, or the overall beauty of the product. Price was the only barrier. Cutting the price would inflict hardships we could not survive. Cutting the quality was clearly unacceptable; we could not live with less than our best. I reminded Jonathan of a conversation I remembered from the visit to London. We had spent the morning with the curator of the Worshipful Company of Pewterers at a small two-craftsmen business, Abbey Pewter, two of the finest craftsmen in England. As we went to lunch at the Guild Hall, I asked the curator how the men at Abbey were doing as a business. He replied that it was a struggle. Sadly, quality pewter did not have a wide market. The companies that make trinkets and the cheap pewter that is sold at the seaside vacation spots found a bigger market. But that was pewter mass-produced by machines, not by craftsmen. J. Webster and R. Channer, the owner craftsmen at Abbey Pewter, had found enough market for their quality work to support them, but not enough to expand.

The task for us was to find markets where the quality of our work would be recognized and valued enough that price would not be an obstacle. The challenge would be to find venues where these kinds of customers would have a chance to see our work. If possible, the market would be local, regional, and national. Could we find ways to market on all three levels? In 1993 and 1994, we saw progress at all three.

Feature articles appeared in the *Keene Sentinel,* the *Concord Monitor,* and the *Boston Globe. Yankee* magazine carried a story that featured the pewterers and the product. A book published with the interesting title *Old Masters of New England* devoted a chapter to our history, craft, product, and philosophy, with pictures of each of us at work. Our work was shown in *Early American Life,* along with citations and our inclusion in the *"Directory of Fine Craftsmen."* We demonstrated for nine days during August 1994, and the three years thereafter at the Sunapee Craftsmen's Fair, which was attended by more than forty thousand visitors annually. We participated in Marian Gould's Hancock, Massachusetts, and Wilton, Connecticut, craft shows. Our work began to be sold in the museum store of the Museum of Fine Arts in Boston (MFA), including the two works that were in their permanent collection and several of our other pieces. Three television programs showed us working and highlighted what we produced.

These are written about in greater detail elsewhere, and are mentioned here to illustrate our response to the lesson we learned in our Portland failure to break into a wholesale market. A working philosophy emerged and began to take form. We tried to understand and shape the currents that were most honest to us and most valued by our customers. If there was a hierarchy of values, expressed in the way we were working, the key points were increasingly clear. Quality of work would be uppermost. Very selective reproductions from Early American pewter, as well as new designs of our own, would continue to guide our work.

To be true to the history and tradition of the craft, we would recognize the connection between the craftsmen and the product. People who wanted our work also wanted some sense of us as people and as craftsmen. The MFA store displays the picture of us that had appeared in *Yankee,* father and son holding a charger. It printed its own card to go with the items sold in the store, telling of our work in its permanent collection.

If we pick up a piece of colonial pewter, we instinctively turn it over and look for a touchmark to tell us who made it. If there is such a mark, it is much more valuable than if the maker is unknown, or merely thought to be, or in the style of, some early, known craftsman. Our touchmark indicates that the piece is ours.

Sales and the recognition of our product have grown steadily from the beginning of the partnership. We still forage widely for ideas, delving ever more deeply into the volumes we have accumulated on the history and current practice of the craft. As I planned this chapter, I asked Jonathan to jot down some of his memories, reflections, and observations on our partnership. I began the chapter with the beginning of his memo; it seems fitting to close with his final comment:

> Looking back, I'd have to say that the thrill of creating pewter is more exciting now than I had imagined it might be when we first began talking back in 1988–89. The product I've designed and created has been especially rewarding for me. The designs that percolate in my head are a constant source of motivation for me as well.

A later chapter—Tankards and Teapots—provides an illustration of some of the ideas that were "percolating" and the very special results when he turned them into reality. The partnership is alive and well, and growing steadily, which bodes well for the future of Gibson Pewter.

Becoming Known

NEW HAMPSHIRE CROSSROADS

Not long after an article about me appeared in the *Concord Monitor*, I had a call from someone at Channel 11, the PBS station in Durham, New Hampshire, saying they wanted to do a program on us for *New Hampshire Crossroads*, a weekly magazine program of half an hour, usually consisting of three segments. It was hosted by Fritz Weatherbee, a New Hampshire version of Alastair Cooke—urbane, cultured, literate. His voice and presence somehow managed to fashion the segments into a whole program, a weekly introduction to special people, history, and events as varied as theater, timbering, artisans at work, and sled-dog racing.

The *Monitor* article that had caught their attention was a nearly full-page cover story of the "Focus" section, with a large picture of me working at the lathe, taken by Dan Habib, one of the *Monitor's* most gifted photographers. The article, by Sarah Hodder, had as its headline, "Head, heart, and hands," which the writer used to introduce my philosophy of life as she was introducing the work with pewter. I had come to that philosophy from experience, and it was a matter of life influencing philosophy rather than the other way around. I had come to value the work and joy of the mind: contemplation, the intellectual journey of humans, in both the East and the West. I had also had a strong attraction to what some would call an understanding heart, or feelings and sensibilities attuned to whatever is deeply human. Valued also have been the creative uses of the hands. In Michelangelo's *Creation of Adam* in the Sistine Chapel, God is reaching out to Adam, and it is their hands—actually their fingers—that almost touch. The Old Testament psalmist writes with awe, "When I consider Thy heavens, the work of Thy hands. . . ."

The writer/cameraman assigned from *Crossroads* to produce the segment was Steve Salniker. When he arrived it was clear immediately that he had positive feelings for all three dimensions of life and wanted to incorporate them into the story he would tell with his camera. He asked to see some of my writing about the practice of the craft, selected a passage, had me read it into his recorder, then used it as a voice-over for a continuous action of forming a centerpiece vase on the lathe. He later had me tell a story on camera about two of our pewter hearts that had been taken to India by a friend, a story told in the chapter "The Pewter Heart," then had me hold the heart in my hand as the camera zoomed in for a close-up.

Steve's two visits and eight hours of shooting to get a seven-minute segment turned out to be a good experience. He arrived in a truck filled with specialized equipment for lighting, sound, and filming. For a time he asked questions, studied the machinery, looked at the space, evaluated the existing light. He then had me turn on the shop equipment to see it in motion and measure its noise.

The large cases of equipment were carried in and lines run for the lights. The tripod for the camera was set up in its pyramid form. Then began several short segments picturing different things in the shop, with each requiring some movement of the light, testing the light, then shooting. When it came to the filming of a piece of pewter being formed on the lathe, I selected the centerpiece vase, a dramatic piece to watch as a continuous action. The lathe faces the window, and there was no room on the other side to set up the camera. To get the shot Steve wanted meant taking out the window and setting up the camera "looking in." The trouble for that setup turned out to be more than worth it. It was a riveting part of the story visually, and the voice-over was given greater power by its placement there.

Another difficult segment was filming the spinning of the fruit bowl, our Stevens Metal Award winner. I was to form that bowl with our apprentice, Seth Bowley, assisting by pressing the follow stick behind the metal, matching the position of my forming tool. This pinching of the metal as it spins keeps the metal from rippling. To get this shot, and to show both the forming of the bowl and the intensity of our spinning effort, Steve worked again from across the lathe, this time from below, shooting across the bowl and up into our faces.

Steve also shot a segment on Chris Beard, our other apprentice, as Chris was buffing the fruit bowl on the fast, or power, buffing machine. I have described elsewhere Chris's intensity in this process, and his choosing to work with his body above the buffing wheel. By his placement of the camera and the shooting angle, Steve captured the focus, power, and concentration of the apprentice at work.

When it came time to portray our general work, another cameraman might have settled for a slow panning shot of the shelves where our pewter is displayed. Steve studied the work at some length and then asked me to tell him about special pieces. He singled out the historic replicas, shot them separately, then did cluster groups and a special close-up of our large chalice, a piece that has gone to church leaders on five continents.

After the first day's shooting, I was tired but exhilarated. From Steve's care in his work, his selecting things around the shop to shoot in addition to the pewter, and the wide-ranging conversation we had had, my respect for him and his craft was high indeed. I also found myself looking again at things that had caught his attention: the random arrangement of the chucks on the shelves, tools lying about, the gently vibrating handle of the lever used to lift the motor and change speeds of the lathe. I was seeing familiar things in a new way, a reminder that art is often an instruction in seeing.

Steve came back a second day after analyzing his film from the earlier shoot. He knew what he wanted to do to fill the gaps in the story he was trying to tell. The shooting went well. When he finished, and had reloaded the equipment into his van, he came back to where I was standing on the ramp of the barn to see him off. He shook hands, then, feeling a need for more emphasis, gave me a hug. "It has been a pleasure to work with you!" he said. As he drove away, I found myself a bit drained, but feeling good about what he had done. I would not see the results for several weeks, but I was confident of its quality. Steve had not worked like someone doing an assignment; it was clear that he valued the objects he was filming and appreciated the craft that had fashioned them. As he was painstaking in his effort to get a good result, so too was he quick to value careful work in a craft he was seeing for the first time.

The show was aired on a Friday evening, and repeated on Sunday and Monday. I watched all three, seeing new things each time, and my respect for Steve kept growing. Certainly he was good at what he did. When I told him so, I also made a request. Would he send a print of his film to the Museum of Fine Arts, in Boston, for its archives? He had shot sequences of the spinning and buffing of the fruit bowl, one of our pieces now in the museum's permanent collection. He agreed, and they were delighted to receive the video. He sent us a copy as well, and it has been used frequently to show family and friends the way his craft of filmmaking interpreted our craft of pewter making.

There were telephone calls, and mail, and people who came "to see for themselves" after the program was aired. Some who called were men nearing retirement age who wanted to know how difficult the craft was to learn, and how difficult it might be to get instruction. Some wanted to know

Special commission for the centennial of the University of New Hampshire.

whether I gave lessons. Others called requesting our brochure, or asking if they could bring their groups to watch a demonstration. The show was popular enough that it was aired several times over the next few years. Each time, there was response from viewers. More than that, I have found that with each viewing, I see new things in the show.

It was on one of the repeats that it occurred to me that Fritz Weatherbee, in his introduction, had echoed my philosophy as represented in the *Monitor* headline, "Head, Heart, and Hands." He began, "Pewter is an alloy. And the person we are about to meet could be called an alloy. He is an author, [he held up a recently published book of mine], a pastor, and a pewterer." The camera panned to a view of our barn, and the show began.

THE MASTERS GROUP

There is an element of loneliness in the practice of a craft. The focus on work, the solitary studio time, the creative moments that come from what is inside rather than what is external, the paucity of people who have equivalent experience even if they practice the same craft, each and all make the pursuit and practice of the craft a severely individual experience. The more accomplished the craftsman, the fewer the number of people who will understand the intricacies of what it is that makes his or her work special. Still, there are various levels of sharing and camaraderie among artisans. One measure of sharing can be seen at craft fairs, and the limits of that sharing are obvious when the fairs are larger and more selective.

There is an annual fair at Codman House, a dwelling dating from 1740, in Lincoln, Massachusetts. The fair is a benefit managed by the Society for the Preservation of New England Antiquities. More than one hundred modest spaces for craft booths are designated on the grounds of the mansion. It is a one-day affair; the craftsmen arrive, set up quickly, and see a stream of fair-goers from ten to five. A music group plays throughout the day, and two or three artisans are scheduled for talks about their crafts in the Carriage House. A children's craft corner engages the young in simple projects, and tours are conducted through Codman House for part of the day. The mood is festive, people visit the booths, the music is loud and popular. With two of us tending the booth, each is able to take a walk-around tour to see who and what is there. There is scant time to consider the work offered, and only rarely time to talk with the artisans showing their wares.

The first time Jonathan and I went to the Codman House Annual Artisans' Fair of Crafts, I was impressed with a handsome display of dried flowers and saw one arrangement that struck me as just right for our granny vase. I offered to exchange one of my vases for the arrangement I liked and the offer was accepted with pleasure and the comment, "But your vase is worth more than that arrangement." I responded that an item is worth what someone is willing to pay for it, and that I was happy with the exchange. Those flowers were a bright spot on our shelves for the next year or two and drew attention to the vase in a way that made it compete more successfully for the notice of visitors to our shop. That brief exchange at the fair, and the words "Nice work," or some variation of that, between artisans looking briefly at one another's work, was the extent of the fellowship or sharing during the day. It reminds me of the experience of pilots on tugboats in a harbor, tooting or waving at one another as they pass, doing their separate work. There was, of course, a minor but meaningful bond with the other artisans that set us off from the visitors. We were behind the tables that held our work and others were there to see what we had made. One felt a bond with the creating group even though their names were not known. A woman selling wares that prompted my comment, "Nice work," said, almost apologetically, "I didn't make it. My husband did. But he couldn't be here today."

The standard for admission to the fairs organized by Marilyn Gould is quite a lot higher. We have enjoyed being included for several years in two of her fairs: one in July each year at the historic Round Barn of the Shaker colony in Hancock, Massachusetts, and the other, in November, in Wilton, Connecticut. Artisans come to these fairs from all over the country. Making the rounds of the displays, you can see some of the finest work being done anywhere. There are as many personality types as there are crafts, and the pressure of time and the press of people make it impossible to get to know any of the artisans more than superficially. Those in adjoining booths are another matter, though, and over a three-day show, familiarity with the work and the personalities of neighboring artisans grows steadily, and in parting, we say with sincerity, "See you next year," or "See you in Wilton." Later we may see them, or their work, pictured in a magazine, and the recognition makes the magazine article more personal.

Over time and association, the Sunapee Craftsmen's Fair builds a web of personal networks made up of a mixture of knowledge of the artisan and regard for his or her work. There is a genial camaraderie during the setup period when all are in the same race to get organized and ready for the fair itself. Names may not be known but faces are familiar, as is the usual question during the first few days, "How's it going?" Exchanges take place at the water cooler, the coffee urn, and when taking a short lunch break. At first a few, and then gradually others, have caught enough of our interest that we go to their booths and study their wares and update what has been going on in their life and work. This happens with only a handful of the more than 150 artisans present. Like the Codman House experience, there are two groups here, those who show their work and those who come to see it. Our sense of belonging to the first group is strong but seldom articulated. The badge you wear identifies you. If you demonstrate your craft, as Jonathan and I have done, you do not merely show your work, but you also show how you make it. This raises your visibility to fairgoers and to fellow artisans as well. However, all of these "fractions" of relationships do not add up to the whole of deep or sustaining friendship.

During the last quarter of 1990, a group formed in south-central New Hampshire that would attempt to unite personal sharing and fellowship with periodic marketing events. The moving spirit was Anneke Rietsema, helped by her husband, Jaap (Jacob), and Cindee Kenney. William Thomas, Peter Sabin, and I were added quite early, and Naomi Lindenfeld, Susan Bliss, and Thomas Harkness a little later. While the prospect of some creative marketing was attractive to all, it was clear to me from the beginning that the venture was being driven more powerfully by a desire for meaningful sharing and mutual support. The discussions of the name and the purposes of the group were intense and engaged everyone present. Three themes emerged as dominant: mutual sharing, quality of work, and creative marketing.

The name for the group was not settled upon until the third meeting. Identity was important, and name should signify as much as possible about us. It was quickly agreed that the word "Masters" was appropriate. We were all juried members of the League of New Hampshire Craftsmen, which was a certification by our craft peers. Anneke wanted the name Seven Masters, which was the informal understanding we shared about the size of the group we desired. To be more descriptive of what we were masters of, a subtitle was quickly agreed upon, Creators of Usable Art. The consideration of maintaining an actual number of seven and being locked in to it made us select the name The Masters Group.

The first brochure went beyond a description of the group to identify the kind of clientele we desired. "The Masters Group is an association of artisans in a variety of media. They enjoy mutual sharing and stimulation as each seeks to achieve the highest quality possible in his or her chosen work. They seek to be special without being elitist. Their guiding concern for quality is a deeply personal matter that flows naturally into their work. They seek a clientele who care, as they do, for products that allow no shortcuts, or make no compromises, that could impair quality. As individual artisans with limited output, they have 'special occasion' marketing events. These are often exhibits, or shows, 'hosted' in private homes and limited to invited guests only."

The first such show and sale took place in Avon, Connecticut, in the home of the Rietsemas' daughter, Annelieke Schauer. This was a good setting for our first venture, and an excellent learning experience for the group, working together in such a congenial atmosphere. We knew already that we enjoyed meeting together and had established a level of trust in planning. Now we found that we worked well in execution.

The next show took place in the "sheep barn" at Stonewall Farm, the Rietsemas' home on Windsor Road, Hillsborough Upper Village, October 12 to 14, 1991, a Saturday to Monday, noon to five, Columbus Day weekend. An article in the October 7, 1991, *Chronicle,* described the artisans and told what would be available:

> The exhibition will have examples of hand-built porcelain, using a Japanese technique called "Nerikome," of combining colored clays to create patterns, done by Naomi Lindenfeld, a founder of the Brattleboro Clayworks, a potters' collective. There will be weavings, including Navajo styles, rugs, wall hangings and blankets by Anneke Rietsema, who, with her husband, is "hosting" the exhibition-sale. The hand-thrown stoneware is by Peter Sabin, of Warner, an independent Studio Potter for 25 years, who had a recent joint exhibition at the Smithsonian Institution in Washington, D.C. Unique baskets are by Cindee Kenney of Hillsboro, whose "native" baskets are made from black ash trees found near her home and which she shaves and handweaves in traditional ways. She received the "Best in Traditional Design Award" at the 1990 Living With Crafts exhibit at the Sunapee Craftsmen's Fair. Her "Root" baskets are particularly acclaimed. William Thomas, also of Hillsboro, is well known for his reproductions of 18th-century American furniture and other period designs. His emphasis on fine joinery to ensure the longevity of his work produces what will assuredly become heirlooms. Raymond Gibson, of Hillsboro Center, a master pewterer, has work that has gone to every part of the United States and to a dozen countries abroad. He does replicas of well-known American pieces as well as his own creations that carry on and extend the tradition of fine hand-crafted pewter.

The group worked hard to prepare the old sheep barn for the show. Some hanging gates had to be removed, and some stalls became natural boundaries for different exhibits. I committed the work of my apprentices, local high school students, to the project; they did some of the heavier lifting in the cleanup. Spirits were high, and attendance was better on Saturday and Sunday than on Monday. The weather was bright and clear. The experience was positive, though the profits were cut into by the printing costs for the brochure promoting the event.

After this show Naomi withdrew, citing distance and cost, but expressed her gratitude for the sharing and the association. Richard Harkness, a Suncook, New Hampshire, glassblower, joined the group and was a genial and positive presence.

Making a chuck for a Yates (1772) bowl replica. And holding the original to check measurements while turning wood to size.

The next sale and show was scheduled in the sheep barn for September 19–20, 1992, eleven AM to five PM. This time guest artists joined us: Susan Bliss, Joppa Road, Warner, New Hampshire with ceramics; and Roger Scheffer, of West Unity, New Hampshire, a maker of Windsor chairs. The two days worked better than the previous show of three days, but the number of visitors fell short of our expectations. The group enjoyed the sharing that took place between seeing customers, and our interest in the blown glass became the source of an invitation to the group to the Harkness studio. A covered-dish supper date was set for Election Day, with spouses or significant others invited.

We gathered early for a demonstration by Richard of the glassblowing process, and when he finished, he offered—challenged—us to give it a try. He rolled a bit of molten glass onto the end of the blowpipe and handed it to me. I tried to proceed as he had done, but found the wind requirement too great, which in itself prompted a number of jokes. Others had varying degrees of failure; all had a heightened respect for the craft and for Richard's facility with it.

After a social time with a variety of drinks and hors d'oeuvres, with one ear tuned to early election speculations by the TV newsmen, we had dinner accompanied by a wide-ranging discussion of life, crafts, religion, politics, and comments on the good food that had been prepared. Returning to the living room after dessert, we learned that the nation had a new president-elect.

This gathering was the last for the group. Continuing friendships had been formed or strengthened, and bonds were valued by all who had been part of the group. Anneke had been the moving force uniting the group. Now, health problems curtailed her activity, and then a fast-moving illness hastened her death. We gathered with her family and a group of neighbors and friends for a memorial service that I conducted, assisted by her son, Kaes, a high-ranking officer in the Air Force, who gave a moving tribute to his mother.

The experience of the Masters Group illumined one or two things for me. There is a value in sharing with other artisans that is unlike other friendships. A quality of "knowing regard" stimulates and strengthens each person's efforts. We desire to be worthy of the regard, while being confirmed in our self-confidence by the knowledge that the regard exists. During the final show, Roger Scheffer, who was seeing our pewter for the first time, suggested that we compete for entry in the annual *Early American Life* contest to select the two hundred leading "traditional craftsmen" in America. Jonathan and I entered and were chosen. I had not known of the contest before, and without Roger's confidence in our work, I doubt that I would have entered. We have been named to that directory every year since.

THE STEVENS METAL AWARD

The winter of 1992 was not a good one for me, regarding health. Between Thanksgiving and Christmas I had a bronchial infection that developed into pneumonia. I coughed until I felt that my lungs would collapse. Unable to shake the malady in spite of strong medications ordered by my doctor, I sat up through many nights in a reclining chair, sleeping fitfully, if at all, and watched gratefully as the sun struck the snow-covered tops of the pine trees at the edge of the woods. A new day might bring a turn in my condition and a step toward recovery. For days that seemed endless, the illness hung on with little or no signs of improvement.

When there were quiet spells between coughing spasms, I could gather energy and think about my plan to enter a new design completed some weeks earlier in the competition for the Stevens Metal Award. While I had made several pieces that I liked, and that others praised, this was the first time I had felt inclined to put my work forward in competition. The Stevens Metal Award was, to my knowledge, the top metal award in our region, and it was open to craftsmen in all the metals. For pewter to compete against silver, gold, and other metals heightened the glamour and the challenge of the contest. The creation of the fruit bowl that I wanted to enter is a story in itself.

There are several ways to go about the design and creation of a new piece. It can begin with a pencil, a felt tip pen, and whatever you choose for the sketch or drawing. Or it can begin in the shop, looking at the shapes of existing chucks and thinking about variations or modifications of the forms that are there. I had accumulated two or three dozen hand-me-down chucks in wood and metal not previously used in our shop. If we were to use a metal chuck, we were bound to its form for, at that point, we did not have a metal lathe to alter it. The wooden ones were another matter. They could be put on the lathe and redesigned with wood-turning tools. They were of seasoned wood, and tapped and threaded to go directly on one or another of our adapters, which attach to the lathes. It was one of these older chucks that provided my beginning for the fruit bowl.

I knew that I wanted a large, low bowl with gentle curves. Among the hand-me-down wooden chucks was one with some promise. I could see the size of the bottom I had in mind and part of the first curve. After that, I would be on my own with a technique called spinning in air. I would not be spinning the metal down to a chuck, but, rather, forming it as it turned on the lathe, shaping the form with wooden turning tools on both sides of the metal at once, guiding it into the shape desired. It required strong hands and wrists, and particularly so in this piece, for I had decided that it would be turned in a thicker or heavier metal than we normally spin. Many bowls have their edges turned back or under and therefore doubled in thickness, and most of the historic basins and bowls were cast with a thick rim. I wanted no rim thickening, yet I wanted it stable and durable. That required thicker metal throughout the piece, which meant that it would be harder to form, especially if spinning in air!

I attached the hand-me-down chuck to the Prybyl, the largest and most powerful of our lathes, cleaned it, made a small adjustment in the beginning curve of the base, and found a follow block for the tailstock that was a bit smaller than the bottom of the bowl about to be spun, in order to give room for the spinning tool to form the curve from the beginning at the bottom. The follow block was faced with leather to keep it from scarring the pewter and to keep it from slipping during the turning process.

I began the spinning with a metal forming tool and watched as its highly polished surface moved outward from the edge of the base of what would be the bowl. The thick metal began to move, but slowly. Its surface lubricated with tallow, the tool glides like the blade of a skate on ice, and the weight applied to the handle held under my arm and close to my body could be increased as needed to make the metal move. Nothing is done abruptly in the spinning process. The lathe has an evenly running speed, determined by the placement of the belt and the pulley ratios. There is a sense of cadence in each speed, and I hear the speed as well as see it in the sound of the lathe at work. The polished tool pressing on the metal now spinning at two thousand revolutions per minute forms the focus for my attention, and I can see, hear, and feel the work being done in contact with the slowly forming shape. I move through the first curve using the shape of the chuck as the guide, while the metal from the chuck to the rim of the spinning disk is carried, like the brim of a hat, out to the edge. When I have reached the limit of what I can do on the chuck, I must change to spinning in air to form that hat brim into the remainder of the bowl.

At the change to spinning in air, I put away the metal spinning tool and take up two strong wooden tools. Then another pin is added to the tool rest, for I must lever two tools now, instead of one. The tapered points of the wooden spinning tools work on two sides of the spinning disk and guide its shape, much as a potter will raise a wall of a bowl by pressing the spinning clay inside and out to shape it. The potter works the clay directly with his or her hands. The pewter spinner will place the wooden tools over the tool rests, arranging their points opposite each other where he wishes to guide and form the pewter. A stronger pressure is exerted on the side that will move the metal upward into the shape of a bowl, while the metal is supported, steadied, and guided on the other side by the second tool which prevents the metal from rippling or distorting.

I stand close to this process, looking down at the spinning bowl. In my right hand is the forming tool that is moving the metal; in my left is its mate, supporting the inside surface as the metal moves. The movement is one of stroking the metal from the center to the outer edge, keeping the tools moving evenly and smoothly. A steady kind of strength is required, and a sustained draw on energy that leaves the hands, wrists, arms, shoulders, and chest tense and tired when the task is completed. But with the buildup of fatigue, there is an accompanying rise in excitement as the desired form materializes. When it goes well, when there is exertion but no struggle, when intention and effort achieve the result desired, there is a feeling of cooperation and unity of spinner, machine, and metal. We have a saying in the

Norman Stevens presents the "Stevens Metal Award—1992."

pewter shop about certain tasks that require extra skill and concentration: "One has to be in a 'state of grace' to do that!" I believe the sense of that saying is not only that there is something extra required, but also that when it happens and brings a sense of fulfillment, you sense a dimension that is beyond your habitual capacities. I liked the first fruit bowl and recognized a grace of line and proportion that prompted me to make three additional bowls in the following weeks. One of those I placed in the Concord shop of the New Hampshire League of Craftsmen, where we offered some of our product. Then I became ill. Time passed and I was no better as the deadline for entries approached. I finally decided that it was impossible for me to get to the shop and prepare one of the finished bowls for entry. One possibility remained. If the bowl at the Concord shop had not sold, I could ask Janet Dow, the director, to take it to league headquarters and enter it for me. I hesitated, then called her, explaining my situation. She was shorthanded at the moment but would get it to the league office later in the day.

In the weeks that followed, my health returned slowly and I was able to work part time in the shop. I received word that my piece had been accepted for the show. I knew it was now on its own, awaiting the judging. The exhibition was held at St. Anselm's College in the Chapel Gallery; the awards would be given on opening night. When the day arrived, we had heard nothing and assumed that this meant I had not won. Still, I wanted to view the piece on exhibit and see how the show was arranged. But the day was risky, with snow predicted for the afternoon or early in the evening. We worked in the pewter shop, going occasionally to the back window of the barn to look out to the hills to the south. The signs were not encouraging. I said to Jon that we should not go. We could see the show when the weather was better.

But I had mixed feelings, and as I went yet again to the back window, Jonathan said, "Let's eat an early dinner and get going. I'll drive." That settled the matter. We cleaned up and had dinner, then headed for St. Anselm's, going over the hills through Deering, Weare, and Goffstown. The sky was thickening as darkness settled, and random flakes of snow fell. We had not been to the college before, but the way was clearly marked, and once on the grounds, the directions guided us to the gallery and the proper parking lot. Just as we entered, Janet Dow was leaving. When she saw me she held out her hand and said, "Congratulations!" "For what?" I asked. "Didn't you know?" she said. "Surely they told you. You have won the metal award."

It seemed too good to be true. After I saw some of the other entries, it was even harder to believe that I had won. My bowl was handsomely exhibited in a glass display case with several other mixed-media pieces. Some woven fabric lay across part of it and two or three small pieces surrounded it. The lighting was good, and the high, bright finish was eye-catching.

I made the rounds and saw the work of friends, looked at the prizewinning pieces in the various categories, and returned several times to my own piece. Someone pointed out Norman Stevens, who had endowed the award in honor of his wife, Nora. At the appointed time, visitors gathered in the most spacious part of the exhibit, a few introductions were made, an early leader of the league reminisced about stages of the league's history. Then the prizes were awarded. Jonathan stood to one side as my name was called and I went forward to receive the award from Norman Stevens, who presented me with a certificate and an envelope that contained the monetary prize. That meeting was the beginning of a friendship that would grow in the years to follow.

Norman Stevens had been the librarian at the University of Connecticut, and was honored by having a gallery built and named for him, attached to the main library. For the dedication, arranged by university staff, the winning work by each of the recipients of the Stevens Metal Award was requested for exhibition. When I saw pictures of the opening of the gallery, there was the fruit bowl in a glass case just inside the gallery entrance. It would have been one of the first items seen by visitors.

On the night of the award, Jonathan and I found, as we were leaving, that snow was falling. We made what we assumed was the wiser choice, to avoid the back roads, and drove home on the highways by way of Manchester, Concord, Henniker, and Hillsborough.

THE MUSEUM OF FINE ARTS, BOSTON

Visits to the Museum of Fine Arts in Boston over the years have been memorable. Our homes in Providence and New Hampshire were close enough for occasional visits, yet far enough away that we did not go casually. Special exhibitions drew us to the MFA and while there we would also revisit a nearby favorite, the Isabella Stewart Gardner Museum. In May 1974, the MFA mounted a major exhibition called "American Pewter" honoring the fortieth anniversary of the Pewter Collectors Club of America and released a fine book, *American Pewter in the Museum of Fine Arts, Boston,* with an introduction by Jonathan Fairbanks, the curator of the museum's Department of American Decorative Arts and Sculpture. As host, Fairbanks conducted the Pewter Collectors Club in their visit to the show. The book is remarkable for the quality of the photographs by Daniel Farber, who, as the book notes, "developed a system of photography that makes pewter look like pewter."

Although a member of the Pewter Collectors Club, I did not manage to attend the celebration of its anniversary. Its banquet was addressed by Charles F. Montgomery on the collection members were to visit . He was one of the outstanding pewter scholars in the country, famous for his book, *American Pewter*, and for his curatorial work at the Winterthur. Later he was professor of art history at Yale, and curator of the Garvan and Related Collections of American Art at the Yale University Art Gallery. He also knew Mrs. Stephen S. Fitzgerald, who had given the museum the pewter on display, and his talk included many interesting references to her and her collection.

We spent an afternoon at the museum not long after the show opened, and were impressed by the range and quality of the pieces. By then a number of artisans were familiar to me and recognizing additional pieces from known makers added to my sense of their work. Striking work that was new to me added names to remember, and became the source of a growing appreciation of the craft, and of the individuals who had practiced it.

Each visit to the MFA has reinforced a memory of my first visit. After hours of busy looking, in gallery after gallery, being drawn by the collections into cultures around the world, I started down the broad stairs as it became time to leave, stopped, and—looking at the flow of people moving in different directions,—was struck with a powerful sense of wonder, that so much of human creativity and achievement had been brought to this place, housed so grandly, preserved with such care, and made available to so many. What an incredible congeries of human vision and effort was necessary to create, and sustain, such vast human treasure: Truly awe inspiring—or, as our children would say, awesome.

It may be some residue from such past feelings that made me reluctant to follow a suggestion by our daughter-in-law, Barbara Shamblin Gibson, wife of our oldest son, Cyrus. After she learned about my winning the Stevens Metal Award, and had seen the bowl, she urged me to offer the bowl to the museum, along with other pieces of my work, for their consideration. Jonathan Fairbanks, the curator, had been the judge of the show and exhibition and had chosen my work to be awarded the Stevens prize. Barbara and Cyrus were graduates of the Rhode Island School of Design, she in photography and he in sculpture. At this point she was head of the art department of Salve Regina College in Newport, Rhode Island, and his construction company was building some impressive homes in the Newport area.

With their encouragement I wrote to Jonathan Fairbanks, telling him something about myself and about our pewter. I reminded him of the bowl to which he had awarded the prize, and described some other pieces we were making that I thought special, including one or two that were unique. I offered to bring any or all of those described for his inspection. His assistant called and arranged a date for our visit and asked me to bring several of the pieces I had mentioned.

Jonathan drove us to the museum on a bright summer morning, getting us there in time for our ten o'clock appointment. We parked as directed in a reserved space near the main entrance. When we carried in our large box, we told the guard at the turnstiles why we were there and whom we were to see. He called the office and a staff member came to guide us through the labyrinth to our meeting place.

Jonathan Fairbanks greeted us warmly, was affable, smiled easily, and after a few pleasant exchanges opened his desk, took out a pair of white cotton gloves, and asked what we had brought. He was generous in his praise of the design and the workmanship. He warmed my heart especially when he took the fruit bowl, turned it one way then another in the light, and said, "When I first saw this at the show, I said to myself, 'This is the work of a master.'" He asked about the technique used in spinning it and was surprised when I told him that the chuck over which it was spun shaped only the first third, and that the remainder had been spun in air. But I added that now that I had the design, a full chuck would be turned in hard wood, perhaps rock maple, so that I could make them more quickly and with greater consistency of design.

When he looked at the child's cup with a birch grain lining, we had a long discussion of that "first" in pewter design. He confirmed my statement that it had not been done before: "At least I have never seen it," he said. He asked me about how it was spun to imprint the grain, and whether I could make a beaker in the same design and about twice the height of the child's cup. I told him I had done that a number of times and that it would be easy to do. He wanted two of them for himself, and he thought that the uniqueness of the piece was important for the museum collection.

Jonathan Fairbanks wanted to submit the wood-grain beaker and the fruit bowl for consideration by the museum's acquisitions committee. He said that he would recommend them, but that he did not sit on that committee. It would be several weeks before they met, which would give us time to send him the beaker. He called the office staff to come and see the work and they were a friendly and enthusiastic group. The younger staff looked at the child's cup and apparently made mental notes, for over the years there were numerous telephone calls asking us to send one for a new child in their group or their circle of friends. Jonathan then phoned the Museum Store to talk to the person in charge of buying for the store. Failing that, he promised to make the connections for us and encouraged us to follow up with the store. That was to prove a bit slower in coming about, but several months later its first order was received, and the relationship grew steadily thereafter.

We returned home heartened by the warm reception we and our pewter had received. The beaker was made for the museum to consider, and the two beakers Jonathan Fairbanks had ordered were mailed to him. A staff member in the curator's office called and ordered a set of eight. We continued to hold our breath a bit, waiting for the committee to decide about our pieces. A curatorial assistant sent me a copy of the recommendation Jonathan Fairbanks had sent to the Museum's director that, after a long introduction about me and my work, ended:

> Currently, the Museum of Fine Arts American pewter collection consists of works dating from the mid-eighteenth century to the third quarter of the nineteenth century. The acquisition of these two very fine works will be the first contemporary work in pewter and wonderful additions to our contemporary metalwork collection. Their acceptance is highly recommended.

I have noted earlier that a call came in midafternoon some weeks later. The committee had met and voted unanimously to take our pieces into the permanent collection. One of the staff in the curator's office called me "unofficially," to say that the official notification would be sent in a few days from the museum director's office. On October 28, 1992, the director, Alan Shestack, wrote,

> I am very pleased to accept, on behalf of the Trustees of the Museum of Fine Arts, your gift of a fine contemporary pewter fruit bowl and beaker. Your work splendidly carries on a venerable old tradition and will add an important dimension to the Museum's pewter collection. . .
>
> . . . On behalf of the Board of Trustees, Jonathan L. Fairbanks, and the staff of the Department of American Decorative Arts and Sculpture, I wish to thank you for your generosity and the enrichment you have brought to this institution.

The elation has been described earlier, and I deemed the event a marker or milestone in my life. There was the joy of knowing that the work would be there; the phrase "Permanent Collection" has a solid, lasting sound to it. For me, it also seemed a confirmation and validation of the years of effort, of the journey that brought me to that milestone. It was not the end of the journey, but a marker on the way. A challenge, too, to keep growing.

A new chapter began in our relationship with the museum as the Museum Store, with its two satellite branches, began to sell our work. The two pieces of their collection, the fruit bowl and the wood-grain beaker, plus our centerpiece vase and apple bowl, were the initial items they selected. A card was published to go with the pieces. It begins, "The father and son team of Raymond and Jonathan Gibson of New Hampshire has been named by *Early American Life* among the 200 finest traditional craftsmen in America. Whether cast, spun or hammered, each of their handmade pieces is crafted with painstaking care. The Museum of Fine Arts, Boston recognizes the Gibsons' innovative designs, and our American Decorative Arts Department is proud to include their fruit bowl and wood-grain beaker in its permanent collection." Then a triptychlike addition to the location of our work showed the color picture printed in *Yankee,* with Jonathan and me holding a large platter in such a way that it reflected our faces, and side bars that give biographical data on each of us.

In 1996, Jon brought his interests and skills to bear on developing a line of mugs and tankards that would be a mixture of Early American works and of his own variations on traditional designs. Models, and then molds, had to be designed and made. The body of each would have to be spun on large chucks, carrying the metal a long way, and doing it so that the thickness would be maintained for strength and the side would be so smooth that no tool marks or unevenness would mar the finish. Tops would have to be designed, flat or double-domed, and a thumb piece made separately and soldered in place, with a hinge feature anchored at the top of the handle. It required a significant proportion of his time as the project expanded. An early confirmation of his success came when he had a prototype displayed at the Sunapee Craftsmen's Fair and found that Norman Stevens, who had endowed the Stevens Metal prize, had selected it as his "Christmas present of choice" in the hearing of his wife, Nora.

Further confirmation came in connection with the MFA. We knew that it owned an original Samuel Hamlin mug. Jonathan arranged for us to take a trip to the museum and have access to its storage area, with an assistant curator present as we studied some of the pieces, with special interest in the Hamlin. Jonathan took a pad and measuring instruments, and we spent an intensive three hours in the cavernous room with row upon row of steel-frame shelving platforms on which treasures were stored. A filing system, not unlike that of a library, led the curatorial assistant to pieces we named from the picture book mentioned earlier. Jon took careful measurements of the Hamlin mug, and notes on other pieces that interested him.

When we returned, Jonathan set to work and produced a replica that would have passed for an original if he could have magically added two hundred years of patina. An order followed from the Museum Store. The mug was well received and will doubtless have regular continuing sales.

Within three months there was a call from Patti Doten, a feature writer for the *Boston Globe,* asking Jonathan if she could come for pictures and an interview for a story she was writing. The article appeared on January 16, 1997, filling most of the cover page of the Globe's "At Home" section. It was titled, "The pull of the past—three New England craftspeople who specialize in re-creating other centuries." There was a picture of the Hamlin mug on the cover page of the section, and a picture of Jon spinning in the follow-up of the story inside. The author had selected a furniture maker, a ceramicist, and a pewterer. It was a long and well-written story with good photographs of the artisans and their work.

THE PEWTER HEART

In addition to being a bright presence, daughter Lauren helped in many ways in the pewter shop during the 1970s and early '80s. She helped in finishing plates, platters, and chargers with careful hand rubbing, by hammering bracelets and napkin rings, and by managing the corner "store" in the barn, where she met customers. Also, from time to time she created something that had not occurred to any of us.

She created a pewter heart that put into play a sequence that has continued to the present. She carved a heart-shaped piece of mahogany and from that we made a plaster cast. The wooden heart was pressed into the soft plaster. When it was cured and hard, the wood was lifted out. It was really a half-mold, and the pewter was poured into it and cooled as one watched. Pewter shrinks a bit as it cools. We could see the edges solidify first, and the center last. The contraction causes some wrinkles and sometimes small pockets in the surface. The surface tension causes the edge of the heart to be rounded. The soft luster of the metal is pleasing to the eye and the touch is soft in the hand.

We could finish the hearts a little or a lot; that is, we could make them rough or smooth in appearance. The first dozen hearts were drilled and a leather thong was attached so that the heart could be worn as a pendant. There was something fitting about the rough casting attached to the leather. Lauren scratched her name down one side of the surface with a scribing tool. She wore one around the shop and some of them were sold, not because they were featured, but because people saw them and wanted one.

I claimed one of the hearts that had not been drilled and carried it in my pocket for a time. I saw it each night as I emptied my pocket onto my dresser, and sometimes found myself turning it over in my hand at odd moments. It reminded me of the "worry beads" we had seen everywhere in Greece, especially among older men, which I had at first mistaken for saying the Rosary. They may have had a religious meaning for some, but the common name, "worry beads," indicates that it is perhaps a distraction from stress, or that handling the beads produces a soothing effect.

Sometime in the 1980s we began casting a few hearts at a time and putting them out on the shelves. A smaller number would be drilled and put on a leather or fabric line. Sales were not brisk, but the individuals who took them responded strongly to some meaning, partly hidden, that the simple heart seemed to represent. Some were bought by young people in love and used as a bonding gift.

A friend, Gordon Sherman, took two with him to India. When he returned he came to the shop and told me how he had used them. He had spoken at a number of places and began each address by holding up the two hearts and saying to his audience something like the following: "I want to take something of you back to the United States when I return. I am going to ask you to pass these two hearts around and each of you touch one of them, and then return them to me." Perhaps he wove the heart theme into his talks. The world does, surely, need more heart. Gordon handed me one of the hearts, saying, "I want you to have this. It has been touched by five thousand hands."

I stamped that heart with a capital "I" to remind me of India, and to keep it from getting mixed with others and lost. I began carrying this special heart in my pocket and telling friends about it, showing it, and then letting them hold and feel the smooth warm surface. Often I would say, as I handed it to them, "It has been touched by five thousand hands!" If a small group were listening, they would pass it around and someone would say, "Five thousand one, five thousand two," and so on as the heart went around. I have never counted, and could not guess how many have touched it, though one I remember well.

A friend who is very "New Age" in her thinking and sensibilities was visiting several months after Gordon returned the heart to me. I decided to hand her the heart without telling her its story. I turned to cross to another part of the shop when her voice stopped me. "Raymond," she said, "where has this been? I have never touched anything with so much energy in it." I told her the story and watched her smile as she replied, "It doesn't surprise me a bit. I knew it had a special story!"

When PBS Channel 11 did a segment on the pewter shop and showed me working and reflecting on the work, the program director asked me to tell the story of the heart to the camera and then hold the heart in my hand for a video close-up. After the program was aired I received several friendly calls and a number of letters. A theme that was repeated in the responses was a warm reaction to the story of the heart: "It made me feel good." "I was touched by the story of the heart." "There is so much sadness and tragedy in the world, it's good to hear something like the heart story."

"They're all different." The speaker was a woman in her middle years who was looking at a row of the hearts in front of the pewter displayed on a wide shelf in our shop. "Different, but not all different, I told her. "I have nine clay molds. If you look carefully, you can match them with look-alikes that came from the same mold." They are also poured from a ladle by hand and that varies the size from one to another even in the same mold. "But they're not very different," she replied. "Why do you have nine molds that are nearly the same?" That prompted a story.

There had been a feature article in the *Concord Monitor* with two excellent photographs taken by Dan Habib. For one of the pictures Dan had crawled under the lathe on which I was spinning a stem goblet, getting a picture of my hands and the goblet seen from below, my face looking down toward the work, with the ceiling boards in the roof above. It was a dramatic picture, and a wonder to me that everything was in focus, from the goblet to the ceiling. That night I had a call from Dan telling me he was getting married "a week from Saturday." He had talked to Betsy, his bride-to-be, and because they both came from traditions where wine was part of the

For one of his pictures for the Concord Monitor, *Dan Habib crawled under the lathe.*

wedding service, they wondered if they could secure one of my stem goblets in time for the nuptials. I was happy at the suggestion and finished the piece over the weekend. Betsy came on Tuesday to pick it up. She turned a heart over in her hand without saying anything. That night, another call from Dan.

Betsy had an idea about putting a pewter heart at each place for their guests at the dinner following the ceremony. Dan knew the time was short, but wondered whether I could get them done by Friday. I said, "Sure, Dan," before I asked the number of guests. There were to be one hundred and fifty. I told him I would begin early on Wednesday and would call if problems developed. I didn't tell Dan that I only had one mold, that it was plaster of Paris. Or that it takes minutes to pour a heart and then have it cool enough to remove it and repeat the process. Or, more troubling still, that I didn't know whether the plaster mold would hold up through that many castings. Before going to sleep, I decided to begin by making a mold that would allow me to cast several hearts with each pouring.

The day was clear and dry. The plaster of Paris mixed well. I hurried to set three rows of three hearts each in the soft surface that was steadily growing harder. In pushing the hearts into the surface of the mix, no two of them were seated exactly the same. While the plaster set, I started the furnace and began melting metal. The hearts had to be removed carefully to preserve the shape and keep a smooth surface. Eight of them parted well. Production could begin after baking the mold long enough to remove any excess moisture.

By eleven o'clock, the production of hearts began. By late afternoon we had enough and a margin to spare. But much work remained. Each had to be worked on the belt sander and a buffing wheel to be finished. On Thursday morning my apprentices set up the necessary machinery; one sanded and the other buffed. When they brought the first five for my inspection, I had an idea. I went to the hand-stamping equipment and set two letters divided by a dash, "D-B." Would it print on the slightly curved surface of the hearts? It did. I phoned Dan at work and told him about the possibility. "Do it!" The twelve-pound box of pewter hearts was ready on Friday and presented to the guests on Saturday. In the pictures I received of the happy couple, one showed them holding the stem goblet that had been used in the service.

That is how I came to have more than one mold. And there is a sequel to the story. At noon several weeks after the wedding a young man came into the shop: "Are you the one who made the hearts for Dan and Betsy? I've lost mine. I really liked having it. It was such a personal reminder of the wedding. Can you supply another?" I found that the type was still set in the holder and quickly stamped another heart, sending him happily on his way.

Over time, special meanings were sometimes attached to the hearts by those who bought them in our shop, often becoming the source of exchanges and reflections on life. None of the hearts we have made has been perfectly symmetrical or finished. It reflects a sense of reality and metaphor at the same time. Once as a customer spent a long time examining one by one the hearts in the small basket on our shelf, I commented, "None is perfect." She kept looking, and when she selected one, I was surprised to see that it was not one of the more perfectly formed ones. "Like life," she said a bit ruefully, "sometimes it takes its bumps and bruises. This one is just right!"

A couple from the Midwest who were part of a small support group at their church bought enough hearts for each member of the group. Sometimes young people, newly in love and looking for a symbol, will each select a heart and have me put their initial on it, and then exchange them. And so all sorts of relationships and bonding find a simple symbol.

I think of the children, who, when given a heart and are allowed to sit on the high stool beside the workbench and watch as I stamp their initial on it, have wonder in their eyes as they look at the soft, satin sheen and trace the letter with a finger. They may look up and smile, and often their eyes are shining. Sometimes when I hold the heart I carry in my pocket and turn it in the light, I close my eyes and try to imagine the faces of the individuals in India who held this heart in their hand. That was years ago now, and half a world away. How, I wonder, will humans find the ways to bind the world more closely except with the best instincts of their hearts, and in Lincoln's words, "by the better angels of our nature?"

AFTER *YANKEE*

Steve Fowle's call reached me in the pewter shop—fitting, for what he had in mind: "I've been asked to do a six-hundred word piece on you for *Yankee.* I'd like to watch you work and ask some questions. Watching will be as important as talking." "Fine," I said. "When?" We agreed on a schedule.

Several times over the next week, he watched the work in progress, listened to my conversations with customers, browsed in my books on the history and craft of pewter, and asked questions that made me see my work from another angle. He talked with Jonathan, son and partner. He gathered enough material to do several articles. We wondered what he would write.

The photographer, Doug Mendell, was a very different experience. Where Steve had stayed on the sidelines as we worked, pictures had to be posed and held, shot from several angles and with different light and cameras. His attention to detail was impressive, and the lighting equipment resembled a movie set. At the end he took Jonathan and me to the front of the barn, opened the sliding doors, had us hold a twelve-inch platter just below our faces, and kept shooting, always encouraging us to look a certain way until he got what he wanted. We were doubtful; he was pleased. The result—a remarkable shot the editors liked so much that they used it for a full-page picture.

Before the article appeared, we told friends about it and were deluged with advice, some of it rather frightening: "Just the two of you? Can you hire help? Can you farm out production?" "Get an answering service or you'll be on the phone all the time." We heard stories of a man who rehabilitated old wood-burning stoves. After a story about his work, he was swamped with inquiries and orders until he was booked for months ahead.

A marketing executive from the Midwest looked at our shelves and into our storage cupboards, walked around our modest work space, and shook his head sadly, like a doctor who didn't enjoy telling his patient the diagnosis. "What are you thinking?" I asked. "Too small a funnel," he said, "for what will try to run through it."

As publication day neared, I wondered whether we could handle what might result. Jonathan, with youth and cheerful optimism, reminded me that if we faced a surplus of demand, that was a problem we had been hoping for: "Let's take it as it comes."

Then the issue was published and we saw the article. Steve, Doug, and the editors had done surprising and good things. The story was informative and warm, the visual material striking.

The phone began to ring. But not "off the hook." Friends near and far called to say they had seen the article and to offer congratulations. Some callers wanted a catalog. Others wanted to discuss or order pieces shown in the magazine. It was mid-October and the Christmas orders did not accelerate until November.

Calls were diverse. Some wanted to talk about the father-son element, a craft being passed on to the next generation. Several older men wanted to explore the possibility of learning the craft. Numerous calls sought repair advice or services for damaged pewter. One, just back from the Orient, had bought several pieces from a company that exports regularly to the United States, and wanted my estimate of their value. Others wanted to describe family heirloom pewter pieces and have us date them and estimate current value. One storied heirloom "brought over by ancestors in the 1600s" was photographed for me to confirm date and place of origin. Should we collapse a family legend by reporting "mid-to late 1800s?"

We were soon carrying more packages to the UPS. Jonathan took most of the phone calls and I did most of the packaging and shipping. On an early Saturday in November two women arrived from the coast of Maine, surveyed the shelves, and declared, "We saw you in *Yankee* and have come to do Christmas shopping. We need five gifts, around $100 each, and no two alike! Can we manage that?" Within the hour we had. The pace quickened by Thanksgiving. We planned carefully, knowing that December would be the real test. And it was. Calls increased and when turnaround time did not allow for sending a catalog, items were selected from Doug's *Yankee* pictures, or by asking Jonathan for suggestions. All Christmas orders met their deadlines, the final two going by overnight express.

Using a fifteen inch disk, the salad bowl is a challenge in spinning. A thick metal is moved a long way on a steady, graceful curve.

We became accustomed to visitors introducing themselves with, "We saw you in *Yankee.*" Callers would also identify themselves that way and set a date for a visit. Individuals called for groups: "We go somewhere, see something, then have a meal together. May we come see you working?" One group filled a bus and more than crowded our shop.

The article mentioned my chalice that had gone to five continents. A committee from a Massachusetts church came to see it. They ordered one: "We want to dedicate it before Christmas." They later sent pictures of the order of service for the dedication, which included a copy of the article from *Yankee.*

Mention was also made of the prize fruit bowl that is in the collection of the Museum of Fine Arts, Boston. That prompted a number of orders for presentation gifts for individuals on special occasions, or for couples being married.

Jonathan had suggested that we mark all orders and sales slips related to *Yankee* so we could see what the impact was on our business. Our first tally came with year-end accounting. From October 15 to January 1, *Yankee* related sales were double all our other sales combined for the same period.

The funnel was large enough. We were able to keep up. It required more careful planning, redesigning our working space, innovation, and expediting some production procedures. However, these were an acceleration of a process we had already begun in handling the increases in our business volume.

There were other and more valuable results. We made a lot of new friends, some of whom have become regular customers. We discovered, soon after the appearance of the article, that the mere fact of our inclusion added a dimension to our status that we could not define and did not foresee. Nor could we anticipate the carrying power of the article. We had been told that *Yankee* has as long a "shelf life" as any magazine published. That point was driven home to us two years after the article appeared, when a couple rode in on a huge motorcycle, pulling a small trailer with their camping gear. They were from the West Coast. "We read about you in *Yankee,"* they said. "We file articles like that and when we plan trips, we link the places we have chosen in planning our itinerary." Their large order was sent west by UPS and timed for their arrival home a month after their visit.

The picture Doug had taken of Jonathan and me holding the platter in such a way that both our faces were reflected in its bright surface has been made into a triptych, and is displayed in shops where our pewter is sold. It is also the lead picture on our Web site, which includes ten panels showing our work.

CHANNEL 30—CRAIG SHIVELY

It was between nine and ten on a weekday morning; work was well under way when we received a call from Craig Shively of Channel 30, White River Junction, Vermont. Were we working? Could he come and shoot footage for the six o'clock evening news? We invited him to come along, and after he had hung up, we wondered how he could travel that far, do some shooting, return, then edit his footage before going on air. But that was his problem.

His entrance added a lot of energy to the pewter shop. Tall, lanky, with bright eyes, and a winning smile, he had a way of working that wasted no time. He looked things over, asking questions as he went from one workstation to another. Then he brought in his equipment, set up the camera, attached the battery pack for power, adjusted the light, and began shooting a spinning sequence. Seeing that he would be working into and through the lunch hour, I told Susan, who invited him to eat with us.

Working with Craig was a study in intensity and focus. He moved quickly, handling his camera with a sense of sureness about what he wanted and what the camera could do. The questions did not stop. Pewter was new to him and he sought to saturate himself with information. He worked with Jonathan for a time and then with me. He had very different questions for each of us. He kept the recorder open and built quite a body of questions and answers to use as voice-overs for the work he was putting on film.

At lunch he was a charming guest, taking an interest in the post-and-beam construction of the house, Susan's flower gardens seen through the large windows, and Cy's rusted-steel sculptures standing in the fields in sight of the house.

After lunch it was back to the barn. Craig picked up the shooting and carried it forward at a brisk pace. Then he went outside to shoot footage of the barn—on the north side showing the entrance, behind and below the barn, picking up the farm machinery, weathered barn boards, and the open area where the rubbing table for pewter finishing sought the best light.

Watching him work with the camera, my respect and admiration grew at the inventiveness of the angles and positions he chose. When I saw the result later, it was even better than I had thought it might be. In one shot he placed the camera within an inch or two of the edge of a large pewter disk that was rotating at more than one thousand revolutions a minute. Another shot was through a small window from the nave of the barn, using the window to frame a view of Jonathan at work in the buffing room. When he edited that sequence, the voice-over was his question to me about Jon that prompted this response: "If I didn't have him as a son, I would want him for a friend."

After two o'clock I began to look at my watch and wonder how Craig would manage. He seemed intent on what he was doing; he was not rushing to get away.

Just after three, he finished a shot and began packing his equipment. I asked whether we could secure a print of his shooting for our video files. "Sorry," he said, "that's against company policy." Then he added, "I'm allowed to send a print of what we air, and will be glad to do that." Then he was gone.

How he managed to get back to White River Junction, edit the three hours of shooting into a three-minute spot, get the voice-over coordinated, and integrate it with the regular news sequence is beyond my imagination. He did it, however, and in a week or so, a package arrived and we saw the results of his day in our shop. Jon and I were not only impressed; we each felt that of all the exchanges with us, he had selected some of the best lines for the voice-overs. The camera work was excellent, with good light quality, smooth transitions, and a consistent air of informality in the way his story unfolded. We were delighted to have the copy for our archives.

When I called to thank him for the tape and for the quality of his work, the secretary at Channel 30 said Craig was away on his honeymoon and would be back in another week. He had not mentioned his upcoming marriage. I got his home address and we sent a wedding present of a centerpiece vase, a piece he had admired when in the shop. Later a note arrived from the bride expressing their pleasure with the vase, and saying that Craig had told her about our shop with much enthusiasm.

I did not see him again for more than a year. Jonathan and I were demonstrating at the Sunapee Craftsmen's Fair in 1995 when I saw Craig putting down his camera gear at a table near our tent. I hailed him and we had a brief catch-up on what we had been doing. He was there, he said, on a special assignment, and could not pick and choose random items at the fair. Then he said, "I've owed you a letter for much too long, and I apologize. That piece I shot in your barn won a statewide prize for special feature last year. I kept meaning to call or write you about it, but I didn't do it. The station was very pleased, and they have been giving me more leeway now in seeking stories on my own. If you and Jon think of a good story sometime, I'd enjoy working with you on another one."

EARLY AMERICAN LIFE DIRECTORY

I was unaware of *Early American Life (EAL)* until it was mentioned by Roger W. Scheffer, a guest exhibiter at a show and sale of the Masters Group. He suggested that we enter the competition for a place in its directory of fine craftsmen. It was, and is, a splendid magazine and I could have benefited from reading it earlier. It has since changed its name to *Early American Homes*, with much the same focus and consistent high quality. Happily, it continues the annual directory, a service to readers and artisans alike. *EAL* explained how craftspeople were chosen in the following statement:

> Every year we select a new group of independent judges who have had extensive exposure to both antiques and skilled contemporary craftsmanship. We ask them to review each description card and the photos you provide and to assign a numerical rating from one to ten, ten being the highest possible score.

> The judges use the following criteria to evaluate entries:
>
> 1. Fidelity to period style, whether the work is a reproduction or an adaptation.
> 2. Quality of craftsmanship.
> 3. Ability of the work to maintain or increase its value over time, in other words, to become an antique in its own right.
>
> All entries will be anonymous. The judges will have only your photographs and your brief description on the separate card provided, so your entry photos and brief description of your work must speak for themselves.
>
> The judges have the choice of giving a numerical rating for each criterion or a combined overall numerical rating. Most judges choose to give a combined overall rating. The decisions of the judges are final.
>
> After all the entries have been rated, they are arranged from highest to lowest scores, and the top 200 are accepted for publication in the directory and are notified by mail.

When the judging was complete, *EAL* would choose from among the photographs submitted by the winners a widely representative group of craft pieces and invite the artisans to send these items to be pictured in an article in the issue that would publish the "Directory of Craftspeople." It involved a lot of work for the magazine staff of the magazine, but the result was an annual directory and photographs of fine work being done by contemporary craftspeople from all over the country, in a variety of media.

The entry into the competition presented two problems: getting good photographs, and defining ourselves and our craft effort. Anyone who has attempted to photograph pewter knows it is not easy. The soft color and texture of the metal require a special quality of light that must be so evenly distributed that there are no "hot spots," or shadows. As an amateur photographer, I have worked in the high, clear light and air of the Acropolis, using wide-angle and telescopic lenses; and on my stomach in our hilltop meadow looking at wildflowers through a barrel lens attachment and shooting within a few inches of the blossoms. But pewter is special, and very difficult. I have been somewhat consoled to see that the professionals I have asked for assistance struggled—sometimes failed—and had only partial success generally.

The second problem was to put into words some description that seemed accurate, that did not claim too much or too little. All the years and work somehow distilled and typed on a four- by-six card? Impossible! I once heard a rabbi say that there was a brief ceremonial comment after the reading of the Torah, as he was rolling up and replacing the scroll, that could be translated, "That's not all it says here." What could we say to the judges who would have five photographs and a four-by-six card? But then it occurred to me that the Apostles' Creed could be typed on a card that size, and that statement is the core description of a diverse religion that is nearly twenty centuries old. We ended with a compact statement that indicated what? how? and why?

> We make pewterware in replicas of well-known traditional styles as well as our own designs. Plates, platters, chargers, beakers, goblets, tankards, cups, porringers, candlesticks, chambersticks, bowls, basins, spoons, and chalices are fashioned with museum-quality standards.
>
> We cast, spin, and hammer, depending upon the piece. We work in somewhat heavier-gauge metal than most so that our pieces are both elegant and sturdy.
>
> Our pieces have gone to thirty states and twenty one foreign countries. Our chalice has gone to church leaders on five continents.

We sent in our entry, feeling a bit small in a large country, wondering how we would fare in the judging. The judges for 1993 were Steve Miller of the Landis Valley Museum; Sherry Phillips, of the Sticky Wicket shop; David Shayt, of the Smithsonian Institution; and Caroline Sloat, of Old Sturbridge Village.

The letter came, announcing that we would be included in the directory, and it asked us to send two of our pieces—our chamberstick in the style of Roswell Gleason, and a porringer replica of one made by Gershom Jones,—to be photographed for the issue of *EAL*. Our work would be photographed in a museum setting and become part of an exhibition at the Landis Valley Museum Visitors Center from March 27 to April 30, 1993.

After I saw the issue and the photographs from the museum, I wrote to the curator and asked whether there would be any interest in adding one of our works to its collection. The answer told me about his operation. There was an "under glass or don't touch" set of objects that were antiques. Other pieces in the collection were the "working" or educational part of the program, and these pieces were used by the guides and in courses about different periods and crafts. They would like to have our chamberstick for that. I agreed, and expressed my pleasure that the work would have that kind of use. I made a special request: Could I give it in memory of a longtime friend, John Rowe Workman, a classics professor at Brown University? He was from Lancaster and devoted to the area, returning "home" whenever he could for extended visits until his death.

In due season I heard from Vernon S. Gunnion, curator of collections for the Landis Valley Museum, Pennsylvania Historical and Museum Commission. He wrote: "Thank you so much for your gift of the pewter chamberstick to Landis Valley Museum. I know the guides will appreciate and enjoy using it. The piece is so well made. I will indicate on the catalog card that it is in memory of John Rowe Workman. Thank you for thinking of Landis Valley Museum."

With our appearance in the "Directory of Traditional Craftsmen," requests for our catalog began to arrive. There were calls and orders for the chamberstick and porringer pictured in the magazine.

A new chapter was written in the relationship with *EAL* in the 1994 competition for entry into the directory. The magazine would consider retailing the craftsmen's work of those who so desired. The judges chosen that year were Robert Shaw, curator of the Shelburne Museum in Shelburne, Vermont; Philip Zea, curator of Historic Deerfield, Deerfield, Massachusetts; Don Carpentier, craftsman and creator of Eastfield Village in East Nassau, New York; and John Curtis, former curator of Old Sturbridge Village. Again we were listed in the directory. This time we were asked to send a fifteen-inch charger to be pictured.

We entered the marketing experience with *EAL* offering the large porringer and large and small Queen Anne spoons. To this would eventually be added our granny vase and a tall beaker with a line. We would receive orders with mailing addresses prepared by *EAL's* "fulfillment house, Kable." After several orders had been sent, a bill was rendered. With two entities between the craftsmen and the customers, it was a bit cumbersome, but the procedures smoothed out as the proper software was designed and put to use. After two years, the program was discontinued.

The experience with *EAL* added a dimension to our life and work. As orders were filled and the address labels attached, it became clear that we were no longer local or regional, but national. We had, of course, had visitors from all parts of the country and from many places overseas. Now, a fine magazine with a national circulation had taken note of our work, pictured it, and was the source of sales from all over the United States.

July 21 to 23, 1995, *Early American Life* created a Festival of American Arts, an invitational show featuring "more than fifty of America's finest traditional artisans selling and demonstrating their work." In her welcome to the show, Mimi Handler, editor, set out its purpose: "*Early American Life* magazine has been deeply involved in American traditional craftsmanship—old and new—for a quarter of a century. We've showcased the best of it in the pages of every issue and for the past decade paid particular attention to exactly the kind of work you will see at this show. Quantity as well as quality has grown immeasurably in those ten years. By presenting the first show that attempts to define quality, comparing the best of the old side by side with the best of the new, and offering a variety of fine objects all of which grow from American traditions, we can support this growth."

The show was held at the Rye Town Hilton, Rye Brook, New York. At the entrance to the great hall under a welcome sign there was a wide display that paired a number of carefully selected antiques with modern work that was either a replica or evocative of that same style or theme. Among a dozen pairings, one case held a Gershom Jones porringer and our replica of it. Within the room they managed to create some fifty booths displaying the work of the craftpeople invited. Somehow, in spite of the diversity, the whole came together as a powerful statement of tradition, creativity, and quality workmanship.

On Saturday afternoon Robert Shaw, former curator of the Shelburne Museum, moderated a forum on the question "Are Today's Crafts Tomorrow's Antiques?" with a distinguished panel of experts on antiques and crafts. Another, and very informal, continuous dialogue was under way among the artisans as they discussed their work. These were often brief exchanges but, like the small pieces that make up a mosaic, pictures and ideas formed as a result of them. Are these merely fragments, or do they together enhance our capacity to understand and respond? In his brief introductory article in the show's program, Robert Shaw begins, "When we look at an object—any object—we bring the sum of our knowledge to it, and the more we know, the better and deeper we see."

Our relationship with *Early American Homes* has continued to be a good one. A number of pictures of our work have drawn attention to us and our product. It is a fine magazine, and a source of pride to have our work shown in it. To be a continuing part of its directory has meant that we have been affirmed by some of the most distinguished judges of colonial crafts in America. It is a source of pride, yes, but also a challenge. I think of the saying of Confucius that uses the image of rowing upstream, "not to advance is to drop back."

CHANNEL 9 — KRISTEN HAENEL

Soon after the article appeared in *Yankee,* Kristen Haenel called from Channel 9, the biggest TV station in New Hampshire, to say that she wanted to do a segment for its news program to be aired just before the six o'clock news that same day. It was a reasonably open day in our schedule and we invited her to come along. Our experience with TV newspeople had always been positive. We have also found that the truism is actually true: A TV news story is the best kind of advertising a business like ours can have. Newsprint stories, when accurate and well written, are also helpful. However, television transports people into the shop, where they can see more in a few minutes than a news article can describe in a long column. And they see it with their own eyes, not in the pictures created by the reporter's language. We welcome them all, of course, and looked forward to meeting Kristen.

She arrived by herself, and I marveled at how well she was able to handle the heavy, bulky, often awkward equipment. She used a tripod to bear the weight of the camera, making it more unwieldy but giving it good stability for shooting. She was clearly adept and experienced in the technical aspects of her trade. After analyzing our layout and operation, she decided on two interviews, the first with Jon, then one with me. Then she would take a number of shots to show the shop, machinery, and product.

Kristen's first question to Jonathan was a big one, going to the heart of his decision to return to pewter: "Jonathan, what is there about your work here that makes you do it?" They had set up for the interview in the wrapping room, with Jon sitting on a stool by a big table, a wide window behind and a number of pieces of pewter on the table waiting to be packaged and mailed.

The question was out of the blue, and listening from the adjoining room, I was moved by his answer. With a gesture toward the windows behind him, looking out into the meadow with apple trees and up the slope toward the stone wall, he said, "It is a wonderful setting in which to work." Then, reaching over to the table behind him, he picked up a large salad bowl and held it in front of himself, toward the camera. Looking down at it, he said slowly, "This didn't exist yesterday." A long lecture on the joys of creativity could not have articulated half as well what he conveyed in his brief response.

Kristen asked a series of questions about how he had learned the craft, and about working with his father. Jon and I have had numerous instances in which this dimension of our situation is singled out, questioned, and occasionally celebrated. There is a residual memory of earlier times when it was more the rule than the exception for the son to follow in the father's business. This is increasingly lost in our contemporary way of life, but the memory of it touches some deep responses. Some of the letters and calls we received after the *Yankee* article focused on this part of our story. Jon referred Kristen to a picture hanging in the front of the shop showing the two of us. He was seven, and doing some simple task in the shop. "I started early," he said. "And it is still helpful, if I have a problem, to have my teacher close at hand."

When Kristen interviewed me, she moved the camera into the sales area so that I could talk about particular pieces as well as the craft in general. She set up the tripod beside a table-high cabinet that held pewter, and on the top of which pewter was laid out in a display on a cover of green felt. The door to the nave of the barn was open behind her as she looked into her viewfinder and began her questions. We were just settling into the conversation when a bat fluttered into the room through the open door, in a downward curve by her legs, between the legs of the tripod, and under the cupboard, finding the darkness there that would make it more secure. "What was that?" asked Kristen, having seen the motion in her peripheral vision as she looked through the camera's eyepiece. "A bat." I said calmly. Startled, Kristen reacted sharply. "What! A bat?" I laughed and said, "That's Elmo, a young bat that forgets to stay with his elders during the day up in the rafters of the barn. He flies around once in a while and just happened to find the open door." The camera had not stopped running and with a smile Kristen went on with the interview.

Later she had me sit at the end of the shelves on which the pewter was displayed as she panned from one item to another, singling out individual pieces or groups of pieces like the four sizes of Paul Revere bowls in a stair-step arrangement.

Kristen asked me about my philosophy of life as it related to my work in crafts, leading me to outline the "head-heart-hands" theme I had articulated for the print articles that appeared in the *Concord Monitor,* the *Boston Globe,* and the *Keene Sentinel.* She was taken with this. When the segment was broadcast later that day, Kristen was on-camera with the announcer for the late-afternoon news, then showed her story, ending with the exchange in which I had spoken about the head, heart, and hands. The studio camera went to Kristen and the announcer, as he picked up my comment and added, "That would not be a bad idea for most of us in our work."

I found the work Kristen had done to be balanced and satisfying. She had been a bright, friendly presence in the shop as she worked on her story. I thought it a fine bit of symmetry to begin with Jon's comment about the salad bowl, "This didn't exist yesterday," and to end with the larger context in which all creative work takes place, whether it is writing a book, nurturing the human good in an individual or in society, or creating in any of the myriad arts or crafts that use the head, heart, and hands.

More than two years had passed when we heard again from Channel 9, Manchester, this time asking Jonathan to bring some work and appear in a "show-and-tell" segment usually featuring something special in New Hampshire. What follows is Jonathan's account of the experience.

"When the receptionist in the main foyer at Channel 9 buzzed me through the security door into the newsroom, the flurry of activity swept me in like an incoming tide. As I walked through the newsroom—a new, multilevel complex laden with phones and desks and millions of dollars of audio and video equipment—it struck me cold: I was about to go on live television. The twenty-five-pound trunk I had carried in with my product and props felt like one hundred pounds all of a sudden.

"A nice young woman escorted me into the TV studio and pointed to the area where they film "Made in New Hampshire" Monday afternoons before the evening news. The woman who organizes the segment had invited me down several weeks earlier for the purpose of promoting Gibson Pewter.

"My area consisted of a fake wall with fake art-work and a three-by-six foot table with a black, floor-length linen cover. It was all assembled in a matter of seconds. I was early, which worked out well because I had about a dozen pieces to unpack and polish. I had also brought plenty of props to help shed light on how we make our pewterware. I felt this would be necessary early on. After all, this was TV and I had four minutes of it to use as I wished.

"Steve Cooper, the anchorman for the 5 PM broadcast, came over and introduced himself and said we would be going on live in about half an hour. Once I was set up, I sat and watched the day's news being broadcast live. I also studied the studio, which consisted of a broad news desk; several room settings, which looked like fancy living rooms, where they shot talk shows; and finally, a well-equipped kitchen where the cooking segments were filmed.

"During the course of the afternoon news hour, Steve would visit each of these room settings with different guests. The "Made in New Hampshire" segment aired in the middle of the hour. When my time was about to arrive, Steve announced the segment with Gibson Pewter just before breaking for commercials. He then popped out of his seat and joined me behind my table.

"He hooked up my mike as he asked a few quick questions about the pewter. Before I knew it, we were back from the commercial break and it was three, two, one and bang. On came the lights and the camera moved in close. I'm sure I looked like the proverbial deer in the headlights for at least a few seconds, but then I felt right at home. As a matter of fact, once I began talking to Steve, I forgot we were on-air live.

"I remember talking about the pewter and how it was made. I brought some tools, which I used to help illustrate the spinning and casting techniques. I even brought a chuck and a pewter disk so the audience could see what the raw material looked like. The boom camera floated all around and got some great shots of the pewterware on the table as we talked. I was most pleased to see later on tape the wonderful shots of the Bradford tankard and the Will teapot.

"When I finished describing the production methods and product line, Steve asked me to give Gibson Pewter's phone number for the viewing audience. He then thanked me for coming, shook my hand, and headed back to the news desk. I packed slowly, making sure not to forget anything, and then departed. I felt good about coming and even better about Channel 9 for featuring one of New Hamphsire's smallest companies. Gibson Pewter was very large in scope that afternoon, thanks to *News 9.*"

* * *

Susan and I watched the program from home, feeling a bit nervous for Jonathan in a situation new for him. However, when the show started, and he picked up a piece of pewter and began talking about it, we relaxed and followed the quick exchanges and explanations with increasing pleasure and pride. It was a good day for Jonathan, for Channel 9, and for Gibson Pewter.

THE NEW HAMPSHIRE ANTIQUARIAN SOCIETY

Pewter has a way of moving a person around in history. We do not live simply in today, or, put another way, every today gets interrupted by something that takes us to another time. "What is the date of this piece?" a customer will ask about something brought in for identification, or about an older piece displayed for accent with our own wares. A cleric is looking at chalices and singles out one he finds of interest. I am pleased with his choice, for it is one I have enjoyed creating. "That is in the style of the earliest pewter chalice surviving from the Colonial period." I tell him. To be exact, it dates from 1744, the work of Joseph Leddell, Jr., New York City, working dates circa 1740–54. He made that chalice for Christ Church in West Haven, Connecticut.

In recent years we have had an annual reminder of things past by our relationship with the New Hampshire Antiquarian Society, located in Hopkinton, a town with a main street where building after building is beautiful, early, and well preserved. The antiquarian society is not a contemporary organization to celebrate the past, but, rather, an older creation by early residents who realized that things were changing and that something was about to be lost that should be remembered. Their story leaves a legacy.

In 1859, three friends formed a club whose purpose was "conversation, for comparing ideas, and literary research and improvement." They named it the Philomathic Club, a philomath being a lover of learning. They soon were joined by four others. They met in each other's homes, discussed books, and wrote and shared articles that were sometimes published in various New England journals.

It is interesting to speculate about what they read and discussed. The *Atlantic Monthly* had been founded two years earlier with James Russell Lowell as editor, and all the famous New England authors contributed to it. That same year *Harper's Weekly* started up under the editorship of George William Curtis. A model for their talk or conversations might well have come from the recently published work by Oliver Wendell Holmes, *The Autocrat of the Breakfast Table.* Famous as a conversationalist, Holmes found a perfect forum in free talk on any subject that comes to mind: poetry, painting, sports, books, trees, intellect; all this and much else is grist for the "autocrat." If they were looking for the most recent best-seller, Charles Dickens's *A Tale of Two Cities* was newly released, the third most popular of the sixteen works by Dickens that became best-sellers in America. Did they discuss, and in what tones, the work by Elizabeth Barrett Browning, *Aurora Leigh,* condemned in Boston as "the hysterical indecencies of an erotic mind"? In 1860, Emerson, at the height of his writing power, released his *The Conduct of Life*, based on lectures he had given about science, evolution, the uses of wealth, the importance of culture, faith, and art, and a reconsideration of Transcendentalism. Henry David Thoreau could have contributed to their discussion of the slavery question with his *A Plea for Captain John Brown.*

Whatever the range of their discussion, there developed another dimension in the life of the group. One of the members, Silas Ketchum, was a collector whose interest was infectious, and collecting was added to their activities. In the post Civil War period rapid changes were occurring; home crafts were being replaced by purchased items and farms were being abandoned for city life. His journals indicate that Silas Ketchum felt the need to preserve something of the world he had known and its way of life. The group's collections grew until they needed a special space.

As the group was enlarged, its purpose expanded to include the preservation of local and genealogical history. The name was changed, and the New Hampshire Antiquarian Society was incorporated in 1875. The group was too big to meet comfortably in each other's homes, even the more spacious ones, and the growing collections of records and artifacts needed a home of their own. In 1890 the group had a new home, a building given by Mrs. Lucia Rollins Long in memory of her husband, Dr. William H. Long. Designed with the needs of the society in mind, a great hall upstairs with a twenty-five foot domed ceiling could accommodate the group meetings, and a stairway leading to displays running the entire length of the room, and the galleries could exhibit their collections.

The first floor held the offices, a library, and the archives of books about everything having to do with the history and life in the town from earliest times, including town reports dating back to 1737. The building is a treasure-trove of artifacts and records, and is visited by those seeking genealogical information about forebears, as well as by those who wish to know more about tools used, books read, and the texture of lives lived in this locale.

Just over a century later, in February 1992, we received an invitation to participate in a benefit show and sale that would open with a champagne reception in June and end in late August. The show included a wide variety of media and the work of thirty-three of the finest artists and artisans of the area. Sixteen of our pieces were displayed tastefully on two large pedestals enclosed by glass walls and cover. The opening reception was crowded and the guests enthusiastic.

Soon after the show opened, I went back to see the display without the press and crush of the crowd. I took my camera to record for our scrapbook the way our pewter was displayed. The exhibit, called "Tomorrow's Masterpieces," was a fine one. Walking about the room, with its high ceiling, I found myself elated by what I was seeing, and marveling at the creativity demonstrated by those represented there. It was important to the sponsors of the show to point to the future, to affirm that these works, or at least many of them, belonged to the future and deserved to survive. The founders of the society would have been pleased by this kind of thinking on the part of their successors. Standing in the middle of the show in the great, high-ceilinged room, I looked up and realized that I had not examined the collection from the previous century. As I climbed the gallery stairs, I could feel that I was between the times, that both were periods in which things created in this community were valued and celebrated.

While looking at the collection I came upon a display of three bronze molds for casting pewter spoons. They were behind glass, and it was impossible to tell their condition until I could hold them in hand, open them, and examine their casting surfaces and the fit in the way they came together. One was of greater length and apparently in better condition than the others. It occurred to me as I was making my way to the first floor that there might be a community of interest here. We could tie the past to the present and project it into the future by using those molds again. The society had several items for sale—books and pamphlets. Why not pewter spoons cast in a mold from its collection?

As I spoke of my idea, Kathleen Belko, the executive director, listened with interest. The molds could not be removed from the museum without permission from the board of directors, who would have to approve the plan to sell the spoons. Her face said more than she was putting into words. There was a growing light in her dark eyes and she was thinking ahead to how it might work. "You have a way to keep the molds secure?" she asked. "Yes," I answered. "We have a combination safe in the shop." She promised to get an early response from the board.

Two weeks later the molds were entrusted to my keeping. My expectations turned out to be correct. Two of the molds were of inferior make, of metal that was rough, imperfectly formed and finished. They may have been community molds, jointly owned, passed around in an area and used for recasting damaged pewter. Kerfoot's comment is apt:

> Spoons, like porringers, were subjected to a strain under which they were ill-calculated to stand up. Add the fact that they were little thought of, and it is small wonder that few early ones have come down to us. It is quite likely, however, that more of them were made here, marked or unmarked, than of any other pewter form in use at the time. This belief is largely based on the quantity of molds of pewter spoons that one used to see banging round in forgotten corners of old junk shops. In fact, it is more than probable that

> "rolling your own" was the spoon order of the day in most outlying communities. It must be recalled that, although pewter spoons broke at the waist and pewter dishes got holes melted in their bottoms, the material they were made of could be used over and over, provided only that one had the necessary implements at hand and a modicum of skill in using them. (Kerfoot, *American Pewter,* p. 45)

Hornsby, writing much later and having access to much wider research, notes, "The importance of spoons is confirmed by the large number of spoon molds, from the United States especially, that have survived. The production of spoons in the nineteenth century was enormous. One company alone, the Meriden Brittania Company, made more than 3,700,000 spoons in one year." (*Pewter of the Western World,* 1600–1850, p.146.)

The third and largest of the three spoon molds lent by the antiquarian society was of good metal and nicely made. Its sides closed securely, promising a good seal and a minimal parting line. It was of the rat-tail design, with the "tail" reaching from the handle underneath the bowl of the spoon to reinforce the joint. It is not easy to date a mold with precision. It appeared identical to a mold that I had used earlier whose owner was certain it dated from 1791.

I put on my "extra eyes," as I called the headband with magnifying lenses that could be pulled down in front of my glasses, doubling the size of the mold visually as I examined it for problems in the inside surfaces. A dent, a deep scratch, any imperfection would "print" on the pewter. The surfaces needed cleaning, but were otherwise in good condition. I proceeded carefully, using a softening agent and a cotton cloth, repeating the process until the bright bronze surface promised a good result.

It would, of course, need a lubricant to make the pewter flow easily into the whole length of the spoon-shaped cavity, and to make the pewter part from the mold when it was opened. The traditional way to lubricate the mold was to use a candle to "lampblack" the surfaces from the smoke as the mold was held just above the flame. There are other traditional coatings made by mixing pumice powder, red or yellow ocher and egg white, or a mixture of black lead and graphite. These are brushed on a warm mold and allowed to dry.

I have written elsewhere about watching a Dutch pewterer work in his shop in Delfshaven. He was casting small basin porringer bodies. The mold was very hot from the repeated castings. Periodically, he would dip the two halves of the mold into a large container of a hot, red liquid, no doubt containing red ocher, and when he removed it, the heat in the mold evaporated the liquid quickly, leaving an even, reddish surface from which his castings parted easily when the mold was opened.

When the time came to try the spoon mold, I lampblacked it and heated it by running a number of test pourings, knowing that it would not yet produce a full spoon. It would, however, increase its temperature steadily, and each casting would take more metal and the spoon would be a bit more fully formed, until a complete spoon resulted. Then it was a matter of rhythm. The repetition of the casting kept the mold hot and the metal flowing. If parts of the spoon were imperfect, adjustments could be made in the angle at which the mold was held. Near vertical sometimes works better than exactly vertical, because it allows the air to vent as the metal flows in. If one spot on the spoon repeatedly comes out with a distortion, there may be a problem with the lubricant. It is better, I have found, to stay in rhythm for a number of castings, even if all of them are imperfect and returned to the melting pot. The problem will often smooth out or just disappear. Then you will have a long series of successful castings, or keepers, as we call them.

Once out of the mold, four-fifths of the work remains before the spoon is finished. It will have a "parting line" around the edges where the two halves of the mold joined, and this will be more pronounced along the sides of the handle. This line must be removed, usually using a file. In the days before the introduction of modern specialty tools and buffing wheels, there was a saying among pewterers that "everything depends on the file."

Before, or just after, the parting line is removed, the sprue must be cut away and the area shaped as needed. The sprue is the opening at the top of the mold into which the metal is poured. Some metal will remain in that opening and harden with the spoon as it cools. This "extra" metal must be cut away carefully, so that the shape of the tip of the spoon's bowl is preserved.

After the parting line and sprue are dealt with, the final work is done in smoothing the entire spoon, top and bottom, and removing any surface irregularity. This can be done by hand, with emery paper and steel wool or their equivalents, or by using a number of abrasive buffing wheels. The finish can range from soft satin, or matte, to a high gloss resembling silver. Colonial spoons were in the satin finish and, if they survived for a time, developed a patina that is dear to the heart of collectors.

When I informed Kathleen Belko that the spoons were available, her initial order was for two dozen. They were offered in a handsome, cotton-filled white box, and are popular enough that reorders are regularly received. It was a short step from that beginning for the antiquarian society to buy a dozen different pieces of our pewter at a discount and include it in its small "museum store."

After our participation in the show and sale for a second year, I was invited by Kathleen to speak about my work to the antiquarian society; the program also included Ira Frost, speaking about his bird-carving work. On September 14, 1993, we gathered in the high-domed hall, this time with neat rows of chairs where pedestals had been for the exhibitions. It was a memorable evening. How many gatherings of the society had been addressed in the 103 years since the building was dedicated? Had there been a pewterer somewhere in that history showing his molds and telling about his work?

I had decided against a slide show, for I wanted to watch the faces of the audience as I spoke. I took a number of examples of Early American pewter, some old molds, and a few samples of our work. After a brief introduction, it was a show-and-tell program, as I took piece after piece and explained what was special about it, how it was used, what it produced. I ended with one or two brief "human interest" stories of occurrences in the shop with apprentices or visitors. There was a spirited question period, full of interest and goodwill. The following day Kathleen wrote a note saying that the presentation "was very appropriate for our audience and was enthusiastically received."

Each year we look forward to the announcement of a new "Tomorrow's Masterpieces" show and the invitation to participate. Both Jonathan and I pick the best of our new work to exhibit and eagerly anticipate seeing the work of other artists and artisans in the area. We make our way to the opening in late afternoon, looking at the lovely old houses on Main Street with their early-summer blossoms. It is easy to recall that there was a brief time when this town was one of four sites at which the state government met, and that until a single permanent site was chosen, this town was a contender for that honor. Its neighbor, Concord, was selected. Part of me is glad that Hopkinton was not chosen, for it would have destroyed one of the most handsome and well preserved of New Hampshire's towns. I enter the show, remembering Silas Ketchum and his friends of the Philomathic Club gathering to share ideas and to conserve the things they did not want to lose from their world.

MARILYN GOULD — HANCOCK AND WILTON

If you attend a quality crafts fair, you may see a hundred or more beautifully designed booths, each as carefully constructed as a theater set all designed to enhance the craft on view. Moving through the fair and looking at the booths, you cannot imagine the process that put them there.

Vans, all kinds of trucks, trailers, and other conveyances must get to the door or doors, be unloaded and moved away as quickly as possible, and parked as close as possible to the fair site. The craftsmen coming to the fair may have driven hundreds of miles. They will be given an unloading time, as the inflow of vehicles, with their unloading and parking, is carefully scheduled. When the fair closes, usually at five o'clock, after a busy and draining day, the entire fair is dismantled at once. Booths are taken apart, product is carefully packed, then the vehicles are maneuvered through the maze to the door for loading. The long journey home in the dark begins at the end of a strenuous day.

As I have watched this in-and-out madness, I have thought of childhood experiences when an anthill had broken open and the hundreds of ants would scurry in all directions. People who study ants find meaning and purpose in the way the frantic action assesses the damage, then begins the needed repairs. So it is with the setting-up process at a fair. In the center of what resembles chaos, creating as much order and efficiency as possible, is the fair director. In the midst of the frenetic activity, it is impossible to believe that in just a few hours there will be a sense of calm readiness; small final touches will be added to carefully constructed and attractive booths. Let the visitors appear.

The key to a fair's quality depends, more than anything else, on the director. The half- dozen elements that come together in a successful crafts fair are: setting; access; parking; layout; workable flow patterns of visitor traffic; good, multimedia publicity; and, most important of all, quality crafts, handsomely displayed. The director must manage all of these things well. He or she must relate to the exhibitors selected, encourage them to provide attractive booths, and create the structures and schedule that can get one or two hundred craftsmen, their booths, and product in through the available doors and ready for visitors at the opening bell. In our experience, which has been limited to New England, no one has played this many-faceted role better than Marilyn Gould.

I called her after seeing an article in *Early American Life* about the schedule of a select list of quality craft fairs. Hers was to be held in the historic Shaker Round Barn, in Hancock, Massachusetts. It was an area I knew well, having served a parish in nearby Pittsfield during the 1950s. Although I had passed the Hancock Shaker buildings for eleven years, I'd never been on the grounds or through the buildings. I knew the Mount Lebanon Shaker buildings to the west, just over the Lebanon mountain, at the Massachusetts-New York border, where I had served a small rural parish for eighteen months. We could look up from the churchyard to another great stone barn and the buildings then being used by the Darrow School, and would attend seasonal celebrations there to which the community was invited.

I was late in calling and could have been dismissed summarily. However, when Marilyn discovered that the craft was pewter, she wanted to discuss the matter further. When she had heard enough to be assured of the quality of the work, that we had been juried by others she knew and trusted, she said that she would put an application in the mail and would welcome the prospect of a pewterer in the show. As the paperwork was done, the realization grew that we were facing a bigger task than just taking a load of our product to market. We had to "showcase" it in a way that would enhance the individual pieces of pewter and create a larger sense of the craft as we practiced it.

From the many ideas that we considered, we settled on this theme, "Museum-Quality Pewter." It was a reminder of the historic nature of the craft, affirmed our commitment to quality, and allowed us to display the pieces of our work that were, in fact, in a museum. We designed our booth with three pedestals of different sizes, fitted with Plexiglas covers to resemble a museum case, and added a table with shelves behind for the greater part of the display. The table was covered with a fitted, black cotton cloth reaching to the floor, which provided storage space underneath.

Our booth would be ten by ten feet, and posed a challenge: How to display our pewter, yet leave room for the movement in and out of customers? On the walls we planned to hang color prints showing our pewter being made, and a handsome lithograph of a seventeenth-century pewter shop. Overhead lighting had to be designed that would illuminate the pedestals and the product on the table and shelves, yet provide an overall softness. Pewter is difficult to photograph; it is also a challenge to light in a way that lets the viewer see its surfaces without glare or hot spots.

When all the components were built, we marked the booth size on the floor in the nave of the barn and worked out the arrangement of the parts, trying to imagine it in a line with other booths in a larger space. It was a revelation to see how little, yet how much, space is contained in one hundred square feet. It would be compact, but it appeared to be workable. Now it remained to plan how we would pack the parts to transport them safely. The three pedestals were designed to fit together like a telescope, saving much space, as were their Plexiglas covers. We were in a new situation and were determined that there would be no last-minute crises. We tested each process in the friendly confines of the old barn until we were comfortable with them all, including loading the van to make sure we could carry everything we planned to take with us. We were ready when the fair date arrived.

Part of the excitement of our first fair was its location, in one of the most famous barns in the United States, the Round Barn of the Hancock Shakers in western Massachusetts. This design dates from the second half of the nineteenth century. The few that were made were scattered over most of agricultural North America. In his *An Age of Barns,* Eric Sloane advances an interesting theory that these groups:—the Shakers, the Holy Rollers, and the Quakers,—were all perfectionist groups:

> Farmers made circular designs on their barns, and their wives sewed circular designs on quilts. The Shakers used the circle in their "inspirational drawings" . . . they took delight in round hats, rugs and boxes; and they made round drawer-pulls and hand-rests for their severely angled furniture. There is a saying that the round barn was intended "to keep the devil from hiding in corners." (New York: Funk & Wagnalls, 1967)

The Round Barn in Hancock was first built in 1824, and had various problems until 1865, at which time the barn that is there now was built on the old foundations. This barn attracted widespread attention and provided a stimulus to development of the form. It had two levels. For purposes of the fair, the entire first level could be used for booths. The second floor was a balcony around the circle with a vast room offset from just inside a large earthen ramp. In older times, that ramp was used by hay wagons; for purposes of the fair, it was used to unload the crafts brought by the exhibitors assigned to the second floor. Our booth space was in the offset room, and we could walk out to the balcony and look down on the booths below, or walk around the circle and see those on our level.

We arrived in good season and awaited our turn to back up the ramp and

At the Hancock Fair, the partners after the strenuous setting-up process is completed.

unload. When everything was moved into our space, the van was driven to its parking place. It was a hot July day and the few windows were open. Large fans circulated warm air. The feverish activity around us added excitement to our own efforts. Things went smoothly, thanks to the practice we had done in our own barn.

More interesting than seeing our own booth being assembled was watching the neighboring booths go up. Each was very different, not only in craft, but also in design. Directly across from us was a joint exhibit of furniture and silverware. The two craftsmen put together a room interior, with lighting fixtures overhead and on the walls. There were sturdy pieces of furniture on which were displays of handcrafted silver pieces of impressive designs, beautifully executed. We would become friends during this show and see them in later years, here and at other locations.

We met Marilyn Gould, whose composure was a tribute to her competence and experience. With clip-board in hand, she was at the busiest spot, keeping the unloading sorted out, welcoming craftspeople, and answering questions from all sides. She had one assistant, and provided a few young helpers to aid with lifting and carrying in crafts and set materials. Her manner was reserved, her decisions quick and decisive. There was no question about who was in charge.

We arrived just after noon on Friday. An outdoor dinner had been arranged for any who desired, following a tour of the Shaker buildings that made up the colony, along with extensive gardens. Tired though we were from traveling and setting up, we found the tour informative and the picnic barbecue filling. We met a number of artisans. Some had traveled a long way to be there—from Pennsylvania, Ohio, Kentucky, Missouri, and North Carolina, among those I remember.

Our lodging was provided by good friends, Art and Stasia Bell, former parishioners when I was a pastor in Pittsfield. Catching up after thirty years, with only Christmas cards between, was a revelation. I was amazed at how strong the memories were and how easily we picked up the strands from years before when they had attended some of my seminars. We spent Friday and Saturday night with them, had breakfast on Saturday and Sunday, and took them out to dinner on Saturday evening. In addition to the updating and sharing, it was a welcome break from the intensity of the fair and a chance to come back to our booth refreshed.

On Sunday morning, I opened the *Berkshire Eagle* at breakfast and was not surprised to see an article about my presence at the fair. I had been called by Darienne Hosley, a reporter for the paper, during the preceding week, for a brief interview. It was a long and well-written article, detailing my ministry in Pittsfield, a brief summary of the years in Providence, and an account of my retirement activity with pewter. The headline was "Ray Gibson turns from pulpit to pewter," and began with the following:

> When Raymond E. Gibson came to Pittsfield in 1951, he was the new, 28-year-old pastor of South Congregational Church and had a lot of energy to share. He quickly emerged as a strong community leader during his 10-year stay, reaching beyond his congregation to speak out against discrimination.
>
> Now, more than 40 years later, Gibson has again brought something to share with the community—but this time it's something you can see, touch and take home with you: pewter.
>
> Gibson is taking part in the Americana Artisans Craft Show, which opened yesterday in the Round Stone Barn at Hancock Shaker Village and continues until 5 o'clock today. He and his son and partner, Jonathan, are among roughly 100 craftspeople exhibiting and selling their traditional works.

> From his home in Hillsborough Centre, N.H., Gibson has become a respected craftsman. In the July/August issue of *Early American Life,* he and his son were named among the top 200 traditional craftsmen in the country.

The two days were full of new experiences, tending the booth and meeting customers, and during the second day, in part the result of the newspaper article, a number of former friends came to the show to see us, renew ties, and recall the sharing we had done in the 1950s. Watching the fairgoers move past the booths was a study in itself. The range was from intense focus and seeking to an appearance of walking in a fog. Those who turned into our booth to look, ask questions, and comment on our work ranged from a few knowledgeable collectors of pewter, to those whose first question was, "What is pewter?" In between were those who knew a little, were curious about how it was made, whether it contained lead, and what certain pieces, like porringers, were designed for.

It was July in the Berkshires, and the fair had been well advertised. Between the Adams Memorial Theater in Williamstown, Tanglewood in Lenox, Jacob's Pillow in Lee, delightful inns, and some resort hotels, there was a tourist population that was culturally informed, well educated, mobile, affluent, and active. Numerous lakes and ponds were ringed with summer homes, some of them quite grand. We had enjoyed our decade in the Berkshires, and it was good being back here.

The most memorable moment in "selling" did not happen in our booth, but, rather, in the booth directly across from us. The silversmith had sales and orders, but the furniture maker none as the fair came near closing time. Then I saw a couple approaching who stood out from the flow of people. They were well dressed: She was petite and beautiful, he was trim and a head taller than those around him. His stylish cowboy hat made him seem taller still. As they came abreast of our booth, she saw the highboy in the booth opposite, tugged at his sleeve, and they turned in to look at it. It was a splendid piece. Jonathan and I had been admiring it, and understood that it was priced around $10,000. The couple pulled some drawers and considered the workmanship, then stood back and took in the full design. Soon I heard his rich baritone ask, "You like to have that, honey?" Her smile gave the answer. He nodded to the artisan and they quickly settled the details of the sale. Luck had struck as quickly as a rattlesnake. When the buyers departed, we and other booth holders around moved in to congratulate the craftsman. It was twenty minutes until closing. He had made one sale, but it was the largest of his offerings. The shared joy of the other craftsmen in that sale was symbolic of the spirit and goodwill among the exhibitors. It was represented regularly throughout the show in the question we asked each other, "How is it going?"

When five o'clock came, the reverse of the unloading began, only this would not be regulated by a schedule. The procedure called for the booths to be completely dismantled and all product packed and ready to move before a vehicle could be brought to the door. Then it was a matter of putting the vehicle in line, taking your turn backing up the ramp to the door, loading as quickly as possible, and driving away. Marilyn and her assistant were in the doorway area, regulating the flow and saying good-bye to exhibitors. We, like many of these, parted with the words, "See you in November!" That would be the fair at Wilton, Connecticut, held in a high school gym and geared to the Christmas season.

We broke up the long drive home with a stop for dinner just before leaving Vermont, then continued on the final leg of the journey. We spent part of the trip asking ourselves what we had learned that fine-tuning could improve. It had been a good experience. Exposure to so much fine work, and sharing with other crafters, fuels our own will to excellence and sustains us on the journey. I remember the words of Hippocrates (460–357 B.C.): "The life so short, the craft so long to learn."

SUNAPEE III — AS DEMONSTRATORS

At the beginning of the 1990s, I found that going to the Sunapee Craftsmen's Fair was as exciting as always, but now it was lacking an element I had enjoyed in the past. No pewterer was demonstrating the spinning process. I discussed the situation with the staff at the League of New Hampshire Craftsmen, and told them that although it would be difficult to move our heavy lathe, I was willing to explore the possibility if they liked the idea. It had been a number of years since Fred Pulsifer had demonstrated, and his death ended a very popular attraction. Their first response was to suggest a three-day period that would include the opening or closing weekend. Logistically, that seemed too much effort for such a short demonstration. It would take two full days' disruption of our shop on each end, before and after being there. That would commit seven days for only three days' exposure. Also, I had two young apprentices, and wondered about our ability to move the heavy lathe and other equipment.

When Jonathan moved to New Hampshire and joined the pewter operation, the idea became more feasible for us and more attractive to the league. We could demonstrate both spinning and casting and, with the help of an apprentice, do some finishing, all in one tent. We made our presentation and indicated that it would be possible for us to make the effort if we could demonstrate for the full nine days of the fair, as Pulsifer had done. They agreed, and we began to work on the layout of our machinery and the presentation of our craft.

It proved to be an interesting role-reversal from all previous experiences at the fair. As an attendee, you look at others and the work of others, and if they are demonstrating, how they work. If you are demonstrating, you are observed, questioned, or briefly noticed and passed by. When I made a joke about its resembling a zoo, where we were the animals, Jonathan responded that the analogy was apt; people go to zoos to see something they will not see anywhere else.

Our sequence would be to get ready, get there, and get set up, all before the first visitor reached our tent. Getting ready meant selecting the necessary machines and tools, alerting the league to the considerable electrical requirements for our motors and melting pot, and choosing the molds to cast from and the chucks to use in spinning. Getting there meant renting a U-Haul truck of the right size, with a ramp for loading and unloading the lathe and tools. Getting set up was to be a part of a beehive of activity as more than 150 booth holders were bringing in their products, and often with elaborate booth appointments. An incredible assortment of hand-drawn conveyances are used by craftspeople, each adapted to what is being carried in. A mood of hurry and concentration does not keep people from waving or calling greetings as they pass. The excitement is contagious.

Our tent was in a good location, near the administration building at the north end of the grounds where the shape funnels toward a footbridge leading to a series of expansive parking areas. People will stream across that bridge and find us early. Some will stop and become engaged; others will make a mental note to come by after they have made the rounds. We have placed the lathe at right angles to the oncoming fairgoers, and they will see Jonathan behind it, giving his attention to a spinning disk. As they come closer, they can see that metal is being formed. The crowd gathers. Jonathan talks as he works, explaining and responding to questions. If their

Jonathan spinning a centerpiece vase at the 1997 Sunapee fair.

eyes move downward below the work, they see a sign explaining that the lathe is 110 years old. To their left, facing east, they may see visitors watching as I pour molten pewter from a small ladle into the top of a spoon mold, as I explain the temperature of the metal and the age of the mold. I open the mold and lift out a full, new spoon; inspect it to see if it is, in fact, whole, that every part of the mold has been filled; pronounce it a "keeper"; and put it with the others on the table beside me.

For nine consecutive days we will be in place, doing something for the visitors to see, always seeking to inform without being tedious and to work without mishap. Each day begins with an early breakfast at home, then loading the few chucks and tools too valuable to chance leaving overnight in our tent. Each one has a lunch pail and rain gear if the day looks threatening. Once we have driven the twenty-six miles and entered the fairgrounds, there is lots to do to get ready for the crowds. The walls of the tent hung overnight must be removed and stacked. We must secure electrical connections and turn on the melting pot. Books and pictures on the craft and history of pewter are arranged on a display table. All the silicone molds are checked and dusted with talc, and the bronze molds are lampblacked over a candle. There's a short walk to the nearby craftsmen's lounge where coffee, tea, and apples are available, then exchanges with others about how things are going. Back to the tent we go as the loudspeaker announces the "Fair is open!"

Time passes at a variety of speeds. It is never the same in the morning as in the afternoon, and it varies from day to day. Overcast and rainy days are slower, as are hot days with little air stirring. Bright days with a gentle breeze, a good flow of people, and spirited exchanges with people asking good questions pass more quickly. However the day goes, we are tired at its end. The fifteen-or twenty-minute break for lunch, Jonathan and I alternating, is welcomed as much for the relaxation as for the food. Then, at five o'clock, the blacksmith goes to the center of the fair, usually followed by children, and blows a horn; turning in each direction, he blows it again. Now comes the putting away, the tidying up, packing the things that will go home with us, hanging the side walls to the tent, then across the bridge to the van and the ride home. During the day, between four and six thousand people will have attended the fair, and the actual count will be posted on the bulletin board by the fair office tomorrow morning.

So went our days in August 1994, our first year to demonstrate at Sunapee. We did not have a booth to sell our product. However, each year the fair has a large tent, called the Shop at the Fair, that sells items for demonstrators or other league members who do not have a booth. It is a cooperative booth staffed by two or three full-time individuals and a number of volunteers. Because Jonathan was often demonstrating the popular centerpiece vase and I was casting spoons, among other things, the Shop at the Fair sold those items for us. It was, we decided, a good thing to have done and we planned to repeat the following year. The leaders of the league reported good visitor response and welcomed the word that we were willing to return.

In 1995 we had a booth, run by Jonathan's wife, Camille, in a big tent near our demonstration. Camille worked with us in the booth design, and did the sewing of the black cotton walls that were fitted to the metal frame we had ordered. She designed the display and the storage of product under the display table. In the demonstration tent we enlarged our presentation to include the finishing of the pieces Jonathan was spinning. Our two apprentices, Jake and Ryan, worked at the finishing, while Jonathan continued spinning and I did castings. We took a second, smaller lathe, a Walker-

Turner, designed for wood turning but a good machine for removing any lines left from the spinning operation. A centerpiece vase would be held between centers and turned at about eight hundred revolutions a minute as the emery paper smoothed the surfaces inside and out. The second apprentice would buff the piece. Or, between vases, they would work at finishing the spoons I had cast. Having the young helpers attracted more young people to watch us at work, and older people expressed their pleasure at seeing them learning a craft.

Having a booth at the fair added work and excitement. Camille, artistic and gifted, helps with the presentation of the product, has a winsome way with people, and knows enough about the product to answer most questions. When the questions are too technical, she can point to our tent and tell the person to ask the pewterers.

As people saw us working, we would invite them to see "all our product" at our booth across the way. There was a young person, a child of a league staff member, who became very interested in the work and leaned on the table to talk with me as I was working. He also rounded up other youngsters his age and brought them to watch. He became familiar with all the molds and knew what could be cast, and encouraged me to show them how to do this or that casting. There was one mold, in hard rubber, that had been made in Ireland and produced a spirited, small colt with his head and tail up in an alert position. It stood an inch tall and had four very slender legs. It was a tricky mold to use, and the chances of getting all four legs complete in any cast were slim. The mold had to be hot and well powdered to work, and the first two or three usually came out of the mold with at least one leg incomplete. The casting would be held over the melting pot for a second, then dropped back into the mix.

I devised a game with the children to get me through those early castings when it was up in the air whether a full colt would result. I would ask for four volunteers from the young people watching, and then assign a particular leg to each. I would ask them to think "right front" or "left back," or whatever the leg assigned, over and over as I poured the metal. They would get very intense and still as I proceeded with some little ceremony to fill the ladle and pour the molten pewter into the mold. Holding the mold in my gloved hand, I would ask them, down the line, to name the leg assigned. Then I would open the mold, shielding it from their sight while I looked to see whether we had a four-legged colt. If not, I would take the small pliers and grasp the edge of the small platform that was always cast with the legs

Raymond casting at the 1997 fair at Sunapee. The children took special delight in the casting of a small colt.

and body of the colt and pull the whole out of the mold, holding it upright for them to see. If one leg or more were missing, I would say, "We must think harder next time!" put the incomplete colt back into the melting pot, and prepare for the next attempt.

Very often a small crowd of adults would get caught up in the drama, with greater attention to the children than to the casting, or so it seemed. On the next try, with a warmer mold, the likelihood of success increased. The ritual would be reenacted and the mold carefully opened, again out of their sight. The result might be a very near miss, and I would hold up a colt complete except for an ankle and a hoof. "Almost, you're doing better," I'd say, "Next time we'll get it. Concentrate!'" And the cycle would be repeated. This time, as I opened the mold, I would look at it, see that it was whole, and smile a big smile as I began to remove it. They would all be beaming in anticipation as I raised the colt for inspection. You could hear the adults breathe a sigh of relief and sometimes they would applaud, sharing the enthusiasm of the youngsters in what was a moment of triumph.

When I took up a bronze spoon mold during the day and began to cast from it, I knew that there would be between four and seven castings before I'd achieve a complete spoon. The bronze has to heat to a temperature around 300 degrees Fahrenheit before the metal will remain liquid long enough to fill the entire cavity of the mold. The first two or three do not even resemble a spoon; they look like a stringy twist of metal down the center of the mold. Once, when an artist was watching me at this stage, she saw me put one of those pieces back into the melt. She asked me quickly, "Please, would you sell me some of those? I could work them into my small sculptures." Everyone watched with a new and different interest as the next three or four followed in a variety of shapes, but each a bit more of a spoon shape. The artist said that she would be at the fair for several hours, and that if there were more, she would like to come back to get them.

When I started with a spoon mold, I normally alerted those watching that I was not expecting a successful spoon for a half-dozen attempts, while the mold heated up to the point that it would not cool the metal too quickly. The pewter would be poured at something over 500 degrees, and in cooling would begin to turn pasty at about 450 degrees, at which point it would stop flowing. When it reached 375 degrees it would be solid. When the mold is hot, the pewter will not cool so quickly, and will therefore have a better chance of filling the whole mold before turning pasty. I explained all this to those watching as I was in the start-up stage with the spoon mold, usually saying that if I achieved a complete spoon before the seventh, I would consider it a small victory. Sometimes adults would appear to get involved in that contest just as the children did with the legs of a colt.

I enjoy casting spoons in a demonstration, for I continue, after so many years, to have a sense of wonder that the molten metal poured into the mold comes out as a shiny new spoon, a creation that did not exist until that moment. I also enjoy the challenge of pouring molten metal into such a small sprue, and stopping the pour when the mold is full. The metal rises quickly in the mold and I have less than half a second to stop the pour when the mold is filled, or there will be a spillover. Ideally, the pour stops and the surface tension holds a small ball above the sprue, providing a small reservoir available to fill any cavity left by shrinkage below as the metal cools.

I know a number of things about the metal, the bronze mold, the heat transfer, and the like, that I have at the ready when demonstrating, but I decided from early experience not to lecture or talk too much when the actual action is taking place. It distracts from careful observation. Also, it seems better to wait for questions and then tell viewers what they want to know. There is always the question, "What is pewter?" When I answer that, there is often a quick, "What, no lead?" I was amused at our apprentices' reaction to being part of the demonstration. They were bored by having to give, repeatedly, the same answer to a very few questions. I had to remind them that although they had answered the questions many times, the answers were the first time that an individual questioner had heard it.

When the blacksmith's horn blew for the close of the fair on the second Sunday, we were all feeling some accumulated fatigue and were ready, as the saying goes, to pack it in: a fitting image for the heavy work of dismantling; packing both the unsold product and the frame of the booth, the machinery, and tools; loading them into the U-Haul truck; and then heading home. There, we would have to unload and return the truck the following morning. The young apprentices were quick and strong and helped move the work along well. Camille was deft and efficient while protecting each piece being wrapped for the journey back to its place in the shop. I stood in line briefly, then presented our records to the treasurer and paid the commission. The sun was going down as we climbed the final three miles to our hilltop village.

As we began the 1996 preparations for the fair, we worked out an arrangement that would be good for the league and for us. We were given a slightly bigger tent, and we could have our booth for sales under the same roof as our demonstration. This meant that fair visitors could watch the forming, casting, and finishing process and move directly to the display of our finished product. Jake Bowley would be with us doing finishing, and casting spoons when I took a break. Jonathan worked out some new variations on his spinning presentation, and Camille had more space, and better light, for the display. I found a way to enlarge the role of casting.

The league encourages demonstrators to find ways to offer fairgoers an opportunity to get hands-on experience with the craft being demonstrated. I had made a rather tentative beginning the year before, by offering for sale some of the spoons, fresh out of the molds, for fairgoers to take home and finish themselves. I gave verbal instructions for those interested, and occasionally would pick up a small file and show how the parting lines could be removed. A few were interested and took home some of the spoons to finish themselves.

This year, I had prepared instructions on cards about the steps in finishing, placed a sizable sign on the table beside the instructions, and laid out a number of spoons. We invited people to try their hand at finishing their own spoons. As people watched the spoons being cast, they could see the sign and ponder the instructions. A surprising number picked up one or more spoons and an instruction card, then went to Camille, who took payment. There was, naturally, a spillover to the other items being cast. The children wanted the little foals, others wanted dolphins, and of course there was interest in both the plain and the Celtic crosses. All of these items were available in their finished state at the display under the same tent, but the idea of doing part of it themselves was appealing to some.

The principal value in having the whole operation under one tent was the ease it afforded in the information flow. If Camille was asked technical questions about this or that piece, she could have the visitor come around the tent and ask Jonathan or me. Often people would form a question as they looked at a product, and when they came to my table, they'd ask about the piece. If it was a spinning question, they would ask Jonathan.

One dimension of demonstrating that took me back some years was the reversal of my earlier experience, as a pewterer, watching pewterers like Lindsey Shuford and Fred Pulsifer in the sixties and seventies. Now it was our turn to have pewterers watching us. Fred and Judi Danforth, fine artisans from Danforth Pewter, in Middlebury, Vermont,—in the lineage of the Danforths of pewter fame in the 1700s and 1800s, principally in Connecticut,—watched and shared experiences, and made appreciative comments about our work.

As I think back over the four years we have demonstrated at Sunapee, there are numerous memories that come quickly to mind. I recall the excitement of the children seeing the casting process for the first time, and their near disbelief when the molten metal turns into a solid object. I think of a short, stooped man who appeared to be in his seventies or eighties, looking at the spoons and asking me if I thought he could finish one. He stood there by himself, with a gentle, wistful look. I took a spoon and a file and showed him how it would be finished. "I think I could do that," he said. "Do you want one, then?" I asked. "I want six," he responded. Then he said, "It will give me something to do." His comment suggested volumes about his life.

I recall an exchange from the first year, when we had no booth and worked under the general rule that selling was not allowed by demonstrators. It was late afternoon and the visitors had thinned out. I had just taken up a silicone mold for making a Celtic cross. A woman in her middle years stood across the table as I placed a flat steel plate against the mold, clamped it, and prepared to cast. I explained something about the history and symbolism of the Celtic cross, and saw that she was listening carefully. I poured the metal and held the mold as it cooled and solidified. Then I opened the mold and took out the cross with small pliers, still too hot to touch. She leaned forward and started to speak, but hesitated. Then she said, "That's lovely. I would like to buy it, if I may." I explained that there was a rule against demonstrators' selling their product. There was a look of sadness about her as she looked at the cross from which I was now cutting away the excess metal that had filled the sprue. I smiled, and said, "I can't sell it to you, but there's no rule to keep me from giving it to you. Wait a minute and I'll clean it up a bit." I turned on a small rubber grinding wheel, removed the wire edges and sharp corners, studied it a moment, then handed it to her. Her face was serious as she took it from me. "I feel that I should pay you for it," she said. There were just the two of us. I said something I felt sure she would understand: "The price was paid two thousand years ago." She clasped the cross with both hands. As she held it over her heart, her eyes filled with tears. "Thank you," she said. "I will treasure it."

TANKARDS AND TEAPOTS

When Jonathan joined me in 1992, I knew that though he had followed in my steps in learning the basics of the craft, he would go in directions of his own in creative uses of his skills. Indeed, upon his return, his early ventures required skills that I had not taught him,—and had not myself developed. He gathered the tools for hammering, many of them inherited from my mentor, Arthur Barnes, and created a special, small workbench area apart from the flow of our regular production. The work that followed was large and small, with touches of both the traditional and the contemporary, and none of it resembling the offerings already on our shelves.

A large hammered sculpture was called Twin Birch Vase, and depicted two joined birch trunks, growing out of spreading roots. The horizontal lines incised suggested bark; the whole, a vase. First exhibited at the annual juried exhibit of the League of New Hampshire Craftsmen, at the Thorne-Sagendorf gallery in Keene, New Hampshire, it was well received. It was later exhibited at the annual show of the New Hampshsire Antiquarian Society, from which it was purchased and presented to a visiting Chinese dignitary.

Jonathan's smaller hammered work included earrings and bracelets. He made a lot of them because they were instantly popular. Soon there was a specially designed rack on the wall exhibiting some thirty or forty designs of earrings. A line of bracelets—displayed standing on edge—filled a special rack.

Some of his creativity was demonstrated in variations on items already in our product line. Our child's cup and one of our beakers had wood grain imprinted inside. Jonathan redesigned our nut bowl, spinning it over a chuck that he had fashioned, of oak wood with a pronounced grain producing a nut bowl with a very sturdy grain showing on the inside. It caught the eye and had an aesthetic synergy, the strength of trees and the pleasure of their fruit united.

In 1996, Jonathan not only created new products but also brought a new level of craft achievement to the shop. It was a demonstration of skills developed over the years, with rapid acceleration after his return to the shop in 1992. There were several things that added knowledge and experience. He remembers "watching Fred Pulsifer at the Craftsmen's Fair," he says. As a teen he recalls, "I worked over and beyond your right shoulder on the red lathe and wondered how I would copy those spinning strokes rightly. The internship at the machine shop of the Fram Corporation during my senior year at Providence Country Day had me spinning steel and the like." In returning to our shop, Jonathan and I were often spinning on lathes at the same time and sharing ideas about any problems that arose or about techniques that were most effective. We went together to northern Maine to purchase tools from a long-time professional spinner who demonstrated for us. Jonathan described him as one "whose hand had spent a lifetime wrapped around a tool post. . . who spun pewter like a machine. I learned a lot about technique from Felix." Jonathan can agree with the line in Tennyson's *Ulysses*, "I am a part of all that I have met."

Inasmuch as this is the story of his venture and achievement, I asked Jon to write about it. During two months of that winter, Susan and I went to stay in southern Utah, and I missed some of the early steps in Jonathan's significant development of new products, a variety of tankards and a teapot. The teapot and one of the tankards were replicas of two of the most important pieces of colonial pewter. What follows is Jonathan's account of his work, its challenges and rewards, written as if he were explaining it all to me.

❊ ❊ ❊

I'm not sure whether a lidded tankard was ever a logical next step for us. No one ever asked me to make one. When I first saw the black-and-white Christies Auction Catalog [1981], which pictured the pewter from the Jenckes estate (a wonderful collection, with all of the lidded tankards mixed with all of the other valuable, mostly marked, Early American pewter), the creative juices started flowing. I would look at this catalog from time to time and think about which style would please me and the customer.

Thoughts of creating a lidded tankard started as early as '93–'94, but there never seemed to be enough spare time to develop the project. It was not until late 1994 that I started to lay the groundwork for my first quart tankard.

I contacted William Thomas [a local craftsman making furniture who is mentioned in the earlier chapter on the Masters Group] for wood—he gave me two pieces that turned out to be prophetic. Bill used his big band saw to cut me two pieces for mahogany handles. Robert Fowle [bird carver] sharpened several of his best carving knives and delivered them to the shop. He also wished me luck. So with Bill's rough cuts and Bob's sharp tools, I went to work shaping my wooden tankard handle, which would be used as a model for mold making. A disaster occurred at the mold maker's in the heat of vulcanizing the still-wet mahogany, which warped and then charred. I had to start from the beginning to carve and shape a new handle.

Handle #2 was used as a model in a sand-cast mold. It would have been easier to use silicone, but drying required time I did not have, because the pressure was on for the deadline for entry in the league's juried show at St. Anselm's. Sand casting was my only hope. We successfully cast two pewter handles in the sand, which I shaped with the belt sander and files. It took a great deal of time and patience. I shaped the second one by hand as well and sent it off to the mold maker, because #1 was going to the annual juried exhibit on tankard #1, the prototype. Tankard #1 has the moon face on the terminal of the handle; none of the others has that feature. Remember, also, I keep #1 of each new design in my own collection at home.

The double-dome-lidded tankard was well received at the exhibit. Almost a dozen have sold in two years; each one is numbered and all measurements are recorded, as is the owner's name, date of manufacture, and date of sale.

My flat-top tankard with chairback thumbpiece was the second lidded tankard and also an original design, although the inspiration came from a silver tankard that Camille and I spotted at the Hood Museum at Dartmouth College in Hanover, New Hampshire, in the winter of 1996. I came back to the shop and started on a new tankard right away.

Once again, I called upon my friend Robert Fowle for carving/whittling tools and this time also for wood. He had suggested that I use basswood instead of mahogany, as it would be far more friendly to work.

I set out with only one block of wood this time, feeling more confident about the task at hand. I carved a beautiful sweeping handle (much like the silver tankard I had seen at Dartmouth) with a "bud" terminal. This tankard shares the same form as the dome-lidded tankard for the body, but I turned a wooden chuck for the flat lid. I also fabricated models for the hinge and thumbpiece from flat stock and then had molds made from my models.

This first flat-lidded quart tankard is also made in a numbered series and is selling well. It was exhibited at the New Hampshire Antiquarian Society in the summer of 1996. The curator of the Cranbrook Art Museum in Michigan bought #2 for his private collection.

While you were in Utah, I also made the Hamlin Pint Mug and the Gibson Pint Mug. I knew that the quart-size tankards were not going to be for everyone and I wanted to make two nice sixteen-ounce, pint-size mugs that which could be used by men or women.

You will remember our visit with Jonathan Fairbanks at the MFA, when I brought down the two lidded quart tankards, the Hamlin pint, and the plain-handle Melville porringer. That's when Fairbanks got excited and got the store manager to come over and see the pieces. We then went downstairs and looked at the collection.

I also made an unlidded quart tankard, also a numbered series, the winter you were in Utah. It is essentially the dome lid without the hinge and lid. Upon your return, I was beginning my next big challenge, the Bradford tankard.

It posed problems that the previous two had not. The first two tankards were original designs, albeit traditional, but the Bradford was my first quart-tankard reproduction. I was originally attracted to the piece by the beautiful "Stuart" handle on the original. The lines were so graceful and the "boot-heel" terminal or splayed terminal was unlike any other I had seen up to that point. It, the tankard, also had a low flat lid with crenate lip that just looked outstanding.

Upon researching this particular tankard, I discovered that it was not only beautiful, but was also alleged to be the earliest known American lidded tankard in existence. The icing on the cake was that there was only one example, and it was in a museum.

This would be my crown jewel in the tankard line. The lines, the lineage—everything seemed right.

Back to Bob Fowle for some basswood and knives. I carved a wonderful strap handle in wood and made a silicone mold from the wooden carving. Once again, I turned to the flat stock to create hinge and thumbpiece. The lid and body would be formed on the spinning lathe.

The Bradford Tankard. This would be my crown jewel in the tankard line.

Fortunately for me, Charles Montgomery gave the important dimensions of the Bradford tankard, that is, height, diameter top, diameter base, and so on in his book, *A History of American Pewter.*

I had S.K. Machine Shop make a custom chuck for the tankard body. The Bradford tankard has almost straight sides with little taper, but it has a flare at the base molding. I had the machinist leave a small shoulder at the base of the chuck in order to replicate the look of the original tankard body.

So with the critical dimensions and a dozen good pictures of the original, the twentieth century version of the early-eighteenth-century tankard was in the works.

The new challenge with this project lay on top. How was I going to make the crenate lip? The original was cast as such in the mold. I decided to spin the lid and cut the lid by hand after the fact. After all, this was not a piece that was going to be mass produced. It takes a full day to make just one.

When spinning the body, great care is required in drawing the metal down over the chuck so that the sides of the tankard are smooth. The bottom roll creates the look of the original cast base molding. The top is then cut out and the edge rolled, in order to create the top molding look and create a firm platform for the lid. After I roll the top lip, I shape it with skimming tools to get the squared look seen in the old tankards and mugs.

On all the lidded tankards I make, the soldering sequence goes as follows: 1. Solder in the bottom. 2. Solder on the handle. 3. Assemble hinge and thumbpiece. 4. Solder thumbpiece to lid. (This is the most difficult.) 5. Solder the hinge to the handle.

The first Bradford quart tankard was completed January 15, 1997. Even though I had held the pieces together while making it, once soldered together the finished piece exceeded my expectations. It is a beautiful tankard. Someday I'd like to hold the original in my hands.

The Bradford tankard was the inspiration for the lidded and unlidded Stuart twenty-four-ounce tankards. The handles were a shaved-down version of the former and the hinge and thumbpiece were also modified to meet the profile of the scale. The first Stuart tankards came out in March 1997. Their smaller size makes them more attractive for everyday use, and the sales of both are going well. I use my unlidded Stuart tankard at home every day. They are also a numbered series.

The latest and probably not last is the dome-lidded quart with the Bradford handle and ram's-horn thumbpiece. Absolutely stunning piece! I'm sure it will do well too. The first one was made November 24, 1997."

AND NOW THE TEAPOT

The Christies Auction Catalog [1981], already mentioned, which has been around the shop for years, also played a part in the development of the William Will teapot.

The Will teapot was featured on the cover of this prestigious sale catalog. It sold for $14,000 in 1981. The next one to come "on the block" sold, at Sotheby's, in 1988, for $40,000! These facts caught my attention, but the further research on Will and his reputation as the Paul Revere of American pewter made this little pot ever more attractive as a potential reproduction project. When I read that there were only four known examples of the original, the appeal became even greater.

The more I looked at the picture, the more I realized that this was going to be a daunting project. I let it sit for a while.

After my sister Lauren's wedding, in June 1996, I contacted the head of the reproductions department at the Metropolitan Museum of Art in New York, Richard Stevens. I mailed him slides of my work with the hope of getting an invitation to go down to look at their collection and perhaps get a reproduction project with the Metropolitan as well.

I was invited down in June of '97 by Dick Stevens. He had me come in on a Monday, when the museum was closed to the public. Dick took me up to the American Wing with his assistant to look at the pieces that were on exhibit there. Some of the finest examples of American pewter were right there before my eyes, and there, on center stage, above all the rest, was the William Will teapot. Dick knew I wanted to see this piece because I had suggested it as a possible reproduction project earlier in our talks.

They were talking, and the young men in charge of polishing the silver not far away were also buzzing about current museum events.

Somehow though, all of the talk around me turned to silence. It was as if Col. William Will had put his hands over my ears and shut out all of the chatter. I was in awe of the piece and I was "soaking" it all in through my mind's eye.

After leaving the American Wing, we went downstairs to look over the rest of their pewter collection, which was equally impressive. I was grateful to have had an opportunity to see this wonderful collection;—so much rich history now housed behind glass walls.

I thanked Dick for inviting me to New York and for giving up half a day of his valuable time. For him, it was just another "day at the office," but for me it was the inspiration I so clearly needed to complete this complex task.

Upon returning to New Hampshire, I refined my design, having seen the original up close and in person. Fortunately, one of the old books on pewter gave the dimensions: diameter top, bottom, height, and so on, so visualizing the spout and handle in person was quite important.

I made models of the spout, finial, and hinge and shipped them off to the mold maker in Rhode Island. I made the chucks for the lids—top and bottom and the ferrules that hold the handle. The body of the pot was spun over a new steel chuck.

Once the teapot was completed, I decided to finish the set, and started on the sugar bowl and creamer. Each had tapered sides and the beaded edges found on the teapot. Last, I designed a tray large enough to hold the three pieces; it had a single band of beading around the edge. The entire set, when assembled, is a thing of beauty, and I hope that William Will would be honored by the effort.

⁂ ⁂ ⁂

Wm. Will Teapot and Service. I was in awe of this piece (meaning the teapot).

As one who watched Jonathan in much of the development of the tankards and teapot, one observation seems apt. The ability to understand the imaginative creations of others is a great gift. The ability to create such objects with our own hands is yet a greater gift.

In the months of our absence and the two years following our return from Utah, the evidence has grown steadily that Jonathan has lifted us to a new level, both in complexity of production and in the quality of the new wares on our shelves. His replicas from a long-ago era have received an auspicious welcome to the contemporary scene. A picture of the Bradford tankard appeared in the national magazine, *Early American Homes,* as part of its annual "Directory of Traditional Craftsmen." The directory lists the two hundred outstanding traditional craftsmen, selected from an annual national competition; we have been listed for five years. The Bradford tankard and the William Will teapot have made their way to the principal museum in our state. They are arranged in a display case near the main-entrance foyer of the Currier Museum in Manchester, New Hampshire, an invitation to visitors to come to the museum store, where the items may be purchased.

Special Memories

PEWTERERS IN FAMILIES

"Over a span of ninety-four years—from 1707 until 1800—members of the Bassett family were making pewter in New York City, and the metal of Frederick, the last of the line, has epitomized for many collectors the pewter of America."

Laughlin writes of Frederick that he was the youngest son of John, who "died in 1761, leaving to his son Frederick his pewter-making tools and a slave, 'Tom.'" Also, "His father's death provided him with tools and a shop just as he came of age." Though his pewter is not common, it is more plentiful than that of any other New York maker. His workmanship was of the highest order and he was unquestionably one of our ablest pewterers." *Pewter in America* (vol. II, pp. 5-6)

As it became increasingly clear that the future of Gibson Pewter would be in the hands of our youngest son, Jonathan, I found myself, as I read about pewterers in America, taking note of father-son relationships whenever they were described. I was interested in the work of some of the pewtering family "clans" or "dynasties" like the Boardmans and Danforths; however, I became more interested where there was a single line of descent. When we had done variations on, or replicas of, earlier pewterers' work, and were attached to them by knowledge and admiration of their work, it added a further dimension to see the passing on of the craft from father to son. Those selected here are of this group. Some of the stories are heartwarming, others are sad.

Joseph Leddell Sr., whose famous chalice I had used as a model for a smaller design, died in January 1754. He left to his son, Joseph, "all my brass moulds for pewter work and all my working tools" and, quite touchingly, left to a former apprentice, Robert Boyle, the joint use with Joseph Jr., of the moulds and tools that he had bought in England. After the son's untimely death five months later, on May 10, 1754, and because he died intestate, we are justified in assuming that the former apprentice came in to those molds and tools, for he used a nearly identical advertisement of offerings for sale thereafter. (Laughlin, vol. II, p. 4, and Montgomery, p. 191)

William Bradford Jr., born into a distinguished family of printers, learned that trade, but poor health and the confining work prompted him to go to sea, as the salt air and outdoor life of a sailor were widely held to be salubrious. When he became a pewterer is unclear. He married November 25, 1716, and became a freeman of New York City in 1719. His occupation is shown as pewterer, and he remained one until his death. His will was probated in 1759. His reputation for quality of design and workmanship would be established by the excellence of a tankard attributed to him. Jonathan chose that tankard as a model to replicate, and many of these have followed the first one completed on January 15, 1997.

Bradford's fifth and youngest child, Cornelius, served an apprenticeship in his father's shop. Married April 23, 1752, he soon thereafter left for Philadelphia for two reasons. New York had a plethora of distinguished pewterers: his father; Francis Bassett the elder; John Bassett; the two Leddells; and John Will. The second reason was more compelling. In Philadelphia, Simon Edgell had died, and only Thomas Byles, mentioned earlier as the Leddell apprentice given the shared use of the tools left to his son, was working. Further, Cornelius's uncle, Andrew Bradford, had died and left his property to Cornelius, who had been his favorite nephew. A house and shop were waiting. He had learned from his father, inherited from his uncle, and was now launched in a successful business.

Fourteen years later he sold his property in Philadelphia and returned to New York, where he became, in Laughlin's words, one of the most prominent figures of his day, active in the movement toward revolution. He was a dispatch bearer for the Committees of Correspondence as a courier between New York and Boston and New York and Philadelphia. When war began and Washington's troops moved out, Cornelius Bradford was with them. After the war, he returned and took charge of the Coffee House near Wall Street, an establishment frequented by prominent business leaders. He died on November 9, 1786. In his will he characterized himself as Keeper of the Coffee House. (Laughlin, vol. II, pp. 10-12) His acclaim as a patriot and his prominence in public life overshadowed his renown in his craft. As with his contemporaries, few of his works survive. Like his father, he was a superb craftsman. His teapot, made in Philadelphia, is cited by Montgomery as "probably the earliest marked American teapot." (Op. cit., p.173)

One of the greatest, if not the greatest, name in American pewter is that of William Will. Like Bradford, he was known as a patriot and trusted community leader, as well as for his pewter. His father, John, and his brother,

Henry, born in Germany and immigrating to New York City in 1752, were "talented pewterers and are noted for their flat-topped Stuart-type tankards." (Ebert, *Collecting American Pewter*, p.59)

Established as a pewterer in Philadelphia by 1772, Will had to interrupt his work due to the Revolutionary War. He organized a company of infantry called Captain Will's Company of Associators. In 1777, he became lieutenant-colonel of the First Battalion and served afterward in various posts of leadership during the Revolution. After the war, he was elected sheriff of the city and county of Philadelphia and a representative to the General Assembly in Philadelphia in 1785. (*ibid.*)

A History of American Pewter makes a connection between an extraordinary loan exhibition in 1939 at the Metropolitan Museum of Art of 370 pieces of marked American pewter and its effect on Henry Francis du Pont, who had 11 pieces in that exhibition. Du Pont "soon thereafter" began to collect in earnest. Writes Montgomery, "About this time Mr. du Pont learned of the versatility of the highly reputed Philadelphia pewterer Colonel William Will. He set out to acquire other pieces to accompany what was then his most important piece, a dish 16 3/8 inches in diameter—the largest known. Eventually Mr. du Pont was to fill a cupboard with 38 pieces of Will's pewter showing the range of forms made by this talented Philadelphian." (Montgomery, p. 1) The index to this history shows three times as many references to Will's work over that of any other pewterer.

In our shop, the name of William Will took on greater meaning when Jonathan decided to do a replica of Will's drum-shaped teapot, a project that is described by Jonathan in the chapter "Tankards and Teapots." This project not only produced a beautiful replica of Will's work, but also led Jonathan to design and create a full tea set:—teapot, creamer, sugar bowl, and tray—in the same style. If Montgomery is correct, this handsome result should take us back to William Will, in Philadelphia and beyond to China, for "the drum-shaped teapot reveals several subtle relationships. Its silhouette is like that of Chinese export porcelain teapots brought back to the United States with tea sets in the 1790s and the early 1800s." (*A History of American Pewter*, p. 174)

The first porringer that I owned was made by Gershom Jones, of Providence, Rhode Island. It was stolen in a robbery while we were in Europe on sabbatical, and is much missed. Sometime later I was given an almost identical porringer with the touchmark of Samuel Hamlin. Jones and Hamlin were for a time partners and used the same handle mold,

The Richard Lees, father and son, were famous for their small porringers (left) 3 3/4" at the rim. The Samuel Hamlins, also father and son, made the more conventional size (right), 5 1/4" at the rim. Both families worked in the late 1700s and early 1800s.

although each kept his own touchmark. My first replica had been of this porringer form, and a friend in the Providence jewelry business was kind enough to make a silicone rubber mold for me, enabling me to cast the porringer handles.

The partnership between Jones and Hamlin did not survive some disputes that developed when first Hamlin and then Jones left to fight in the Revolutionary War. A legal suit over debts, loans, and shared property was settled in Jones's favor, but with an award of only one-seventh of the amount sought. Jones had two sons and took them into partnership for a time, then that partnership ended and the sons set up business as coppersmiths, founders, and plumbers.

Samuel had two sons. William was an engraver of "at least local prominence, while another, Samuel Ely Hamlin, carried on his father's business." (Laughlin, vol I, p. 96) He worked in his father's shop until his father died, and continued in the trade thereafter. He used the inherited touches and designed a few of his own. It is difficult, in some cases, to know if a piece was made by father or son. Laughlin comments on father and son with the judgment, "Hamlin pewter is of fine quality, and we honor the younger man for maintaining the standard of his father right through the Britannia period. His death did not occur until April 14, 1864, when he had almost reached his eighty-ninth milestone." (*Ibid*, p. 97)

If the first near-replica I had made was of a Jones-Hamlin porringer, one of the most recent is of a Hamlin pint mug, made and described by Jonathan in the chapter "Tankards and Teapots." It is sold by the Museum of Fine Arts in Boston, and was copied from an original in its collection.

In writing this account of the history of fathers and sons, I found myself wondering if ever there had been daughters involved in pewter work. I cannot recall seeing accounts from the colonial period in which a daughter is mentioned. I have two reasons to appreciate the place of women in the craft. Frances Felton, a key figure in the craft renascence since World War II, is a much celebrated pewterer, and was the teacher of my mentor, Arthur Barnes. More important in my own experience, though, are the many important contributions made by our daughter, Lauren, during the founding and the early growth of Gibson Pewter. She has continued to be an enthusiastic supporter of our product and a knowing critic of what we do. In whatever future we build with our enterprise, her legacy is firmly placed in her contributions during the early years, and in our memories of her working with us to build something of which we could all be proud.

As this chapter is about pewter in families, and attention has been given to Lauren, Jonathan, and Christopher, it seems unfair to complete the story without mentioning three others who, though not on the production line, made significant contributions to the total effort.

In the early years of the pewter enterprise, our oldest son, Cyrus, usually had summer jobs and contributed to the cost of his education. He worked as a carpenter's helper one summer; then on a farm in Maine, and still later at a company that reclaimed, melted, and recycled iron and steel.

He learned some of the craft in our shop, and was a great help in other ways. In those years we carried much of the heavy shop equipment to and from the country. He worked with his brothers dismantling the lathe and loading and unloading a utility trailer. They moved it all in and out of a cellar window in Providence to avoid the narrow stairs, and fashioned ingenious ways to move the lathe bed across the floor on rollers, and up a ramp they designed, to the window.

Cyrus has a fine arts degree in sculpture from the Rhode Island School of Design. Seven of his large welded-steel sculptures stand in nearby fields and near the barn, and a powerful casting of a gryphon hangs in the nave of the barn near the entrance to the pewter shop. Visitors who note the casting often go to look at the outdoor pieces from the back of the barn. Some go for a walk into the fields to see them up close. Cyrus has always been a helpful resource for our designs.

Mark, our second son, also spent summers away from the farm working to help fund his education. Trained as an engineer, and gifted in mechanics, he provided welcome help when present, with the equipment, and the machinery.

When we needed a process to finish large pieces in the clean-up stage, he designed, then made, what we call the "Mark Machine." It allows us access to clean up and finish the centers of larger pewter pieces that cannot be reached on the forming lathe because these areas are under the blocks holding them in place as they are spun. In recent years, he has helped us find and use some metalworking specialists who produce the metal chucks we need for new designs.

Finally, and important to us all, and to the enterprise, is Susan. Visitors to the pewter shop often walk to the back of the barn to look at the view to the south, and discover the garden. Repeat visitors will often go to look there before coming into the shop to see the pewter. Occasionally, seeing her working among the flowers, some will go down the back steps and venture into the garden for a closer view and conversation.

A few years ago, a benefit was arranged for a local church. Five gardens on our hill were open to the community for a garden tour and box lunch at the small, nearby, Center Club. Susan and Lauren were hostess to five hundred visitors. Flowers and shrubs were labeled with their botanical, as well as their everyday, names.

Through the years, she has sometimes been asked, "Do you have anything to do with the pewter operation?" Her quick answer was sometimes, "I feed them." That is an understatement. We value her judgment in things literary and aesthetic. Whether in a line of prose or in the lines of a piece of pewter, we trusted always her innate good taste, aesthetic sense, and judgement. When we are working on a new design, her comments are unfailingly helpful and affirming of us and our work.

When Jonathan was quite young, he was often venturesome in moving into new areas of the craft. One day he foraged in the box of throwaway parts that would eventually be melted down and kept as ingots to be used for casting. "Dad, can I have this?" he asked as he came back to me several times. He had two or three stems intended for stem goblets, and some stalks of candlesticks that had small imperfections. He soldered them together, and then cleaned and buffed them. They were quite attractive, and certainly unique. He brought them to his mother and she put them on our dining table, where they are still used. This kind of affirmation is important always, for a craftsman, and for a family.

If Susan is asked today whether she has anything to do with the pewter operation, she sometimes says, "Yes, I'm a design consultant." But she is also so much more!

A SON REMEMBERS

Chris Gibson

"All rise!" came the wake-up call. Fitting command, I thought, coming from a preacher. It always seemed to come too early, especially on a gray morning like this one. I could hear the patter of rain on the roof, inches above my head. What I really wanted at that moment was to put the world on hold and grab two more hours of sleep. That wasn't going to happen, though. Eight feet across the boys' dorm, my brother Jon was lying in his bed, undoubtedly feeling the same way. I rolled yesterday's socks into a tight ball and hurled them at his head. "He meant both of us, bro." "— you," came the muffled response.

I sat at the breakfast table feeling sorry for myself. I thought of my friends waiting tables at fancy restaurants on the Vineyard or Nantucket, or lifeguarding at Second Beach in Newport. That all seemed so far away as I looked southwest toward where Mt. Monadnock should have been. All I saw were clouds. It was one of those slow drizzling rains that I knew would last. Not very conducive to buffing pewter, I thought. Days like today made my job twice as hard. But I was good, and I knew all the tricks. A little damp air wasn't going to stop me. A few summers ago, maybe, but not now. We really had come a long way with this little family business of ours. What had started out as a hobby had turned into so much more.

As I made the quick walk out to the barn, I remembered this was a production day. The idea was to make the same piece all day long. The theory was that we could make more of them in this manner, and today it would be centerpiece vases, one of our more popular items. My dad was at the gray lathe, and had already completed two. "What's the target today?" I asked, already knowing the answer. "Six per hour," came the reply. Jon strolled up to the backup lathe and made a few quick adjustments. Within minutes he was ready to begin a day of what had to be the most boring of tasks—sanding. But he seemed to accept that role the same way I accepted mine. It was a necessary part of the creative process we had grown to love. My friends might be working where the action was, I thought, but they weren't part of something like this.

The buffing area was on the other side of the barn, in its own section. To the casual observer, it must have seemed somewhat makeshift. The primary buffing machine was actually an old electric lawnmower motor, which we had mounted on L-brackets, turned on its side, and clamped onto the workbench. On the main shaft was a cone-shaped screw nose, onto which a variety of wheels or brushes could be attached. Most of my buffing was done with a few different-shaped brushes, and I had my favorites. The secret ingredient was a type of compound applied to the brush, and it was only through trial and error that we found the one that I now used most often. The damp air meant I had to be extra careful not the rush the process. If I applied too much compound, or if I didn't wait an extra minute or so before starting to buff, a dark blotch would appear where you would normally expect a silvery satin finish. The self-imposed pressure of a production run, coupled with this kind of weather, and it was only a matter of time before that happened.

I glanced at my watch and looked at my work tray. Twelve done at eleven A.M. meant I was behind. I looked across at my dad and brother, cranking away. My shoulders were starting to ache and I needed a break. My heart leaped as I looked toward the barn door. Saved by the customer, I thought, as a family of five walked up. This will slow Dad down a little, and maybe I could catch up. My dad was not only a master craftsman, but also a master schmoozer, and the crowds loved his stories. I always believed that our customers felt they were getting a little bit of the Guv when they walked out with some pewter.

Centerpiece vases are an engineering feat unto themselves. The top of the vase has an opening narrower than its midsection, and since it's spun from a single disk over an apparently solid chuck, a person observing the process for the first time can't help wondering how it will be possible to get the piece off the chuck, once it's finished. So it was with the family watching my father at this very moment. I looked over at Jon, who shot a quick glance my way. His smile told me what I already knew—that it would be only a few seconds before my dad, a master storyteller, would start in with perhaps his best ever, the one known as "The Hindu Trance," and undoubtedly told in detail elsewhere in this manuscript. Ten minutes and five "true believers" later, the visiting family was making the predictable rounds to our various workstations. The questions and comments were always welcome on a day like this. After purchasing several pieces, including a centerpiece vase, they departed, and I focused again on the task at hand.

By three o'clock I came to the realization that I would not be able to finish all of that day's buffing. The damp air had slowed me down more than I anticipated. But as I looked at the twenty satin-finished pieces sitting in my work tray, a sense of satisfaction came over me. What had started that morning as nothing more than twenty flat disks of metal had been transformed into something with shape, beauty, and personality. In short, we had created something. I thought of the hundreds of people who visited our shop each summer and wondered how many of them felt the same way about their own lives. I look back today and know that the answer is, sadly, not many.

At four-forty-five I shut down my buffing wheel, covered my work tray, and walked slowly across to the spinning area, where my dad was still hard at work. His large strong hands skillfully guided the spinning tool across the shiny metal. His firm yet gentle touch was evident with each pass. Every move was calculated and efficient, and the result inevitable. Another perfect vase. He shut down his lathe and as he turned to look at me, I saw it in his eyes. I knew instantly what he felt at that moment. He didn't have to say anything. Creating objects of beauty has a payback that can't be described with words. Doing it with your family is icing on the cake.

GROWING UP—PLACE, CRAFT, AND FAMILY

Lauren Gibson

Thanks, Dad, for inviting me to share some memories of the pewter shop. I will start with tankards. There was an early one-of-a-kind followed later by a settled design that was the Gibson tankard written about elsewhere. I was involved in both ventures.

Lauren in her studio forming a bracelet.

The summer of 1977, I was finished with Wheeler and about to head to New York City and begin my years at Parsons. Instead of a typewriter or dictionary, I received our first tankard as a send-off to college. Chris was home that summer; and I remember his being a part of this process. It was my idea to make a tankard and I poured a brick of plaster of Paris into a canister of sand in the crude shape of a number 7. From that piece of plaster, I carved something that I thought looked like a tankard handle. I spent off-hours through the summer working on this project. The result was an extremely crude, large handle, complete with deep pockmarks and the gravel texture of the original mold.

I remember your reaction, Dad, when presented with the handle, and your willingness to make the body to match the monster. I think you were really amused by it, but you still gave it your best effort. You were very anxious soldering in the bottom and the handle. It was a first and I was counting on you not to ruin my tankard. It all came off perfectly. We signed the bottom with REG 1977 and the number 1. I scratched in the name I was planning to begin using that fall, Lauren. We did not use the Gibson Pewter stamp because it was still, in those days, Gibson & Sons. The plaster mold broke before we could cast a second handle. I remember that there were some tugging rights among the brothers as to who should get the first tankard made at Gibson Pewter. The brothers really knew it had been my project they helped with. I still have the piece but think I will return it to Jonny for the shop, and for a good laugh.

The project was a prelude to the Gibson tankard. We started again with a plaster mold, a smaller design for the handle. I sculpted it and cast the first handle for the Gibson tankard. I had learned my lesson from the original one and chose to design a handle that was simple and elegant, similar to the original tankard designs. You made a silicone mold from my model, then a friend used the prototype to sandcast the handles needed until you had a bronze mold made in Providence.

I spent two of my growing-up years away from the farm and that was an adventure, but the best years were spent in Hillsborough and having a job in our own backyard. After the farm was opened up early each summer and the fields mowed, you started production in the pewter shop and we were kept on a tight schedule. Expected to get out to the barn by 8:30, we did not sleep late on weekdays. The routine kept us busy until we washed hands for lunch, hacked around for a hour, and then headed out to the barn for the afternoon shift. We usually finished around 4:30 and had time to play or swim before dinner. I can't remember ever missing a clear evening on the back terrace. After dinner we'd amuse ourselves with books or TV or music. You created an environment that we didn't have to leave. We had companionship, art, music, work, and play. We shared two meals together each day, we entertained your friends and you and Mom entertained ours. The neighborhood was in on the action as well; all our peers worked in the business with you and learned the skills that you taught us. You housed Billy Potter and Kevin Mullaney for entire summers. It was an enlightened place to grow up in, and nothing compared to it in the vicinity.

If the farm wasn't the center of the universe in the summer, it surely felt as though it were. If you spent the summer there, you'd witness a steady stream of visitors, overnight and weekend guests and occasional visiting work parties of a dozen or more unpaid laborers who worked for beer and camaraderie. If we weren't expecting guests, we counted on customers or visitors to the pewter shop. Everything came to us, and when a brother returned home, usually with a friend or girlfriend, you wondered why they would ever leave. We didn't go on vacations to exotic beaches or drag a trailer through National Park systems. We went home whenever we had the time to get there. The pewter shop kept us on the property with a job, and we developed a work ethic to deliver a quality product with the family name. It was fun and hip and exclusive, with an inclusive clause: "You must come back—you hear?"

We were encouraged to pursue our interests. I did jewelry and hammered metal over anvils and once made a pair of cuff bracelets that must have been five inches wide, a commissioned work for a customer who admired the bracelets I wore. I made conch-belts, a modern version of the traditional Native American designs, heavy but spectacular. I cast hearts and strung them with leather cord, the latest trend in the city, and signed each piece with my name and the year. I made napkin rings,—hammered and soldered them. For a while the paint room was my studio, with a great view, a private office to escape to.

I walked the length of the barn a hundred times in a day, from the buffing station to the soapstone sink, to the shop and back to collect the next piece. Occasionally Chris would get an entire tray of pewter for me to finish and I'd carry a wooden tray for those rounds. Days that we made coasters were the worst. Not only would there be hundreds of them at a time, but we usually made coasters on rainy or colder days when we would not be out of doors. It was the type of job you hunkered in for. My fingers would get cold on wet days washing hundreds of coasters in the rainwater collected from the roof of the barn, and my hands ached after half an hour and didn't stop for the rest of the day.

My workstation at the end of the barn had the best view, and while I would hand-finish plates, chargers, or salad bowls, I'd look to the mountains in the

Lauren greeting visitors in the pewter shop. Her way with people won many friends.

distance, over the clothes drying on the line, across the fields, down the valley and away up the distant peak, greet my mother walking with a basket of laundry or freshly pulled or plucked vegetables from the garden. I watched birches bend with coming storms and willows hula as clouds turned green. I hung damp gray washcloths on every drying stand and dowel, the back of chairs, or on the railing at the end of the barn. They'd dry stiff from hard water, most days, in no time at all. My view afforded me glimpses of the future I dreamed of and the time to daydream of boyfriends I had yet to meet and of all the fun ahead of me. I readied myself to move on with my young life from there, looking out onto those mountains beyond the laundry on the line.

You do not know how great it was for me to work with my family and to have been a part of that production routine. You gave me something to do that I could excel at. No one ever told me that I was the salesgirl; I just took to it. If I needed to do something creative, I was encouraged. Of course nothing is perfect, nothing in adolescence could be, and, yes, there were times when my brothers or you would make me angry; or the notion that we were stuck there would depress me, and the tears would roll. The guys didn't like to hang out with their sister and for years the Jeep would roll down the driveway without me. Occasionally I'd get to tag along. But of course I loved working in the shop; I couldn't be left out, I was a part of the action.

I also have some funny memories of my brothers. The guys used to think it was hysterical to scare their sister. Whenever they found a dead bat in the barn they would remove my bar of Lava soap from the wire soap hanger on the wall by the soapstone sink and place the bat, wings extended, face directed at me, and wait for me to wash my first piece of pewter after lunch. I usually ran the water, picked up a small square of green felt from the sink, reached up to the soap dish, ran the felt over the soap, rinsed the pewter, and then dried it off. I can't tell you how many times I fell for their prank, rubbing the furry back of the postmortem creature. I know I dropped a piece or two of pewter this way, a guaranteed laugh for the guys. Jonny, whose red lathe was over in your section of the barn, had a set of mirrors arranged so that he'd catch all the action. I knew something was up whenever I'd see Jonny and Chris standing at Chris's buffing station looking in my direction. But the first time they did it, I almost passed out.

Year after year, I came to recognize our repeat customers. We became a place to go to, a point of interest. When people go to Venice they see glass; when they come to Hillsborough they go to see the Centre and the Pewterer. I was never good with names, but I never forgot a face and from visit to visit I learned people's histories and families. They would come back the next year, the kids with sieves in their hands to catch frogs from our pond. I remember the look on a child's face when I'd reach up to the beam near the front of the barn and magically produce—a swing! I think I stopped to watch you give a demonstration a thousand times; always an "Ooooh" ran through the crowd when you'd move the metal the first inch. I never tired of seeing it done. I never for a second thought it was unimportant. Being up front gave me a lot of confidence with people.

Looking back, the tankard memory stands out. It marked a turning point in our business. It's not that we once sold eight at once, or that they took a long time to finish, or that they were pricey; it's that we had reached another level. The design came together and was stunning, simple, strong: an achievement I am very proud to have helped design and create. It was one of the last summers I spent in New Hampshire, and the creation of our tankard was my last big contribution to the family business.

Thank you for asking me my recollections. I once told you my slogan for the shop, "At Gibson Pewter We Make History Every Day." These stories are twenty and thirty years old and open for revision or someone else's remembrance. What hasn't changed is the metal you moved. Those were THE glory years, working with my brothers and Dad, being able to get home every summer and have a job. I look back on those years and remember that we swam and played; it was when we all knew each other's daily business and fine-tuned being able to annoy one another to perfection. It was in those days that we created an unbreakable bond. We were at our best, with our youth in bloom, and Bunky dropping apples at our feet.

Love, Lauren

REFLECTION

I have worked with pewter for more than a quarter of a century, and it might be expected that the mystery of the metal would recede as my knowledge of it grew. But I have not found that so. As my knowledge has grown, so has a sense of mystery, amazement, and wonder. We see the movement through stages—from molten metal, bright and shiny in the melting pot; then as it is poured like a glistening string from ladle to sprue to enter the mold; then when it emerges solid, sometimes gray, at other times gleaming and mirror-like. We work with the metal in the buffing process, which can end with a variety of satin finishes or a brightness rivaling silver. We can view a collection of pewter covering two or three centuries and marvel at the variations of patina, suggesting that each piece has its own story to tell of its aging.

I read, and immediately agree with, the testimonial by Montgomery at the beginning of his fine history: "Upon my first view of an old pewter dish, I was caught by its color, its character, and its form. Since that day in 1934, old pewter has had a very special appeal which I have tried to put into words and pictures. Indeed, one of my most compelling reasons for wanting to write this book was to illustrate pewter in such a way that others could sense its color, soft sheen, and textural qualities as they appear to me." (*A History of American Pewter,* p. 2)

In a similar vein, Henry J. Kauffman celebrates the response of collectors to the metal: "It is quite apparent that the collecting cognoscenti of pewter objects recognize in them an indefinable 'mystique.' There is about them an aura which no other objects of metal possess, a glamour which is very difficult, if not impossible, for anyone 'on the outside' to understand or define." (*The American Pewterer—His Techniques & His Products,* p. 11)

Vanessa Brett begins her *Phaidon Guide to Pewter* by noting that "for many centuries pewter played an important part in people's lives. It is associated with warmth and good company—long evenings spent by a kitchen hearth, splendid dinners and everyday meals, with the good fellowship of tavern, public house, club or society, with travelers and with church ceremony." (p. 7) There is a note of sadness as she reports that pewter lost its place to china and glass, that it was constantly melted down to be remade into new articles, and, because it took second place to silver, that it was locked in to the same shape because molds were so expensive and "passed from generation to generation of pewterers, too costly to be refashioned, causing some pewter design to stagnate. But it is precisely this homeliness, this continuance of tradition, that is so appealing and which makes the 'feel' of pewter so important an attribute for any collector." (*Ibid.*)

If the metal itself has the power to excite, and sometimes amaze, those who become interested in it may find that its history is intertwined with much they value in the human story. There is surprise at how early the alloy was in use in the West and the Far East. We become aware of national styles, and the modification of styles by interaction or by lineage, as in the influence of English styles on American. In the rise and fall of the pewter trade, we rejoice as it improves upon the woodenware it displaces, and flourishes, and are saddened by its rapid decline with the advent of china and glassware. We may seek out the pewter on display at a museum, or see the pewter that is pictured by Old World masters: Jacopo's *Supper at Emmaus,* showing a flagon and plate (1525); the painter Jan Steen's *The World Upside Down,* presenting a boisterous family scene in which we can see a charger and flagon (1600s); Jean-Baptiste Simeon Chardin's *Back from Market,* showing a large charger (1739). The paintings were not done for the sake of showing pewter; they depict scenes in which pewter would naturally appear.

Pewter has been the medium for meeting and continuing relationships with people I would not have known otherwise, as well as an added content enriching friendships developed in other ways and for different reasons. Among these have been knowledgeable, sometimes even expert, individuals with wide associations with the craft and its products. Some have been collectors, ranging from the casual, who collect pewter among other things, to the intensely devoted who know the periods and pewterers in the history, and will know other collectors also highly committed and knowledgeable. It is possible in such relationships to learn from the exchanges, and they will often appear to be learning special things from an artisan creating new forms or replicating old ones. There is a strong bond with those who, over time, build a collection of our work. When that collection is a full set of tableware and serving dishes, we may imagine a whole family assembled around a Thanksgiving or Christmas feast.

A chalice made in a special commission may create a tie with a worshiping community nearby, far away, or even on the other side of the world. We may never see or share in the sacrament or the group, or we may be invited, as Jonathan and I once were, to the dedication of the chalice and to participate in the service. To work together with a couple, designing their set of pewter as they approach their wedding, creates rich memories as well as their pewter. Just as, with couples long married, when one partner creates a conspiracy of silence about a special gift to be made in secret for the other, there is joy in having a part in their giving and receiving. One family's experience using our pewter for some central rites is so special that I asked for an account of some of her own from a good friend, Elizabeth Hambrick-Stowe. Part of her letter follows.

"We are grateful to own four of your works: a large communion chalice, which I purchased in honor of Charlie's first sabbatical; two goblets; and a specially designed goblet," she wrote. "The latter three were purchased for the confirmations of our three children. I also have purchased three small goblets, which are wrapped away for the weddings of the children.

"Some years ago, I attended a workshop on family concerns at which one of the speakers talked about exercises and *The Blessing Cup,* by Rock Travnikar, O.F.M., a Roman Catholic priest. It shared 24 simple rites and activities to deepen and nourish the spiritual life of families. He had created a resource entitled, 'for family prayer-celebrations.' The concept immediately caught me. As the Foreword states, 'Sharing by cup has symbolized nearly every profound human emotion and divine grace.' The Blessing Cup includes orders in three categories: the Circle of Love (everything from dedication of the Blessing Cup itself to times of achievements, hardship, illness, etc), Milestones of the Christian life, and Seasons and Holidays.

"Our family has used the Blessing Cup as a resource, and over the years have spun off from it our own orders and traditions. For example, we mark the end of summer each year with an extended Blessing Cup that reminds us of all the many varied activities, places, and persons of the past season. Usually the Blessing Cup follows a family dinner, although sometimes it is used as a grace before the meals. We select not only the theme for a particular evening but also the Gibson chalice or goblet to be used. If the birthday is one of the children's, or some significant event is the occasion, his or her cup is the obvious choice. It's nice to have a variety of sizes and styles to choose from.

"This is something of what your pewter chalices/goblets mean to the Hambrick-Stowes," she continued. "I could add that your pewter hearts have gone to college with Anne, and to Germany and to Japan this year, with our son Chuck and my brother Dave and his family. Similarly, as Christmas presents this year the New Hampshire loon was shared with Chuck's host family in Germany as something thoroughly American, and with Dave's wife, Linda, to surprise her with a feeling of 'home' in far-off Kyoto!"

From these, and many others, the well of memory is filled with so much on which we gratefully draw. When I work at the lathe, the buffing wheel, pour the molten metal into a mold, or solder a handle onto a child's cup or tankard, I am too intent on the care required by the craft to wonder where the piece will go or who will own it. Then, again, a letter will come from someone we've never met, who writes, "I received one of your centerpiece vases as a gift and marvel at the finish, and especially the effect of the light on the graceful curve that comes together at the neck." I want to tell him that I have often watched the play of light changing as the forming tool brings the spinning metal down to that curve as I complete the piece. Practicing the craft is to live with a mosaic, an incredible number of pieces, each different from the others, yet the whole forming a picture that adds meaning to our work, and to life as well.

Another part of me prefers the image of a web, the mental picture being reinforced daily by the large webs made by a family of spiders (*Araneus cavaticus*) whose work blocks the top half of the large doorway under the barn. We store the yard and farm machinery there and I often stand amazed by the size and the lengths of the strands that hold those webs together. The morning sunlight, combined with the darker interior space behind them, creates a dramatic definition and clarity.

If I draw mental lines connecting all the people with whom, and places where, our pewter is now, the web is concentrated at the center where it is made. It reaches out to much of the world, the strands thinning as the distances grow. The mosaic affirms the special reality of each individual piece; the web suggests the connections. There is doubtless some hubris in the symbolism that places the center of the web where we are. However, wasn't it William James who noted that by the nature of things we remain the center no matter in what direction we look?

There are two other realms we may visit: the past and the future. We may venture into the past through research and study, and into the future by anticipation and conjecture. When I began a college major in philosophy, the introductory course started with the Milesian School:—Thales, Anaximander and Anaximenes, (birth dates 640, 611, and 585 B.C.)—and worked its way to the Big Three of classical philosophy: Socrates, Plato, and Aristotle. It was a long way back, but soon it became clear that in the realm of ideas and the quest for meaning, much of the furniture of the mind had its initial construction or creation in their dialogues and exchanges. Listening to them (and reading them became an exercise in "listening" to the growth of ideas through such exchanges) was to realize gradually that we live in a "house of intellect" that they had engineered and began to build. The history of thought would be revisions and elaborations on their work. All human achievements may be variations on just such a pattern. When a gifted woodcarver was asked about his beginning, the answer was disarmingly simple: "My father taught me to whittle."

The craft of pewter has a history older than the Greek philosophers. The earliest piece of pewter positively dated, a two-handled flask of circa 1400 B.C. taken from an Egyptian grave at Abydos, is of a quality of metal —93 percent tin, 6 percent lead, 1 percent copper —"that would have been accepted in Britain as a suitable grade for holloware as late as the eighteenth or even the nineteenth centuries." (*The Techniques of Pewtersmithing,* by Charles Hull & Jack Murrell, London: B.T. Batsford Ltd., 1984, p. 13) Studying the history of pewter, we can see the development of national or regional styles, their occasional interactions and resulting influences. In the present century, we see the waning use of pewter accompanied by a growing interest in its history. Collecting groups shared the excitement in finding, identifying, and exchanging information about the craftsmen who fashioned the pieces, spurred on by the knowledge that the older and more rare the item, the greater its value. Historical lore grew steadily, and writing celebrating both craft and craftsmen emerged. Museum collections foster research that is historical and technical.

For me, the engagement with pewter resembles my experience with philosophy: There will always be far more to know than one person can learn. This is no cause for regret; instead I am grateful for realms so vast in possibilities. There is always a challenge waiting, the excitement in pursuing it, and the joy when something new is discovered. In the practice of the pewter craft, sometimes the hands discover a variation on a technique that the mind questions. The result resembles the product of a craftsman who lived more than a century ago. Did he do it that way? It resembles a conversation in which I am reminded of a kindred thought expressed in a Platonic dialogue. While very different, both experiences suggest something about the world, or worlds, we inhabit. Each enhances the present world of our experience by a sense of rootedness in the past.

Edmund Burke was probably correct in writing, "You cannot plan the future by the past." ("Letter to a Member of the National Assembly") Still, most of us hope that the things we cherish will continue, and that the things we especially care about might be enhanced and become meaningful parts of what will be. It was Hocking who wrote: "Duration is a dimension of value." We do not want the world to lose the things we truly value.

When I think of the future of our pewter shop, I hope for both the continued work in making replicas of fine historical examples and the creation of new designs that venture into work as yet unimagined. I rejoice that Jonathan—son, partner, and key to the future—has the careful skills that make the replicas possible, and the creativity to produce impressive new designs.

The final value I celebrate prompts the hope of future friendships as meaningful as those we have experienced. Friendships are a gracious mystery, adding much to life. They begin in a variety of ways, many of them unexpected. The craft has created numerous opportunities and occasions leading to friendships that grow with the years. Some people were mentors and guides in the formative years. Other relationships gathered force with time. Some arose from achievements in which they had a part. Some friends were pewter enthusiasts, who came to see the product and became bonded to us as well. Others were artisans in other crafts, met at fairs, seen only occasionally but always gladly.

We have a repeated experience of visitors from near and far (and sometimes very far), who come into our old barn—a typical farmer's barn from the early 1800s—who, entering our showroom, express near disbelief at what they see. There is a mixture of our own designs, replicas of some of the most notable work of early American pewterers, with one set of shelves of original pewter made by outstanding pewterers of the 1700s and 1800s. In the adjoining space, they see the machinery on which our work is formed, it, too, venerable in age (one old lathe is an American first in its design). The setting and contents prompt discussions of history as well as production techniques. It is for us a wonderful atmosphere in which to work and it gives an endless variety of things to share with those who visit. Often friendships are formed that deepen in richness of sharing over the years.

The barn itself has had its own way of being special. There is a bit of country wisdom about barns: If you have a good foundation and a dependable roof, the barn can last forever. The post-and-beam framework, seen most dramatically in old pictures of barn raisings, gives the barn its strength. The roof protects from weather and water damage; the foundation keeps the great posts and beams, with their triangulated bracing at the corners, level and stable. Visitors who express interest in the barn are shown the marks at the joints, circles and slashes cut into the wood to identify and guide the builders in assembling the beams on the ground before they are levered into their upright position. When we have added partitions, in order to divide into rooms and insulate our work spaces, we have been careful to keep the structural beams visible.

From time to time the suggestion has been made that we might create a more efficient operation by putting up a new building with a concrete floor, more open space, and a proper "factory" layout for the machinery. I find the thought depressing for a number of reasons, the first being that the barn is itself an example of the colonial era, and was standing when pewterers like Roswell Gleason, Eben Smith, and Israel Trask were creating work that we sometimes see at auctions. Further, the barn itself is a work of craftsmanship, and the result of knowing handwork requiring much strength and skill. As we work, the barn is for us another bridge to an older time, when pewter was a larger part of the lives of all. The barn is not only the place where we work, but it is also a vantage point from which we view our world.

From the back of the barn, we look across the pond to a ring of mountains and hills: Crotched, Pack Monadnock, Gibson, Riley, Monadnock. The seasons offer them in a variety of colors: the soft greens of spring, the warm green and tans of summer, the bright palettes of autumn and fall, and the blue-white hues of winter. Within the seasons there is a daily variety added by the gray-white mists before and after rain; the dry, red heat of late August; the glories of autumn when, to quote Hal Borland, "the woods become a hooked rug flung across the hills." On winter nights, the lights of a distant ski slope appear as strings of pearls down the mountain side.

Above the southern range of mountains and hills, the stately movements of distant stars glide through the seasons: Scorpio with its red star, Antares, and all the other familiar constellations. The planets pass in an ordered, but separate schedule and, like the moon with its phases, provide a different order of movement and light. We live within the changing seasons and the larger, changeless order of things, grateful for every opportunity to offer the creations of our life and work, in wonder of the Creation of which we are so small a part, and in awe before the infinite mystery and majesty of the Creator.

And so the end may be an echo of the beginning as I come back to the "mantra" tacked to the wall over the workbench in the lathe room. It is a brief passage from a psalm, one of several places in Scripture that affirm the work of the hands. May it be so for us all:

> . . . let the favor of the Lord our God be upon us;
> and establish Thou the work of our hands upon us;
> yea, the work of our hands, establish Thou it.

Glossary

Booge—The curve of the metal from the base to the rim of a plate, or up the side of a porringer.

Burnish—To polish a pewter surface using a polished steel tool.

Chuck—The wood, plastic, or metal form mounted on the headstock or power side of the lathe, over which the pewter is spun.

Fulcrum Pin—A metal pin that is movable along a series of holes in the toolrest of the lathe, making possible a levering action with the forming tool in spinning pewter.

Headstock—The rotating spindle of the lathe on the power side, to which a chuck is attached, over which the pewter is spun.

Mandrel—A metal bar, used as a core around which pewter may be shaped.

Patina—A surface softening or mellowing of the color of pewter with age.

Planish—To smooth or polish the pewter, accomplished by use of a special forming tool that is flatter than the more curved forming tool.

Sprue Hole—The hole through which metal is poured when casting.

Sprue—The part of a casting that filled the sprue hole. It must be removed in finishing the piece.

Tailstock—The adjustable head for the lathe for holding the centered work against the headstock. It provides the pressure that keeps the metal disk in place during the spinning process.